FEDERICO FELLINI:
CONTEMPORARY PERSPECTIV

Edited by Frank Burke and Marguerite R. Waller

Federico Fellini remains the best known of the postwar Italian directors. This collection of essays brings Fellini scholarship up to date,
employing a range of recent critical approaches, including semiotic,
psychoanalytical, feminist, and deconstructionist. Accordingly, a number of important themes arise – the reception of fascism, the crisis of
the subject, the question of agency, homoeroticism, feminism, and constructions of gender.

Since the early 1970s, there has been a decline in critical and theoretical attention to Fellini's work, accompanied by an assumption that his
films are self-indulgent and lacking in political value. This volume
moves the discussion forward towards a politics of signification, contending that Fellini's evolving self-reflexivity is not mere solipsism but
rather a critique of both aesthetics and signification. The essays presented here are almost all new, and were chosen to illustrate the self-
critical, analytical dimension of Fellini's work, particularly apparent in
some of his earlier and lesser-known films.

This lively and ambitious collection brings a new critical language
to bear on Fellini's films, offering fresh insights into their underlying
issues and meaning. It will have a significant impact on film studies,
reclaiming this important director for a contemporary audience.

(Toronto Italian Studies)

FRANK BURKE is Professor of Film Studies, Queen's University.

MARGUERITE R. WALLER is Professor of English and Women's Studies,
University of California, Riverside.

EDITED BY
FRANK BURKE AND MARGUERITE R. WALLER

Federico Fellini
Contemporary Perspectives

UNIVERSITY OF TORONTO PRESS
Toronto Buffalo London

© University of Toronto Press Incorporated 2002
Toronto Buffalo London
Printed in Canada

ISBN 0-8020-0696-5 (cloth)
ISBN 0-8020-7647-5 (paper)

Printed on acid-free paper

Toronto Italian Studies

National Library of Canada Cataloguing in Publication Data

Main entry under title:
Federico Fellini: contemporary perspectives

(Toronto Italian studies)
Includes bibliographical references.
ISBN 0-8020-0696-5 (bound). ISBN 0-8020-7647-5 (pbk.)

1. Fellini, Federico – Criticism and interpretation. I. Burke, Frank
II. Waller, Marguerite R., 1948– III. Series.

PN1998.3.F45F453 2002   791.43′0233′092   C2001-903774-0

University of Toronto Press acknowledges the financial assistance to its
publishing program of the Canada Council for the Arts and the Ontario
Arts Council.

University of Toronto Press acknowledges the financial support for its
Publishing activities of the Government of Canada through the Book
Publishing Industry Development Program (BPIDP).

This book has been published with the help of grants from Queen's
University and the Istituto Italiano di Cultura, Toronto.

Contents

Preface   vii
FRANK BURKE

Acknowledgments   xi
Chronology   xiii
Illustrations   xvii

Introduction   3
MARGUERITE R. WALLER

1 Federico Fellini: Realism/Representation/Signification   26
FRANK BURKE

2 Subtle Wasted Traces: Fellini and the Circus   47
HELEN STODDART

3 Fellini and Lacan: The Hollow Phallus, the Male Womb, and the Retying of the Umbilical   65
WILLIAM VAN WATSON

4 When in Rome Do As the Romans Do? Federico Fellini's Problematization of Femininity (*The White Sheik*)   92
VIRGINIA PICCHIETTI

5 Whose *Dolce vita* Is This, Anyway? The Language of Fellini's Cinema   107
MARGUERITE R. WALLER

6 'Toby Dammit,' Intertext, and the End of Humanism   121
CHRISTOPHER SHARRETT

7 Fellini's *Amarcord*: Variations on the Libidinal Limbo of
Adolescence   137
DOROTHÉE BONNIGAL

8 Memory, Dialect, Politics: Linguistic Strategies in Fellini's
Amarcord   155
COSETTA GAUDENZI

9 Fellini's *Ginger and Fred*: Postmodern Simulation Meets
Hollywood Romance   169
MILLICENT MARCUS

10 Cinecittà and *America*: Fellini Interviews Kafka (*Intervista*)   188
CARLO TESTA

11 Interview with the Vamp: Deconstructing Femininity in
Fellini's Final Films (*Intervista*, *La voce della luna*)   209
ÁINE O'HEALY

Selected Bibliography   233
Filmography   235
Contributors   237

Preface

FRANK BURKE

Federico Fellini is probably the best known of the postwar Italian directors, and he remains among the most noted filmmakers in the history of the medium. In 1980, while still at the peak of his fame (though not necessarily his career), Fellini was described by CBS's Harry Reasoner as 'maybe the premier filmmaker of the age.' He was awarded five Oscars, and though his reputation declined in the 1980s and early 1990s, his final Oscar was the 1993 Lifetime Achievement Award of the Academy of Motion Picture Arts and Sciences. Nineteen years earlier he had received a similar award from Cannes; eight years earlier, from the Film Society of Lincoln Center (New York City). Perhaps more important, Fellini's work strongly influenced international filmmaking well into the 1990s. In a 1992 *Sight and Sound* survey he ranked first in a poll in which world-renowned directors were asked to name their favourite filmmaker.

This collection of essays has been motivated by a desire to 'update' Fellini's importance by bringing his work into relation with recent critical methodologies: semiotic/poststructuralist, psychoanalytical, feminist, and deconstructionist. (I use the last term broadly to encompass the intertextual thrust of several of the essays below.) Consequently, almost all of the essays in this collection were solicited especially for the project. The two exceptions are my own 'Federico Fellini: From Representation to Signification,' *Romance Languages Annual* 1 (1989), and Marguerite R. Waller's 'Whose *Dolce vita* Is This Anyhow?: The Language of Fellini's Cinema,' *Quaderni d'italianistica* 9.1 (1990), the appearance of which a little over ten years ago helped establish new directions in Fellini criticism.[1]

In bringing contemporary theoretical approaches to bear on Fellini's work, we hope to reverse what has been an unfortunate slide in critical attention to Fellini in the English-speaking world since the early 1970s. Waller addresses this slide in her Introduction, while also suggesting that Fellini's work to a large extent belies the apparent reasoning behind this critical neglect (i.e., an assumption that Fellini's films are self-indulgent and thoroughly lacking in political value). In particular, we have sought to move discussion toward what we might call a politics of signification. We contend that Fellini's engagement with modernism and postmodernism, and in particular his evolving self-reflexivity – which has been read by politicized critics only as self-indulgence – are not mere solipsism but rather a critique and an opening out of both aesthetics and signification at a moment in which politics and the social have themselves become aestheticized or 'virtualized' as simulation. We believe that many of the essays that follow strongly illuminate this self-critical, analytical dimension of Fellini's work.

Because our emphasis is on critical methodology, we have not provided uniform coverage of the Fellini canon. We have included rereadings of some early work (e.g., *The White Sheik*) from new perspectives. But we have emphasized readings of those films constructed on the verge of or within postmodernity, precisely because those are the films that demonstrate best Fellini's continuing relevance as an arbiter of social value. All of this explains why some of the staples of conventional Fellini criticism – *La Strada, Nights of Cabiria, 8½* – are largely missing, their place taken by films such as *Toby Dammit, Amarcord, Ginger and Fred, Intervista,* and *The Voice of the Moon*.

We have chosen not to include interview material, because so much is in print nowadays and thus easily accessible (see the Bibliography).

It may seem strange that in a collection of essays on an Italian film director, there is no native Italian contributor. We did seek to involve Italian writers in our project, but were unsuccessful. Although there is much solid academic work in Italy, it tends to consist of either general critical/biographical introductions to his career or aesthetic analysis focusing on the design and look of his films – often linked to his sketches. We were unable to identify scholars writing, or inclined to write, on Fellini from the critical and theoretical perspectives privileged in this volume. The other recent writing on Fellini in Italy has been non-academic, comprising three types: traditional plot and theme summaries of his films; 'behind the scenes' reportage on his filmmaking; and celebrations of 'Fellini the great auteur' in the wake of his death – coffee table books that bring together images from his films as well as sketches and other memorabilia. This type of writing is more commercial than critical in approach.

Our decision to organize the volume according to theoretical issues within postmodernity meant locating Fellini less within the context of Italian culture and more within a broader context of postwar signifying strategies. We would welcome a volume that addressed the former, especially one that viewed Fellini's work in relation to Italian cultural studies, a field that has emerged and grown rapidly in the past decade.

Note

1 Waller's essay has been somewhat revised for this volume. Two other essays occupy roughly the same historical terrain: Waller's 'Neither an "I" nor an "Eye"': The Gaze in Fellini's *Giulietta degli spiriti,*' *Romance Languages Annual* 1 (1989): 75–80 and my own 'Fellini: Changing the Subject,' *Film Quarterly* 43.1 (Fall 1989): 36–48. However, both have been reprinted in *Perspectives on Federico Fellini*, ed. Peter Bondanella and Cristina Degli-Esposti (New York: G.K. Hall, 1993), and it did not seem sensible to reprint them again here.

Acknowledgments

First and foremost the editors thank all those who contributed essays to this volume. It has been a pleasure working with them and benefitting from their insights, which have made this project rewarding beyond our most optimistic projections.

We thank the Queen's University Vice-Principal (Research) and the Office of Research Services for their generous support of this project. The Social Science and Humanities Council of Canada and the Queen's University Advisory Research Council provided funding that was essential to the research Frank Burke conducted in conjunction with this volume. We are also grateful for the funding provided by the Academic Senate of the University of California, Riverside.

We thank the Purdue Research Foundation for letting us include a revised version of Frank Burke's 'Federico Fellini: From Representation to Signification,' *Romance Languages Annual* 1 (1989), as well as material from Áine O'Healy's 'Unspeakable Bodies: Fellini's Female Grotesques,' *Romance Languages Annual* 4 (1992). We thank *Quaderni d'italianistica* for letting us include a revised version of Marguerite R. Waller's 'Whose Dolce vita Is This Anyhow?: The Language of Fellini's Cinema,' 9.1 (1990). Finally, we wish to acknowledge that Millicent Marcus's essay 'Fellini's *Ginger and Fred*: Postmodern Simulation Meets Hollywood Romance' also appears in her book *After Fellini: National Cinema in the Postmodern Age*, published by The Johns Hopkins University Press, 2002.

For the still photographs from Fellini's films, we thank the Museum of Modern Art/Film Stills Archive, especially Helena Robinson, and the Academy of Motion Picture Arts and Sciences Library. For the Fellini sketches, we thank the Lilly Rare Book Library of Indiana

University and Professor Peter Bondanella, who brought the Fellini archive to the Lilly Library.

To Ron Schoeffel, Anne Laughlin, and the production department at the University of Toronto Press we are deeply grateful for the care with which they have helped bring this project to fruition.

Chronology

1920–38   Federico Fellini was born on 20 January 1920 to middle-class parents in Rimini, a small town on the Adriatic Sea. When he was around eight he ran away from school and joined a circus for a short time (or so he claimed in some interviews). In 1938 he went to Florence, where he drew comic strips for the humorous newspaper *420*.

1939–44   In 1939 Fellini moved to Rome, where he worked as a reporter for three weeks on *Il popolo*. In 1940 he joined the editorial staff of *Marc'Aurelio*. He also began writing sketches for radio and gags for the movies. In 1941 comedian and actor Aldo Fabrizi helped him get script-writing jobs in movies. In 1943 he married Giulietta Masina. He was saved from the draft when an air raid destroyed his medical records. In 1944 Giulietta gave birth to a son, who lived only three weeks. After Rome was liberated, Fellini and friends opened several 'Funny Face Shops' to draw caricatures for Allied soldiers.

1945–49   In 1945 Fellini met director Roberto Rossellini and became involved in the script for *Roma, città aperta* (*Rome, Open City*). In 1946 he worked as screenwriter and assistant director on *Paisà* (*Paisan*). In 1947 he wrote and acted in *Il miracolo* (*The Miracle*, Rossellini) and worked with director Alberto Lattuada on *Il delitto di*

Giovanni Episcopo. In 1948 he worked with Lattuada on *Senza pietà* and *Il mulino del Po* and with Pietro Germi on *In nome della legge.* In 1949 he worked as scriptwriter and assistant director with Rossellini on *Francesco, giullare di Dio.*

1950–65   In 1950 Fellini launched his directing career, making *Luci del varietà (Variety Lights)* with Lattuada. In 1952 came his first solo directing effort, *Lo sceicco bianco (The White Sheik).* In 1953 *I vitelloni* won the Silver Lion Award at the Venice Film Festival; this was the first of his films to receive international distribution. In 1954 *La strada* won the Silver Lion Award, Venice. In 1956 *La strada* began a three-year run in New York City and received an Academy Award and a New York Film Critics Award for Best Foreign Film. In 1957 *Le notti di Cabiria (Nights of Cabiria)* received an Academy Award as Best Foreign Film, and Giulietta Masina was voted Best Actress at Cannes. In 1960 *La dolce vita* received the Best Film Award at Cannes, and in 1961 it received a New York Film Critics Award and a National Board of Review citation as Best Foreign Film. In 1963 *Otto e mezzo (8½)* received an Academy Award and a New York Film Critics Award as Best Foreign Film, as well as a National Board of Review Award as Best Foreign Language Picture. The same year, Fellini was nominated for an Academy Award as Best Director. In 1965 *Giulietta degli Spiriti (Juliet of the Spirits)* received a New York Film Critics Award as Best Foreign Film, a National Board of Review Award for Best Foreign Language Story, and a Golden Globe Award for Best Foreign Language Film.

1965–present After 1965 Fellini found himself being 'reproduced' as an international cultural icon. *Nights of Cabiria* was adapted on Broadway as the musical *Sweet Charity,* with great success. In 1969 *Sweet Charity* was made into a movie starring Shirley MacLaine. In 1970 Fellini appeared as himself in American director Paul Mazursky's *Alex in Wonderland,* a homage of sorts to *8½.* In

1979 Bob Fosse directed *All That Jazz*, a film musical homage to *8½*. In 1980 Woody Allen referenced *8½* in *Stardust Memories*. In 1981, *8½* became the inspiration for the hit Broadway musical *Nine*. In the 1990s Frank Castorf adapted *City of Women* for the Berlin stage, and Fellini's work became the 'inspiration' for, among other things, episodes of the American TV shows *Northern Exposure* and *Third Rock from the Sun*. Most recently British director Peter Greenaway has cited Fellini in his *8½ Women*.

Fellini suffered a serious illness in 1967 that seemed to trigger a mid-life crisis, both personal and professional. He stopped working with Pinelli, Flaiano, and Rondi as his scriptwriters and turned instead to Bernardino Zapponi. A change in aesthetics and worldview was reflected in 1968 in *Toby Dammit* and in 1969 by *Fellini-Satyricon*. In 1971, *I clowns* (*The Clowns*) received a National Board of Review citation as Best Foreign Language Film. In 1974 *Amarcord* received a New York Film Critics Award for Best Motion Picture and an Academy Award and a National Board of Review Award for Best Foreign Language Film, and Fellini received the New York Critics Award for Best Direction. He also received lifetime achievement honours (along with René Clair) at Cannes. In 1979 Nino Rota, who composed the music for all of Fellini's films from *The White Sheik* through to *Orchestra Rehearsal*, died. In 1983 *E la nave va* (*And the Ship Sails On*) received a fifteen-minute ovation at its premiere, out of competition, at Venice.

In 1984, despite all his protestations against television, Fellini filmed TV commercials for Campari vermouth. In 1985 he became the first non-American to receive the Film Society of Lincoln Center's annual award for cinematic achievement. He was also awarded an honorary Golden Lion at Venice. In 1986 he filmed TV commercials for Barilla pasta. In 1987 *Intervista* was awarded a Special Prize at Cannes and the Audience Prize and Grand Prize at Moscow. In Brussels a panel of thirty professionals from eighteen European countries

named *8½* the best European film of all time and Fellini
the world's best director.

In 1992 Fellini filmed TV commercials for Italy's
Republican Party and Banco di Roma and was ranked
first in popularity in a *Sight and Sound* survey of international film directors. In 1993 he received an Academy
Award for Lifetime Achievement. On 31 October of the
same year, Fellini died. His death was followed five
months later by that of Giulietta Masina.

La Città delle donne/*The City of Women* (1980). Snaporaz is more interested in Katzone's sexual equipment than in his own wife Elena. MOMA

La Città delle donne/The City of Women (1980). The last major woman figure Snaporaz encounters in his dream – the inflated Madonna/soubrette, Saint/ Whore – a cultural cliché if ever there was one. Fellini Archive, Lilly Rare Book Library, Indiana University

Fellini's Casanova (1976). Casanova and the *bambola meccanica*. Academy of Motion Picture Arts and Sciences Library

Roma (1972). Nowhere is the signified of spirituality more hollowed out than in the clerical fashion show. MOMA

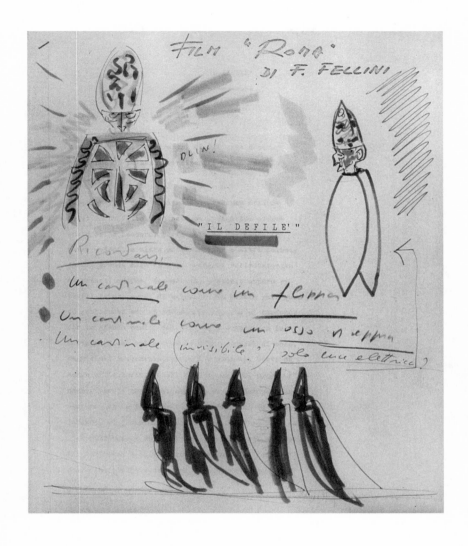

Roma (1972). Vestments made of mirrors and electric lights move of their own volition without anyone inside. Fellini Archive, Lilly Rare Book Library, Indiana University

VOCE

Le mitrie... La tiara... Il ca
mauro...

46. a 60 a·disposizione regia.
Ed ecco apparire, abbaglianti,
maestosi, vescovi e cardinali,
con immense vesti rosse, e al-
tissime mitrie, carichi di col
lane, tempestati di diamanti,e
anelli; alcuni sono altissimi
e ischeletriti, altri tozzi,
grassissimi come rospi, grotte
schi fra gli ornamenti splendi
di. Il coro aumenta di podero-
sità; fra l'incenso e i vesti-
ti così vistosi, s'è creato per
incanto un clima di alta cerimo
nia religiosa; sembra di assi-
stere a una messa solenne, o a
qualche altro grandioso rito
in San Pietro.

61.   entra,
Alla fine, su una portantina altissima,
portata a spalle da quattro sa-
cerdoti e circondata da chieri-
ci coi flabelli, entra un vec-
chissimo cardinale che tiene ab
to...

Roma (1972). The spectacularity of bejewelled ecclesiastical garments escalates to Fellini's quintessential visual representation of the hollow phallus within the religious realm. Fellini Archive, Lilly Rare Book Library, Indiana University

La Città delle donne/*The City of Women* (1980). Snaporaz umbilically hangs from his ideal Madonna-as-whore balloon woman. MOMA

Lo sceicco bianco/The White Sheik (1952). A brief appearance by a Chaplinesque Giulietta Masina underscores the performative nature of gender. MOMA

La dolce vita (1960). The opening shot subverts the opposition of present to past without violating documentary realism. MOMA

Toby Dammit (1968). The midnight run recapitulates the supercharged, suicidal male action/adventure imagery of the period. Fellini Archive, Lilly Rare Book Library, Indiana University

Amarcord (1973) opens on the circular space delineated by the town's cyclical celebration of the end of winter. MOMA

Amarcord (1973). The motif of the maze appears in *Amarcord* as paths shovelled on the piazza. MOMA

Ginger e Fred (1985). Pippo falls after Amelia, and Pipo must 'face the music and dance,' when electrical power and the audiovisual values of TV are restored. MOMA

Intervista (1987). Fellini plays 'Fellini' in a personal and highly idiosyncratic tribute to Cinecittà, the studio where the director spent most of his working life. MOMA

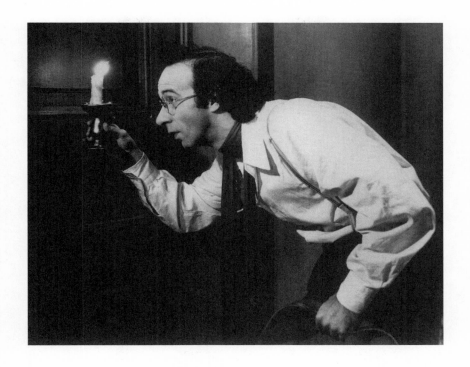

La voce della luna/The Voice of the Moon (1990). Ivo's fascination with the world 'beyond' – with the hole leading elsewhere – mirrors the regressive fantasy of a return to the maternal realm. MOMA

La voce della luna/The Voice of the Moon (1990). Participation in the hi-tech global village does not imply the acquisition of a more cosmopolitan outlook. MOMA

FEDERICO FELLINI:
CONTEMPORARY PERSPECTIVES

Introduction

MARGUERITE R. WALLER

My path leads to the creation of a fresh perception of the world. I decipher in a new way a world unknown to you.

– Dziga Vertov[1]

I don't think my films are misunderstood when they are accepted for different reasons ... This diversity of reaction doesn't mean that the objective reality of the film has been misunderstood. Anyway, there is no objective reality in my films, any more than there is in life.

– Federico Fellini[2]

Fellini: Film Form and Film Sense

If one were to search for an analogy, however inadequate, for Federico Fellini's distinctive way of deploying the cinematic image, one might come close with the recent cyber-novelty, virtual on-screen creatures called 'Artificial Life.'[3] These little electronic beings, 'living' out their 'lives' in cyberspace, have the power to challenge the very foundations of our philosophical beliefs. They are invented in the sense that they are computer generated; yet their programmers cannot foretell, nor can they control, the outcome of their programming. The programmer merely sets the stage, on which the properties of the AL program then emerge. AL has attracted enthusiasts not as an *object* of vision, but as an *optic* through which to challenge assumptions about what we non-digital creatures are and how we came to be. The more interactive our relations with AL, the better. The shapes on the screen grow more provocative the more provocatively the AL programs are written, and the programs can be written more provocatively the more there is on screen to respond to. The process is also recursive in multiple ways. The programs themselves are written to self-transform rather than to achieve a teleological endpoint (which complicates notions of likeness and unlikeness, identity and difference), while human subjects and AL figures change their significance in relation to one another. Thus, subject/object, seer/seen distinctions between human and computer screen come undone. As the computer-generated screen image interacts with the programmer/spectator's self-image, each in a sense produces the other in a spiralling interactive counterpoint.

The editors of this volume of contemporary perspectives on Federico Fellini have been motivated by their conviction that on a grand scale – comparable to that of early Soviet filmmakers such as Sergei Eisenstein and Dziga Vertov – Fellini has displayed a profound and original engagement with film as a technology of perception and tool of analysis.[4] Though his foci are different – not the complex interactions among matter, energy, motion, and production, or the brilliant mechanics of the human body, that excited the revolutionary Soviet filmmakers, but rather gender and sexuality, psyche and spirit, subject construction and cultural production – Fellini shares his predecessors' inventiveness in devising camera positions and editing strategies that are instantly recognizable as his own and at the same time startlingly unorthodox in their social, political, and ontological implications. Whether it is the *Man with a Movie Camera* montaging a new Moscow or Fellini and his crew trying to archaeologize a rhizomatic Rome, the camera involves us in seeing a new world and seeing it in a new way (Vertov 18).[5] Fellini's rigorous love affair with kinetic visual images as a medium of creative investigation has left us with a body of work whose transformative challenges film critics are just beginning to come to terms with. Fellini's films, as the essays in this volume testify, not only anticipate but also extend qualify, reconfigure, and even deconstruct the most innovative contemporary critical/theoretical discourses.

To offer an example, one of the most consequential ramifications of Fellini's particular relationship with his medium involves the status of his images. If one leaves behind mimetic paradigms of constructing/reading film images (as Frank Burke in 'Realism/Representation/ Signification' argues that Fellini did), the status of these images becomes impossible to determine in any stabilizing way, even as determining their status becomes of the essence to the films' characters and spectators. Wanda, Gelsomina, Cabiria, Marcello, Guido, Giulietta, Amelia (aka 'Ginger') and Pippo (aka 'Fred'), Marcello (again), and others all suffer to varying degrees from a lively uncertainty about what they are seeing and how they are seen. Spectators, if they are open to this paradigm shift, confront this same instability and the responsibilities it brings with it. Let me offer two brief examples of the logic and vast implications of Fellinian ambiguity.

In the elegant living room of Steiner, the excessively rational, intellectual friend and mentor of Marcello, the journalist in *La dolce vita*, a young woman of colour wearing a sari sits cross-legged on the floor singing and accompanying herself on the guitar. An old colonial anthropologist holds forth on the 'Oriental' woman as the essence of true femininity, hinting that his fieldwork has included intimate investigation in this area. Steiner and Marcello, oblivious to the feelings of Steiner's wife and Marcello's girlfriend, enthusiastically lionize the old man. Some moments later, Steiner's two young children, a boy and a girl, appear. Steiner interacts very directly with his son but very little with his daughter, whom he refers to in the third person. Steiner's differential response to his children also silences his daughter's own voice. He would dismiss the question she once posed to him – '*Chi è la madre del sole?*' (Who is the mother of the sun?) – by aestheticizing it as 'poetic' (and nonsensical), failing to hear in it, as we may, a challenge to his Olympian stance toward a messy world. Several beats later, Steiner and Marcello repair to the terrace to speak of their despair over the state of the world and of their own inability to work out a viable relationship to it. Meanwhile, the singer – for a few moments framed in the centre of the screen, begins a new song. As she sings the words 'look away' (in American-accented English), it becomes obvious that she is not Asian at all but rather African American, not 'Eastern' but rather a particularly loaded signifier of 'Western' culture. Furthermore, the words she is singing evoke another text in which a revolution in the seer's relationship to the seen is called for. This moment in *La dolce vita* knots intertextually with a tense passage in Dante's *Inferno*, Canto IX, in which Virgil orders Dante the pilgrim to turn away and close his eyes, and Dante the poet exhorts the reader to look beneath the 'veil' or 'screen' of his lines for an important '*dottrina*' or teaching.[6]

The hypnotic pacing and rich layering of Fellini's long, complex scene are *there* on the screen. Not present in any literal way, but not absent either, are the hypertextual links that one might begin to pursue between and among Orientalism, colonialism, Western constructions of gender and race, Oedipal family dynamics, the roots of U.S. economic and military dominance in the slave trade, the binarism of the Cold War (Steiner refers to threat of nuclear war as the reason for his alienation), bourgeois aesthetics, Canto IX of Dante's *Inferno*, and so on. Fellini here is avoiding explicitness, since any linear, hierarchical organization of these elements would support the version of subjectivity epitomized by the uncomprehending characters, Steiner and Marcello. However, if the spectator follows the sound cue to 'look away' from the two figures who are ostensibly the focus of the scene, a whole new logic displaces the authority of Steiner's and Marcello's perceptions and the legitimacy of their central position. For this new logic to take hold, the spectator's actions, which are really the issue here, may already involve operations such as allowing sound images equal status with visual images, a woman of colour equal status with white men, perceiving foreground and background as equally important, or performing some other concatenation of conceptual calisthenics. In this way the smallest and most casual fissure in the film's glamorous surface can lead not to an interior or secret subtext but rather to a metamorphic reconfiguration of its surface elements.[7] None of these elements is discarded in the process; it is just as important to see how Steiner and Marcello process the world as it is to free oneself from identifying with them. The 'meanings' of the scene begin to emerge, in part, from the differences between the characters' readings of their situation and the alternative readings that viewers piece together.

This highly contingent and unpredictable – but nevertheless readable – interactivity can be further deontologized if the viewer assumes an egalitarian relationship to the screen. Spectators are not engaged by Fellini's films as arbiters passing judgment on the screen figures; nor do the screen figures work narratively or figuratively as moral models or objects of desire. Though viewers often do watch Fellini's films in conventional ways, the disgruntled commentaries of many distinguished older critics attest to the films' power to frustrate such approaches.[8] By 1959 Fellini himself was saying: 'I believe that everyone has to find truth by himself ... I think it is immoral (in the true sense of the word) to tell a story that has a conclusion. Because you cut out the audience the moment you present a solution on the screen' (Harcourt 242). Characters like Maddalena, Emma, Sylvia, and even Marcello tend not to arrive at any sort of recognition or closure; instead they simply drop out of sight. A shocking exception is Steiner, the stony, detached (*distaccato*) father in *La dolce vita*, who kills his children and commits suicide. For the film's other diegetic characters, of course, Steiner's leap to a definitive ending leads only to more questions.

Not only Guido of *8½* or Giulietta of *Giulietta degli spiriti* but even the movie icon Anita Ekberg, the hyperfetishist Katzone of *La Città delle donne* (*The City of Women*), and the compulsive Casanova exist in a fundamentally fluid relationship to those around them, as the essays in this volume demonstrate. These characters are as free as Fellini's spectators to begin seeing and/or signifying differently (or not) than they had a moment before. The oscillations one finds among commentators concerning whether Fellini sees his art as 'salvational' are therefore entirely appropriate. This question keeps being posed, but cannot be answered definitively without destroying the circumstances that allow it to emerge (Deleuze 270). Thus, for example, *Fellini's Casanova* can equally well support both Van Watson's argument (in this volume) that Fellini's 'pallid Latin lover' 'leaves only a legacy of flesh' and Millicent Marcus's reading elsewhere of the aged Casanova as a 'figure for the artist onto whom Fellini cannot help but project all the anxieties and hopes of his creative calling' (*Filmmaking by the Book* 224). The real misreading of the film would be to force these two readers to agree.

A throwaway sequence near the beginning of *Ginger and Fred* facetiously, though precisely, clarifies what might be meant by 'salvation' and what filmmaking might have to do with it. Giulietta Masina, alias Amelia, alias 'Ginger,' has just arrived at the *Stazione Termini* in Rome for her appearance on the television program '*Ed ecco a voi*' when she is whisked away by a production assistant to a minivan equipped with an array of media and communication devices. Among these is a small-screen TV set tuned to the station on which she is to appear. A 'commercial' – really one of Fellini's own satiric *fegatelli* created expressly for the film, though not linked to it narratively – appears on the tiny screen positioned to the left of the production assistant's hand, which is impatiently thrumming on the dashboard. On this screen-within-the-screen a marionette Dante, shown in a wide shot, intones the opening line of the *Commedia*: '*Nel mezzo del cammin di nostra vita*' (In the middle of the journey of our life'). Without any perspectivizing of the sound, the second line, '*mi ritrovai per una selva oscura*' ('I found myself in a dark wood'), is accompanied by an exterior shot of the driver opening the door of the van and getting into the driver's seat. As he puts on and adjusts some headphones, we hear '*che la via diritta era smarrita* ('where the right way was lost'). Then, returning to the first framing, we see a close-up of the marionette wrist on the screen and

hear, 'but with my trusty compass-watch, which I had never abandoned,' followed by 'I quickly found the path again' as the TV set camera zooms out and tilts to a close-up of Dante's face. Throughout these
three shots, the sound of 'Dante's' voice in the commercial is overlaid
with both the diegetic sounds of the driver getting into the van and the
rather insistent 'urban bustle' music that has accompanied Amelia
since her arrival.

The effect on the rest of the film of these fleeting evocations of the
Commedia and of puppetry cannot in the end be calculated, but the
immediate implications are quite concrete. A watch organizes time, and
a compass organizes space, into precisely the kind of homogeneous,
measurable, griddable dimensionality that is required to construct and
maintain the sovereign subject. It is precisely this subject position that
Fellini's films are always at pains to decentre and – as several of this volume's author's persuasively argue – to transform. Clock time and Cartesian space, taken literally, imply the possibility of cognitive mastery –
broadly ironized here by the Dante caricature visibly dangling from
strings pulled by unseen hands – and support the image of a neutral,
individual consciousness. In the immediate context of the film we are
watching, both the homogeneity of time and space and the stable self-
identity of the subject are not merely challenged but manically obliterated. The insertion of the television images among the film images, to
begin with, disrupts the homogeneous space of the film screen. The
human hand is bigger than the entire *mise-en-scène* of the famous '*selva
oscura*,' and in a perverse reversal of the usual opposition of the 'flat'
television image to film's greater depth of field, the TV image leads the
eye in toward an indefinite darkness, while the hand on the dashboard
has a shallow depth of field.[9] When the scene shifts to the exterior of the
truck, that space too is complicated, on the one hand by the ironic synchronization of what is obviously an image of a city street with the
Dante puppet's voice talking about a dark wood, and on the other hand
by the doubling of the frame-within-a-frame motif. The characters looking out the windows of the van rhyme for a moment with the puppet on
the TV screen. When in the third shot the marionette 'Dante' finds his
way again with the help of his compass-watch, these disparate audiovisual spaces are suddenly and arbitrarily homogenized, the televisual
close-up of the marionette bringing it into scale with the hand on the
dashboard. As soon as the two spaces line up, the film characters, neatly
boxed in the van, proceed on their way. But in the visual punchline of
this quick and dirty comic strip game with space, the van travels hori-

zontally, right to left, between a huge billboard and a steaming pile of garbage bags. The billboard, suspended in the background, proclaims 'Roma pulita' ('A Clean Rome'), while the garbage takes up the entire foreground, frameline to frameline.

The director Guido discovered in *8½* that there was no role in his film for *pulizia e ordine* (cleanliness and order) – for the salvation from confusion he had fantasized that actress Claudia Cardinale would embody. A clean Rome, like masterable space, would be a groundless abstraction and a drastic reduction of the rich heterogeneity of urban, televisual, literary, and filmic spaces, not to mention psychic ones. *Pulizia e ordine* are constructions, which the Dante commercial relates with startling economy, not to the fulfilment but rather to the commodification of desire. Because he will never abandon his compass-watch, this Dante will never discover the unmasterable heterogeneity of his own position and will remain unaware of the strings orchestrating his movement – of the puppetry involved in the appearance of autonomous, self-determining consumerism. The rhyming of the human figures in the van with the Dante marionette extends the problematic of desire and subject construction to include Amelia/Ginger and the assorted human *sosie*, or look-alikes – including a transvestite 'Rita Hayworth' and the identical twin doubles of Lucio Dalla with whom she shares her ride.

Furthermore, this grouping is by no means accidental. It is not an example of what has sometimes been construed as the gratuitous inclusion of unusual, eccentric human figures in Fellini's films. Identical twins offer a concise metacommentary on the constructedness and intersubjectivity of identity. Uncannily both alike and different, their likeness is recognized *because* they are different; their difference is remarkable *because* they are so alike. Thus they neatly undo the self/other opposition that grounds stable, self-identitical identity. And as the name of the television show, '*Ed ecco a voi*' suggests, they offer as well a provocative reflection of untwinned selves, constructed just as relationally, if not as obviously so. The fact that the twins are, in turn, 'look-alikes' of a celebrity shows how this fluid interplay of categories of likeness and difference becomes fixed when some form of hierarchical power intervenes. In relation to the media star Lucio Dalla, the twins in the van become relegated to secondary, subordinate, status, mere signifiers of their more exalted signified. Dalla's celebrity – a commodified position crystallized out of its own complicated web of relations – obscures the nonself-identicalness of all three figures and sets up an ontological hierarchy that reduces the rich possibilities of intersubjective connection to the isolating one-way street of imitation and identification – the relation instantiated by commercials.[10] Yet neither the film's spectators nor, presumably, the twins themselves are condemned to follow the straight and narrow path charted by the compass-watch.

The transvestite or transsexual 'Rita Hayworth' trails a rich legacy of further conundra concerning national, ethnic, gender, and sexual subject positionings, extending those posed by Amelia and her partner Pippo's imitation of Rogers and Astaire in the 1940s and 1950s. Rita Hayworth, a.k.a. Rita Cansino and Margarita Carmen Cansino, already defied the logic of the media empire that made her an icon by the time her image on a movie poster played a pivotal role in Vittorio de Sica's *Ladri di biciclette* (*Bicycle Thief*). In *Ladri di biciclette* her image intertextually referenced not only America's cultural imperialism in Italy and South America after the Second World War (the film being advertised on the poster is Charles Vidor's *Gilda*, set in Argentina), but also Hayworth's own colonization by Hollywood. 'Discovered' as a Latin dancer by a Hollywood agent in a Tijuana nightclub in the early 1930s, she had also previously acted in Italian film. After two name changes and two years of painful electrolysis to raise her 'Latin' hairline, she became such a popular 'American' pin-up girl that her likeness 'graced the first hydrogen bomb' (Nericcio 534).[11] Fellini's analogy of 'Hayworth' to a male-to-female transvestite or transsexual (whose vocation in *Ginger e Fred* is to offer sexual relief to imprisoned males) thus pushes De Sica's take on political/cultural imperialism to some of its logical conclusions (Waller 259–60). What appears to be an affair between nation-states could be seen, more fundamentally, as an affair 'between men' (see Sedgwick's so-named study) that involves not just the deployment of sexual desire in the service of domination, but the constructedness of gender from the ground up. In this sense Paolina, the Rita Hayworth look-alike, is more 'real' than a 'real' woman. His/her masquerade as a woman is an accurate depiction of 'woman' as a 'male' construct designed to naturalize, eroticize, glamorize, and distract from other possibilities the constricted 'male' subject positions required by a 'masculinist' system of domination and control that in effect stunts and constrains all of its constitutive subjects (Tyler 42–3).

Dance, the artistic medium of Amelia and Pippo, aka Ginger and Fred, is quintessentially about shaping bodies and choreographing movement. As Millicent Marcus notes in her contribution, 'Fellini's

Ginger and Fred, or Postmodern Simulation Meets Hollywood Romance,' Fred Astaire was famous for insisting that the dance numbers in his films be integral to the development of the relationship between the partners. That Amelia and Pippo had to dance the dances of Fred Astaire and Ginger Rogers, that Pippo had to adopt the 'American' stage name 'Andrew Light' in order to dance Fred Astaire's dances, and that the couple were very successful performing as *Ginger e Fred* on the variety show circuit in postwar Italy, all point to the extremely intimate levels – physical, emotional, and psychological – on which the politics of identity and identification operate. But when Pippo is dancing Fred's dance with Amelia who is dancing Ginger's dance, Pippo and Amelia are not dancing together in the same sense that Fred and Ginger are. As with the Dante marionette and the *sosie*, the structures of relation, the puppet strings, that create the illusion on stage of the right path found or the romantic relationship consummated become more obvious. (When Pippo and Amelia finally do dance on television, Mastroianni makes Pippo actually look like a marionette jerkily performing at the end of a handful of strings.) If, in retrospect, one rereads Astaire and Rogers as themselves enactments of cultural choreographies they haven't authored and don't control, then ironically, the Italian imitators *Ginger e Fred*, like the Italian transvestite/transsexual 'Rita Hayworth,' upstage the authority and subvert the charisma of their illustrious 'originals.'[12]

The baroque 'sculpting in time' (see Tarkovsky's so-named study) involved in this or some other unpacking of the figures of *Ginger e Fred* has as little to do with homogeneous, linear clock time as Fellini's heterogeneous spaces have to do with Cartesian dimensionality. As I suggest in my reading of *La dolce vita*, Fellini does not oppose present and past (another version of the self/other or like/different opposition); he never depicts historical change in terms of stable subjects with stable, linear narratives. As Frank Burke demonstrates in this volume and elsewhere, in the later films this principle contributes richly to Fellini's highly original experiments in constructing the autobiographical subject, a key category – perhaps *the* key category – in the investigation of ontology and desire ('salvation') (Burke, 'Changing the Subject').

Fellini and New Perspectives in Cinema Studies

If intellectual and affective freedom lies for Fellini off-road, within the confused tangle of images, relationships, and modes of perception that escape (temporarily or definitively) from the time and space of phallocentric organization, this 'freedom' radically challenges, as we noted earlier, the viewing habits – not to mention the ontologies – of most spectators. In this regard, I would like to call attention to the intersubjective, intertextual dimension of the essays in this volume. There has been no single conference of which these are the proceedings; however, two annual conferences have provided an unusually congenial environment for the emergence of an intergenerational group of scholars who have formally and informally supported one another in taking on the kinds of challenges posed by Fellini's filmmaking. The Purdue Conference on Romance Languages, Literatures, and Film, hosted every October by the Purdue University Romance Languages Department since 1988 and the American Association of Italian Studies (AAIS) annual conference, held each spring at a different host campus, have provided the enthusiastic, well-informed, and constructively critical audiences that have emboldened many of the contributers to this volume to shed their own orthodoxies and take ever greater risks. The Indiana University conference 'European Cinemas, European Societies 1895–1995,' organized in 1995 by Peter Bondanella, who created the Fellini archive at Indiana University's Lilly Rare Books Library, also did much to foster the recognition of postwar Italian cinema in general and Fellini's cinema in particular as among the most fertile cultural labours of the twentieth century.[13]

The outpouring in 1990s North America of 'contemporary perspectives' on Fellini has seemed disjunct from the pioneering essays of the 1950s and 1960s that secured Fellini's critical reputation. What is surprising is the relative paucity of work on Fellini in the theoretically oriented 1970s. Fellini's filmmaking before, during, and after the 1970s now seems conceptually well ahead of its time; yet his post-$8\frac{1}{2}$ films have been regarded – when they are discussed at all – as romantic, melodramatic, and otherwise reactionary (Burke, 'Changing the Subject' 276; Fellini's Films 311). Christian Metz's essay 'Mirror Construction in Fellini's $8\frac{1}{2}$' (1966) remains a lonely exception, and even Metz, while describing the hall-of-mirror effects of the film itself, does not contextualize that film theoretically. The French philosopher Gilles Deleuze finally broke the mould with his Cinéma 1: L' Image-mouvement (1983) and Cinéma 2: L'Image-temps (1985), though English-language film theory has been slow in registering the impact of Deleuze's attentiveness to film as a philosophical medium.[14]

In 'Fellini and the Crystals of Time,' a compilation drawn by Peter

Bondanella and Cristina Degli-Esposti from *Cinéma 1* and *Cinéma 2* for their invaluable 1993 volume *Perspectives on Federico Fellini*, Deleuze returns to the scene of André Bazin's defence of *La strada* from the attacks of the *Cinema nuovo* Marxists, and to the debate over neorealism. Deleuze's argument also responds implicitly to the question of why 1970s film theory massively ignored Fellini's project. Agreeing up to a point with Bazin's description of neorealist film as aiming at 'an always ambiguous, to be deciphered real,' Deleuze goes on, astonishingly, to hail the innovativeness of neorealism's film language as 'perhaps as important as ... impressionism' (Bondanella and Degli-Esposti 261). For Deleuze, what characterizes neorealist film is what he calls the 'crisis of the action-image' and the birth of a new breed of signs that extend perception not into action but rather into thought. In other words, the optical and sound situations of neorealism do not construct characters who move and respond to movements in the environments they inhabit, as in traditional realism. Instead, characters are constructed as themselves spectators by situations that exceed their motor capacities and thus allow (or force) them to see and hear in ways not subject to the habits of response or action: 'This is a cinema of the seer and no longer of the agent.' In these circumstances the distinction, though not the interaction, between subjective and objective loses its importance: 'We no longer know what is imaginary or real, physical or mental, in the situation, not because they are confused, but because we do not have to know and there is no longer even a place from which to ask. It is as if the real and the imaginary were running after each other, as if each was being reflected in the other, around a point of indiscernibility' (265).

The encounter in *Giulietta degli spiriti* between Giulietta and her exaggeratedly taller, more glamorous mother and sisters, all wearing excessively wide-brimmed hats, is a small case in point. These family figures are clearly to some extent Giulietta's projections, but *for that very reason* they tell us (and her) something about who Giulietta is – about the intersection of cultural and familial influences at which she has found herself. At the same time, deducing something about her position offers us (and her) an entrance into the palimpsest of glamorous images (and images of glamour); these offer in turn a somewhat different take on her position, and so on, as with Artificial Life. Deleuze's crystal metaphor refers to these entrances – to Fellini's visually fascinating spectacles as they are constructed in relation to their spectatorial mirror images, and to the coalescence of these seed crystals into the cinematic sequences of larger crystals.

In *Cinéma 1* Deleuze describes the context of the crisis of the action-image ideologically as well as historically. He speculates that at the end of the Second World War, de Gaulle's France identified itself, however conflictually and ambiguously, with the victors; meanwhile, Italy, not quite defeated in the sense that Germany was, but certainly not part of the winner's circle, could point 'to a resistance and a popular life underlying oppression, although one without illusion' (211). Thus while French cinema at first 'kept itself within the framework of a traditional action-image,' acting in the service of conventional nationalism with its conventional structures of identification and conventional structurations of time and space, Italian cinema had a different kind of story to tell. For its different kind of telling, it developed a new type of *récit* capable of including the elliptical and the unorganized. This different cinematic language questioned 'all the accepted facts of the American tradition' (211–12). A restructuring of space and time followed suit: 'There is no longer a vector or line of the universe which extends and links up the events of *The Bicycle Thief* ... Fellini's *I Vitelloni* testifies not only to the insignificance of events, but also to the uncertainty of the links between them ... Neorealism makes any-space-whatevers proliferate – urban cancer, undifferentiated fabrics, pieces of waste-ground – which are opposed to the determined spaces of the old realism' (212).

What appears within this cinematic horizon could not possibly be 'raw reality' (which would require quite a different set of coordinates), but might be understood as 'its understudy, the reign of cliches, both internally and externally, in people's heads and hearts as much as in the whole of space' (212). Even Fellini's first films, Deleuze points out, are put 'under the sign of manufacture' with all their 'nightclubs, music halls and circuses and all the jingles which console or despair' (212–13).

Deleuze sees a similar mutation of the cinematic image occurring around 1958 with the French New Wave, and around 1968 with the New German Cinema; but for him these two cases – along with the case of Alfred Hitchcock – never negotiated the transition from 'a negative or parodic critical consciousness' (214) to the birth of the new image, which he locates in postwar Italian cinema. In Deleuzian terms, cinema 'had to become truly thought and thinking,' its new mental dimension not the completion or fulfilment of conventional cinema but rather 'a new substance' (215). This metamorphosis of the image threatens much more than identifiable targets like Hollywood hegemony. Its effects ramify indefinitely in every direction, absorbing into its novel geographies not only the cinema characters but also the assorted subjectivities of cinema spectators. It follows from Deleuze's understanding of postwar Italian cinema as a new mode and medium of thought that film theory – deeply absorbed in a linguistically oriented critical deconstruction of dominant cultural institutions (massively shaped by five hundred years of print culture) – has been unprepared for this new mutation, which 'smashes the whole system' (215). As Frank Burke notes in our Preface, it was not until the mid-1980s that the two of us (unknown to each other) began to explore the ramifications of Fellini's metamorphosis of the image. The oldest essays in this collection, both published in 1989–90, are the early fruits of that labour.

In her study of Fellini's antifascist exploitation of the gap between standard Italian and dialect, 'Memory, Dialect, Politics: Linguistic Strategies in 'Fellini's *Amarcord*,' Cosetta Gaudenzi in her contribution to this volume suggests that the situation of Deleuze's Fellini is akin to that of Deleuze's and Félix Guattari's Kafka. Deleuze and Guattari have characterized Kafka's writing as a 'minor literature' (as opposed-not to 'major' but rather to something more like 'national'), which (in Gaudenzi's words) refuses 'to submit to an external entity that would dictate the choices, tastes, and life of its people.' Deleuze and Guattari argue that as a Yiddish-speaking Jew living in Prague and writing in German, Kafka was profoundly alienated from the politics of mimesis and the aesthetics of reference. D. Emily Hicks has usefully compared 'minor literature' to what is becoming known in North America as 'border writing' – writing that emphasizes the differences in reference codes between two or more cultures and the multiplicity of languages within any single language: 'Border writers give the reader the opportunity to practice multidimensional perception and nonsynchronous memory ... by choosing a strategy of translation rather than representation, border writers ultimately undermine the distinction between original and alien culture' (xxiii).

This notion of minor or border writing offers yet another lens through which to view Fellini's absence from Anglo-European film theory in the 1970s. The structuralist-inspired French film theorists, the British theorists affiliated with the journal *Screen*, and many of the founders of the academic discipline of film studies in North America focused mainly on excessively monocultural Hollywood film and on the Oedipal subject positions and modes of pleasure described by the universalizing interpretive discipline of psychoanalysis. Freudian and

Lacanian psychoanalysis, inflected by the imperial culture of Haps-
burg Vienna and the patriarchal, centrist legacies of the French empire,
tend to promote one subjectivity, however fractured, as normative and
prescriptive. Differences from that norm are acknowledged only as
subordinate to, or departing from it, and pathologized, even (or especially) in the case of women and children. The task of the progressive,
psychoanalytically sophisticated film theorist, then, became to discover in illuminating detail, how film does the same. Ironically, that is,
psychoanalysis came to be used to pathologize film texts – even cinema itself – rather than being staged in dialogue with film or as an
object of cinematic inquiry. Perhaps because of the relatively good fit
between Hollywood film and Freudian theory (an astonishing number
of Austro-Hungarians were involved in the founding of the major studios), theorists have not looked to film as a discourse that might denat-
uralize or dehegemonize the psychoanalytic subject.[15] Postwar Italian
cinema and other great cinemas of the world have concomitantly had
to be 'minoritized' (Sedgwick, *Epistemology* 1), positioned conceptually
as the exception – as 'art films' or 'foreign films' in relation to the 'real'
films being made by or in the Oedipal language of Hollywood.

In Deleuze and Guattari's different sense of 'minor,' work like Fellini's makes the universalizing language of Hollywood cinema seem
monocultural and provincial, and challenges film theory to examine its
own gaps and exclusions. With Gaudenzi, Van Watson in his essay
'Fellini and Lacan: The Hollow Phallus, the Male Womb, and the
Retying of the Umbilical' sets the stage for that examination with a
thorough and precise reading of Fellini's corpus as a comprehensive
challenge to the normative authority of Lacanian subject construction.

Carlo Testa's essay on *Intervista*, 'Cinecittà and *America*: Fellini Interviews Kafka,' concretizes the analogy between the position of Kafka,
the anti-*Bildungsroman* Czech writer, and Fellini, the anti-Oedipal
Italian filmmaker, and reminds us that Fellini was the first to see the
Prague writer's situation as profoundly similar to his own. Testa
points out that Fellini read Kafka passionately and in a sense adapted
Kafka's novel *America* to the screen despite (or with the help of) profound differences of culture, language, period, and style. The space
that Testa leaves blank in his diagram of the structure of *Intervista*, to
indicate that the director-within-the-film ('Fellini') never gets around
to shooting his film version of Kafka's *America*, remains empty only in
the sense of Watson's term 'hollow phallus.' The whole of *Intervista* is
Fellini's film version of Kafka's text, in the form (appropriately) of an

'interview' – a genre that has no author. Though the interviewer's desires and frames of reference inevitably influence the selection of issues and the discourse into which the exchange becomes interpolated, the interviewer does not speak for the one interviewed, but collaborates in the creation of a space within which the other voice can emerge. Furthermore, the interviewer and the interviewee need not understand one another particularly well. We never find out what the female director of the Japanese documentary crew interviewing Fellini makes of the visit to the villa of Anita Ekberg. Though the young Japanese documentarist speaks passable Italian, she remarks of Ekberg, 'There are no women like her in Japan.' This, as Áine O'Healy notes, is the deuniversalizing point: Ekberg's incarnation of beauty is culturally specific, in this case decidedly Western (and in fact northern rather than Mediterranean). Testa concludes that to complete or even to begin the Kafka film requires cutting across 'the conventional barriers of narration ... abolishing the boundaries of time and self that artificially separate life from life and plot from plot.' Who is interviewing whom need not and cannot finally be decided; what matters is that the voices and images engage one another and that the patterns of likeness and difference that emerge be honoured.

Rigorously attuned to such patterning in *Intervista*, and orienting herself epistemologically to find it meaningful, O'Healy in 'Interview with the Vamp: Deconstructing Femininity in Fellini's Final Films' spotlights the cultural and temporal limits of the figure of Anita Ekberg as a signifier of ideal femininity in the West. O'Healy begins with the paradox that 'beautiful' women become icons of Womanhood both despite and because of their *unlikeness* to other, ordinary women. She then calls attention to the non-universality of this iconography, which does not 'translate' into contemporary Japanese culture. Linking these two dimensions of unlikeness with a third – the most fundamental – O'Healy points out that Fellini's Ekberg does not resemble even herself. Her younger and older selves operate catachrestically, subverting each other's ontology, when the film 'daringly and unusually' deploys the actress as both feminine ideal and female grotesque. Significantly, in O'Healy's complex analysis here of yet another crucial subversion of oppositions between past and present, subject and object, it is the separate, identifiable figure of the director who disappears. Ekberg, however imperfect, remains available to the camera, while Fellini disappears into the conceptual black hole of a patriarchal subject position whose projections are collapsing in on themselves.

O'Healy, Gaudenzi, and Dorothée Bonnigal all link Fellini's interest in constructions of gender with the history, ideology, and aesthetics of fascism. Bonnigal draws on Millicent Marcus's concept of a Fellinian 'hyperfilm' – a bounded but infinite intertext made up of all Fellini's films – to read *Amarcord* as an evocation of the passageway to maturity of Fellini's cinematic subject. Fellini's itinerary, like Dante's, lies through the personal, the political, and the aesthetic, and centrally involves a meditation on how memory works in this universe.[16] 'Memories and the act of remembering become indistinguishable' when present and past are not opposed. Strategies different from 'othering' them are found for coming to terms with the claustrophobias of adolescent masculinity, the fascist era, provincial life, and the artificiality of cinema.

Gaudenzi is also concerned with memory, politics, and hegemonic enclosure. In her essay on *Amarcord* she shows Fellini brilliantly deploying the Romagnolo dialect to parody both fascist Rome and capitalist Hollywood. She argues that Fellini employs witty and subversive heteroglossia in the film to disrupt sites of cultural unification – an approach with close parallels to the decolonizing linguistic strategies of Pasolini. These sites range from school education (notably the history class) to the *commune*'s offering of 'La Gradisca' to the *principe* visiting the Grand Hotel, the parallel between the two not being accidental.

In her essay on *Lo sceicco bianco*, 'When in Rome, Do As the Romans Do? Federico Fellini's Problematization of Femininity,' Virginia Pichietti presents Fellini as an astute and precocious gender theorist. Drawing on feminist masquerade theory, she delineates the socialization into femininity of *Lo sceicco bianco*'s protagonist Wanda, who finds herself compelled to assume personas scripted for her by everyone from her new husband to the Pope. The friction between her masks becomes the film's point of departure for a critique of a social system diffused through both 'high' and 'low' culture – a social system enforced no less by the torrid *fotoromanzi* to which Wanda is addicted than by the Vatican, with whose authority her husband identifies.

According to Helen Stoddart, Fellini extends his search for different dialects and textualities well beyond the elements that can be captured on celluloid. In her vertiginous reading of *I clowns*, 'Subtle Wasted Traces: Fellini and the Circus,' she contends that the performative mode of the circus is for Fellini not an analogue for what happens on the screen, but rather – and much more challengingly – an all-important collaborator in the creation of non-binary 'border machines,' to borrow Hicks's term (xxvi). Mikhail Bakhtin and Walter Benjamin, the theorist of early modern carnival and the theorist of late modern mechanical reproduction, encounter each other in the pages of Stoddart's exploration of another Fellinian border region – the space between the live performance art of circus clowns and the different kind of simultaneous 'living and creating' of filmmaking. It is their fundamental incompatibility that is significant, Stoddart stresses – the impossibility of having or doing both clowning and filmmaking at the same time. Yet in this space ambivalently of pathos and insight, the film image manages something like the evanescence of the clown act, productively disabling the trope of director as *auteur* and metamorphosing the film images into *momenti mori* of their own production.

Christopher Sharrett in his '"Toby Dammit," Intertext, and the End of Humanism' sees Fellini as at heart, a frustrated humanist. His reading of the pivotal 1968 short film 'Toby Dammit' though, also considers the director's creative involvement with the genres and signification practices of popular culture. Here the 'horror picture' serves as a framework for a meditation on the failure of Fellini's own filmmaking to 'awaken the spectator to the tricks of the cinema, so enamored is s/he of all that is "Fellini."' Part of an anthology of Edgar Allan Poe tales, mostly directed by B-movie master Roger Corman, 'Toby Dammit,' Sharrett argues, is so hyperbolically Fellini that it becomes its own caricature. Sharrett's subtle unpacking of the film's simultaneous indulgence and criticism resonates intriguingly with Millicent Marcus's discussion of the double-stranded *Ginger and Fred*.

Marcus's apt and very productive metaphor – the 'hyperfilm' – encompasses these and the many other border regions given substance by Fellini's life work. Marcus characterizes the hyperfilm as 'an elevated or heightened film' that operates at 'a relatively high level of abstraction' as a kind of conceptual matrix within which to read the individual films. Comparable, I would suggest, to Deleuze's notion of a 'cinema of thought and thinking,' this matrix enables Marcus to locate a theoretically – and perhaps theologically – significant chiastic relationship in *Ginger and Fred* between the story of Amelia's and Pippo's romance and the film's critique of postmodern culture. These two strands have more often been read as incompatible rival elements, but in Marcus's reading they embody Fellini's distinctive movement *across* (in this case) parody and vitality and (in general) genres, genders, conceptual planes, and signifying media. Marcus's notion of the 'hyperfilm,' unlike the entropic 'hypertext' currently instantiated by the World Wide Web, allows and calls for ever more richly recursive and generative acts of spectatorship. A closer analogue than the Web might be the 'greater language' evoked for Walter Benjamin by the relationship between a translation (corresponding to Fellinian spectatorship) and its original: 'A translation, instead of resembling the meaning of the original, must lovingly and in detail incorporate the original's mode of signification, thus making both the original and the translation recognizable as fragments of a greater language' (78).

The editors would like to extend Marcus's metaphor to encourage our readers to engage these essays, too, not only in their specificity but also as fields of (inter)activity. As the metaphor of Artificial Life suggests, readers should feel free to traverse chapters in any order that is productive, and to avail themselves freely of the agendas, methodologies, and epistemologies offered here to construct different configurations and new intertexts that foster the realization of their own critical/creative purposes. Among these may be, and is for us, giving Fellini (and Italian film generally) a more central role in academic film studies. Dudley Andrew has recently described an 'identity crisis' (350) in the field, related, one might surmise, to Deleuze's 'crisis of the action image.' Fellini's cinema emerges from the midst of such moments – compounded of the personal, political, conceptual, spiritual, and artistic – and his films offer an incomparable 'virtual arena' in which to make our way from crisis to the production of new images of cinematic thought and thinking.

Notes

1 Vertov 18.
2 From an interview with Gideon Bachman, quoted by Peter Harcourt (253).
3 Artificial Life has been described by Sherry Turkle as the discipline of building electronic organisms and systems that would be considered alive if found in nature. Still in its infancy (so to speak), AL was initially devised by biologist Richard Dawkins to illustrate evolutionary principles. He developed a program to dramatize how simple structures could evolve into something quite different from an original random form, and was taken aback by the complexity of the organisms that emerged on his computer screen (Turkle, 149–52).
4 In *Kino-Eye: The Writings of Dziga Vertov*, Annette Michelson has assembled and introduced an excellent collection of Vertov's still underappreciated writings on the moving picture optic.

5 I borrow the term 'rhizomatic' from Gilles Deleuze and Félix Guattari, who borrow it from biology to describe a concept of organization that is not centred. Rhizomes, such as the potato, can give rise to roots, flowers, and leaves, but the multiplicity of the contents of the potato itself is not a multiplicity based on sameness and difference. Thus, 'There are no points or positions in a rhizome ... There are only lines,' and 'a mulitiplicity has neither subject nor object, only determinations, magnitudes, and dimensions that cannot increase in number without the multiplicity changing in nature (the laws of combination therefore increase in number as the multiplicity grows' (A Thousand Plateaus 8). The affinities between Fellini's cinema and Deleuze and Guattari's 'anti-Oedipal' theorizing are striking, and are taken up in greater detail by Deleuze in his two-volume work on film as philosophy, Cinema 1, The Movement Image and Cinema 2: The Time Image.

6 In response to a threat by the Furies that Medusa will come and turn the pilgrim to stone, aborting his journey, Virgil turns Dante around and covers the pilgrim's eyes with his own hands (Inferno IX: 58–63).

7 On this level too, Fellini seems to be following the example of Inferno IX. See John Freccero's 'Medusa: The Letter and the Spirit.'

8 Peter Harcourt, for example, characterized Fellini in 1966 as 'a great muddle-headed irrationalist with very strong feelings and no clear thought' (243). 'Much as I respond with enormous pleasure to nearly everything that he has produced ... he is a director of uncertain control over the many elements that his mind ... can with such energy invent' (250).

9 Film images' constant variations in size and scale always threaten the illusion of spatial homogeneity, but the threat is generally domesticated by narrative and continuity editing and by the simple fact that we receive the images sequentially rather than simultaneously.

10 Anne Friedberg discusses more fully the ideological operations of identification in the context of film in 'A Denial of Difference: Theories of Cinematic Identification.'

11 I am deeply indebted here to William Nericco's brilliant discussion of the figure of Rita Hayworth in American film and culture in his article, 'Sordid Meditations on What Might Occur if Frantz Fanon, Rosario Castellanos, Jacques Derrida, Gayatri Spivak and Sandra Cisneros Asked Rita Hayworth Her Name: THEORYCELEBRITY – SHAME.' The actress's appearance under the name Rita Cansino in Harry Lachman's Dante's Inferno (1935) is noted by Amilcare Iannucci (forthcoming) in 'A Century of Dante at the Movies.' For more on the figure of Rita Hayworth in Italian cinema, see Waller, 'Decolonizing the Screen: From Ladri di biciclette to Ladri di saponette.'

12 Gilles Deleuze and Félix Guattari deploy the same puppetry metaphor in the same abyssal way as they pursue their explication of the 'rhizome.' 'Puppet strings, as a rhizome or multiplicity, are tied not to the supposed will of an artist or puppeteer but to a multiplicity of nerve fibers, which form another puppet in other dimensions connected to the first' (*A Thousand Plateaus* 8).

13 See also Bondanella's *Perspectives on Federico Fellini*, co-edited with Cristina Degli-Esposti, and his extensive historical/critical scholarship on Italian cinema, including *Italian Cinema: From Neorealism to the Present* and *The Cinema of Federico Fellini*. The superb scholarly, collegial, and pedagogical example of Millicent Marcus, author of the *Italian Film in the Light of Neorealism* and *Filmmaking by the Book*, has infused both the Purdue and AAIS conferences, directly and indirectly inspiring many of the essays in this volume.

14 David Rodowick's study of Deleuze's film books, *Gilles Deleuze's Time Machine*, was published in 1997.

15 Theoretical studies that pathologize film include Laura Mulvey's deservedly well-known but overused 'Visual Pleasure and Narrative Cinema' Teresa de Lauretis's ground-breaking *Alice Doesn't* and *Technologies of Gender*, and Kaja Silverman's interdisciplinary *The Subject of Semiotics*, and *The Acoustic Mirror: The Female Voice in Psychoanalysis and Cinema*. There are many others.

Amy Ziering Kofman, on the other hand, sets up a mutually illuminating dialogue between Hitchcock and Freud in 'Psycholanalysis on the Couch: Hitchcock's *The Birds*' (unpublished ms.).

16 Like Bonnigal, Amilcare Iannucci notes that the first film the young Fellini saw was Guido Brignone's *Maciste all'Inferno* (1926). Iannucci, building on Ben Lawton and Gian Piero Brunetta, shows convincingly how deeply Fellini throughout his career linked Dante and cinema. The intertextual links and interpretive possibilities suggested by this relationship promise richly to engage scholars in both Dante studies and film studies as Fellini's range and depth as a visual philosopher begin to emerge more fully ('A Century of Dante at the Movies').

References

Andrew, Dudley. 'The "Three Ages" of Cinema Studies and the Age to Come.' *PMLA* 115.3 (2000): 341–51.

Benjamin, Walter. 'The Task of the Translator.' *Illuminations*. Trans. Hannah Arendt. New York: Schocken Books, 1969. 69–82.

Bondanella, Peter, *The Cinema of Federico Fellini*. Foreword by Federico Fellini. Princeton: Princeton UP, 1992.

– ed. *Italian Cinema: From Neorealism to the Present*. New York: Ungar, 1983. 2nd ed. New York: Continuum, 1990.

– ed. *Federico Fellini: Essays in Criticism*. New York: Oxford UP, 1978.

Bondanelle, Peter, and Cristina Degli-Esposti, eds. *Perspectives on Federico Fellini*. New York: G.K. Hall, 1993.

Brunetta, Gian Piero. *Storia del cinema italiano, 1895–1945*. 4 vols. Rome: Editore Riuniti, 1993.

Burke, Frank. 'Fellini: Changing the Subject.' *Film Quarterly* 43.1 (1989): 36–48. Reprinted in Bondanella and Degli-Esposti. 275–92.

– *Fellini's Films*. New York: Twayne Publishers, 1996.

Dante Alighieri. *The Divine Comedy of Dante Alighiere: Inferno*. Trans. Allen Mandelbaum. New York: Bantam Books, 1982.

De Lauretis, Teresa. *Alice Doesn't: Feminism, Semiotics, Cinema*. Bloomington: Indiana UP, 1984.

– *Technologies of Gender: Essays on Theory, Film, and Fiction*. Bloomington and Indianapolis: Indiana UP, 1987.

Deleuze, Gilles. *Cinema 1: The Movement-Image*. Trans. Hugh Tomlinson and Barbara Habberjam. Minneapolis: U of Minnesota P, 1986. Trans. of *Cinéma 1: L'Image-mouvement*. Paris: Les Editions de Minuit, 1983.

– *Cinema 2: The Time-Image*. Minneapolis: U of Minnesota P, 1989. Trans. of *Cinéma 2: L'Image-temps*. Paris: Les Editions de Minuit, 1985.

– ['Fellini and the Crystals of Time.'] *Perspectives on Federico Fellini*. Ed. Bondanella and Degli-Esposti. 260–74.

Deleuze, Gilles, and Felix Guattari. *Kafka: Toward a Minor Literature*. Trans. Dana Polan. Minneapolis: University of Minnesota Press, 1986.

– *A Thousand Plateaus: Capitalism and Schizophrenia*. Trans. Brian Massumi. Minneapolis: U of Minnesota P, 1987.

Fellini, Federico. 'Interview with Gideon Bachmann.' *Film: Book 1*. Ed. Robert Hughes. New York: Grove Press, 1959. Quoted in Harcourt, 'The Secret Life of Federico Fellini.'

– 'Interview with Gideon Bachmann.' *Cinéma 65*. Numero 99 (Septembre/ Octobre). Quoted in Harcourt, 'The Secret Life of Federico Fellini.'

Freccero, John. 'Medusa: The Letter and the Spirit.' *Dante: The Poetics of Conversion*. Ed. Rachel Jacoff. Cambridge: Harvard UP, 1986. 119–35.

Friedberg, Anne. 'A Denial of Difference: Theories of Cinematic Identification.'

Psychoanalysis and Cinema. Ed. E. Ann Kaplan. New York and London: Routledge, 1990. 36–45.

Gabler, Neal. *An Empire of Their Own: How the Jews Invented Hollywood*. New York: Anchor Books/Doubleday, 1988.

Harcourt, Peter. 'The Secret Life of Federico Fellini.' *Federico Fellini: Essays in Criticism*. Ed. Peter Bondanella. New York: Oxford UP, 1978. 239–53. Reprinted from *Film Quarterly* 19.3 (1966): 4–13.

Hicks, D. Emily. *Border Writing: The Multidimensional Text*. Minneapolis: U of Minnesota P, 1991.

Iannucci, Amilcare. 'A Century of Dante at the Movies.' *Dante, Cinema, and Television*. Ed. Amilcare Iannucci. Toronto: U of Toronto P (forthcoming).

Lawton, Ben.'Fellini and the Literary Tradition.' *Perspectives on Federico Fellini*. Ed. Bondanella and Degli-Esposti. 191–202.

Marcus, Millicent. *Italian Film in the Light of Neorealism*. Princeton, New Jersey: Princeton UP, 1986.

– *Filmmaking by the Book*: *Italian Cinema and Literary Adaptation*. Baltimore: Johns Hopkins UP, 1993.

Metz, Christian. 'Mirror Construction in Fellini's *8½*.' *Film Language: A Semiotics of the Cinema*. Trans. Michael Taylor. New York: Oxford UP, 1974. 228–34. Reprinted in Bondanella, ed. *Federico Fellini: Essays in Criticism*. 130–6.

Mulvey, Laura. 'Visual Pleasure and Narrative Cinema.' *Visual and Other Pleasures*. Bloomington and Indianapolis: Indiana UP, 1989.

Nericcio, William. 'Sordid Meditations on What Might Occur if Frantz Fanon, Rosario Castellanos, Jacques Derrida, Gayatri Spivak and Sandra Cisneros Asked Rita Hayworth Her Name: THEORYCELEBRITYSHAME.' *Romance Languages Annual* 3. 1992. 531–40.

Rodowick, D.N. *Gilles Deleuze's Time Machine*. Durham, NC: Duke UP, 1997.

Sedgwick, Eve Kosofsky. *Between Men: English Literature and Male Homosocial Desire*. New York: Columbia UP, 1992.

– *Epistemology of the Closet*. Berkeley: U of California P, 1990.

Silverman, Kaja. *The Acoustic Mirror: The Female Voice in Psychoanalysis and Cinema*. Bloomington and Indianapolis: Indiana UP, 1988.

– *The Subject of Semiotics*. New York: Oxford UP, 1983.

Tarkovsky, Andrey. *Sculpting in Time: Reflections on the Cinema*. Trans. Kitty Hunter-Blair. Austin: U of Texas P, 1986.

Tyler, Carole-Anne. 'Boys Will Be Girls: The Politics of Gay Drag.' *Inside/Out: Lesbian Theories, Gay Theories*. Ed. Diana Fuss. New York and London: Routledge, 1991. 32–70.

Turkle, Sherry. *Life on the Screen: Identity in the Age of the Internet*. New York: Simon and Schuster, 1995.

Vertov, Dziga. *Kino-Eye: The Writings of Dziga Vertov.* Trans. Kevin O'Brien. Ed. and Intro. Annette Michelson. Berkeley: U of California P, 1984.

Waller, Marguerite R. 'Decolonizing the Screen: From *Ladri di biciclette* to *Ladri di saponette.*' *Revisioning Italy: National Identity and Global Culture.* Ed. Beverly Allen and Mary Russo. Minneapolis: U of Minnesota P, 1997. 253–74.

Ziering Kofman, Amy. 'Psychoanalysis on the Couch: Alfred Hitchcock's *The Birds*' (unpublished manuscript), 1990.

1

Federico Fellini: Reality/Representation/Signification

FRANK BURKE

Editors' note: We include this essay, first published in 1989, because it served as one of the inaugurating moments in the discussion of Fellini and postmodernity. It was not intended to map out the terrain for the remainder of the volume. In fact something like the reverse occurred in that we decided to include the essay to complement all the other contributions, after they had been selected. Because of the essay's historical function, there has been no attempt to update it theoretically, nor to make it accord with Burke's recent book-length study of Fellini (see Burke, *Fellini's Films*). The principal changes are a more extensive analysis of *Intervista*, which had not received North American distribution at the time the essay was written, and a discussion of *The Voice of the Moon*, which had not yet been released.

To put my title in perspective, let me briefly hypothesize, somewhat after both Fredric Jameson and Jean Baudrillard, a continuum from reality to representation to signification, using notions now commonplace in poststructural semiotic critique. Traditional aesthetics has tended to place art and language in direct relation to the real, via concepts such as mimesis and representation. Traditional language theory, along with aesthetics, has posited a relationship based on reference, in which the word/artwork is the sign and the real its referent. Within a referential relationship, the word/artwork represents the real. In the past several decades, notions of the real and the referent have tended to recede, and the system of sign and referent has been replaced, in theoretical discussion, by a system based solely on the sign, now split into signifier and signified. Within this system there is no way 'out' to the real. Consequently, art, language, and thought take place entirely within the domain of signification rather than representation. It is conceivable to view Fellini's career along a reality/representation/signification continuum, moving from neorealism to modernist questioning of representation (e.g., *8½*) then to postmodern transformation of the real and the representable into pure sign (e.g., *Fellini's Casanova*).

The above scheme tends, as do all generalizations (especially diachronic), toward oversimplification. Fellini's neorealism was far more 'modernist' than that of some of his predecessors, and one can detect postmodern elements in his modernist work and vice versa. Nonetheless, as a heuristic device, I feel my continuum offers a useful way of talking about changes in aesthetic production, and, particularly, of opening Fellini's later work to constructive discussion.

Representation: The Decline and Fall

Having posited my continuum, let me move to the issue of representation. Aesthetically, the term can connote realism or the presumed imitation of a 'real' world (much of art theory to the twentieth century). Politically, it can imply the reproduction of ideology as though it were real or 'natural' (Althusser). Philosophically, it can exemplify the commitment of Western art and thought to a metaphysics of 'presence' (Derrida).

In all its contexts representation poses problems, but never more so than in its affiliation with reference and reality. Here, the notion of representation has suffered sustained critique at the hands of structural linguistics and semiology, in conjunction with Lacanian psychoanalysis. In persuasively arguing not only that we live encapsulated in language but that language is a system of relations from which the referent is absent, followers of de Saussure have attacked naïve assumptions about referentiality and objective reality. In light of their attack, and in light of the recent writings of Baudrillard, representation like language, becomes a system of relations that does not relate to or 'represent' anything outside itself. (Baudrillard's 'simulacrum,' for example [see his Simulations], is a system of signification without representation.)[1]

Amidst such intense revaluation, modern and postmodern art have become excruciatingly self-conscious. Images of conventional or objective reality have disappeared or been radically disfigured. The process and effects of representation have been foregrounded, deconstructing the illusion that art is about anything but its own modes of production.

To the extent that a representable or objective reality appears to reassert itself (as in much postmodern art), it does so only to highlight the gaps and absences that forever mark the difference between representation and the seeming represented. (The real returns only as a signifier of signification – not a referent – to cite the writings of Rosalind Krauss.)[2]

Movies have played their own distinct role in the drama of representation. As a photographic medium that appears to record reality, film seems to remain tied to the referent or 'world.' However, the history of the avant-garde film, from the 1920s to the present has been in part the history of a critique of representation.[3] Outside the avant-garde, the critique of representation has been central to the European art film movement of the 1950s and 1960s and the proliferating counter-cinemas of the past thirty years (Wollen, Kuhn, Kolker, Kaplan, de Lauretis, Steven, Brunsden, Armes). Moreover, the presumed bastion of realism and reference – the documentary cinema – has been engaged in an extensive revaluation of its own relation to the real over the past three decades (Nichols, *Movies and Methods*, 2:233–287).

While filmmakers have become increasingly self-conscious about their means of representation, film theory – influenced by semiology, psychoanalysis, and Marxism – has become passionately dedicated to identifying, unmasking, and analysing the ideology of reference and realism. The 'classic realist film text' has come under particular scrutiny as a system of concealed and insidious representations (Dayan; de Lauretis and Heath; Cha; Bordwell, Staiger and Thompson; Rosen). At the same time, film theory has singled out alternative cinematic signifying practices as useful correctives to classic realism. In short, the issue of representation has become as crucial to the making and analysis of film as it has been to the production and consideration of other contemporary forms of cultural signification.

When one turns to the history of Italian cinema since the Second World War, representation is again in the forefront. Initially valorized for its seemingly artless and unmediated portrayal of reality, Italian neorealism has been increasingly explored in terms of its manipulation and construction of reality. Theoreticians of Italian film have come to focus on how neorealist films foreground fictional technique, or at least allow for such technique to be foregrounded by the astute critic.[4] And it is common knowledge that many of the major figures of the neorealist movement (Antonioni, Visconti, and Fellini in particular) had left realistic filmmaking far behind by the 1960s and 1970s. The debate about the abandonment of neorealism has been fundamentally a debate about modes of representation: in general terms, Italian Marxists have continued to prefer social realism, while realism of any sort has become untenable for many other intellectuals and artists.[5]

Not only is the movement of Antonioni, Visconti, and Fellini beyond neorealism part of the drama of representation in the history of movies, it might well be argued that this movement constitutes a fundamental rejection of conventional notions of representation. Antonioni's use of a photographer, journalist, and film director as protagonists in his post-neorealist films *Blow-Up* (1966), *The Passenger* (1975), and *Identification of a Woman* (1982), and his employment of documentary form in *Chung–Kuo Cina* (1972), clearly foreground referentiality and representation. (The inadequacies of all three media-related protagonists suggest that Antonioni views reference largely negatively.) And Visconti's re-representation of literary texts in the context of decadence and excess in films such as *The Leopard* (1963) and *Death in Venice* (1971) suggests a vastly different but equally intense encounter with representation.

However, the most insistent among the three graduates of neorealism in his examination of representation is, I would suggest, Federico Fellini. Fellini moved beyond neorealism relatively early in his career, as has been well documented (Bondanella, 'Early Fellini'; Lawton, 'Italian Neorealism'; Marcus; Bazin), so I will focus on later developments. The only thing I would note here is that Fellini appears to have made his two major breaks with neorealism through two films about failed or inadequate reporters.[6] 'The Matrimonial Agency' (1953) marked the move from *I vitelloni* (1953), a film of extraordinary social realism, to the poetic vision of *La strada* (1954) and *Nights of Cabiria* (1956). *La dolce vita* (1960) served as the threshold between a renewed and heightened social realism (*La dolce vita* itself) and the emphatically nonrealistic 'The Temptations of Dr Antonio' (1962) and *8½* (1963). It seems that Fellini used the neorealist/journalistic ideals of Cesare Zavattini[7] to exorcise neorealism altogether.

Fellini and Representation

In talking about Fellini and representation, I feel that at least three things need to be kept in mind: a shift in Fellini's work away from an early, 'transparent' use of cinema, which usually concealed the fact that his films were representations, toward a highly self-conscious foregrounding of film-as-representation; implicit distinctions within his films between experience and representations of experience; and a shift in his work (related to the previous point) from films about 'life' to films about 'representations of life.'

It is the move toward self-conscious cinema – accentuating the artifice and manipulation of film – that makes Fellini's work such a consistent interrogation of representation. (Before that shift his films often employed forms of representation as symbols of characters' willingness to live lives of illusion. Vaudeville or variety theatre serves this purpose in 1950s *Variety Lights*, and *fotoromanzi* (photo novels) in 1952's *The White Sheik*. However, these films do not focus on their own complicity as representations or 'illusions.')[8] My discussion of that move will, however, be assimilated into my discussion of the latter two aspects of Fellini's engagement with representation.

In terms of the distinction between experience and the representation of experience, toward the middle of Fellini's career his work clearly begins to privilege those figures who are able to move from the first to the second. In, say, *Variety Lights*, *The White Sheik*, *La strada*, and *Il bidone* (1955), his characters embrace fiction (read 'illusion') at the expense of meaningful experience; in contrast, Cabiria becomes capable of self-transformation at the moment she can imagine herself as 'Maria' and envision a dream lover 'Oscar' (a moment that occurs, tellingly, at the Lux variety theatre). Moreover, Guido is able to achieve his culminating moment of integration in *8½* principally by imagining rather than living life. (Among other things, he escapes the claustrophobic demands of the real Luisa – who appears for the last time at the screen tests – by inventing 'a spirit' Luisa – the figure in white who can promise attempted tolerance as the film's concluding sequence gets under way.)[9] And both a film set and a circus ring are crucial in this process.

This strategy of representing rather than merely living life recurs throughout Fellini's middle period in the device of voice-over narration. Toby in 'Toby Dammit' (1968), Encolpio in *Fellini-Satyricon* (1969), and Fellini himself in *Fellini: A Director's Notebook* (1969), *I clowns* (1970), and *Fellini's Roma* (1972) do not just experience, they articulate their experiences. Linked to this is the 'second coming' motif that runs so richly through Fellini's work: characters such as Toby, by narrating in the past tense and apparently from beyond the grave, are able to 'come again' through representation – rewriting history and getting right the second time what did not work the first.

In discussing characters who move from experience to representation, I have, of course, begun to trace the shift from films principally about *life* (virtually everything up to 'The Temptations of Dr Antonio') to films principally about *representation*. However, the extent of this shift only becomes clear when we move beyond character to other considerations. For instance, beginning with 'The Temptations of Dr Antonio,' Fellini's career insistently becomes art about art.[10] First there are the films principally about film: *8½, Fellini: A Director's Notebook, I clowns, Fellini's Roma, Intervista* (1987). Then there are the films largely (as opposed to principally) about film: 'The Temptations of Dr Antonio,' 'Toby Dammit,' and 1983's *And the Ship Sails On*. Next there are the films based on literary texts: 'Toby Dammit,' *Fellini-Satyricon, Fellini's Casanova* (1976), *The Voice of the Moon* (1990). Finally there are the films on art forms other than film and literature: *I clowns, The Orchestra Rehearsal* (1979), *And the Ship Sails On*. When we move outside the realm of art, we still remain within the realm of representation. *Amarcord* ('I remember'; 1973) presents itself as a series of reconstructed memories; *City of Women* (1980) is principally a dream; and both *Ginger and Fred* (1985) and, to a significant extent, *The Voice of the Moon* are about the consummate representational medium of our age: television.

Of the fifteen films from Fellini's middle and late periods, the only one I have not included is *Juliet of the Spirits* (1965), which, though not about one specific form of representation, is shot through with many: fantasies, visions, circuses, school plays, performance art (Suzy and friends), psychodrama, and so on.

As I have already suggested, through Fellini's middle period, the emphasis on representation appears to be positive, at least within terms set up by the films themselves.[11] Cabiria and Guido grow through (self)representation, and Fellini himself seems to achieve moments of both creation and reconciliation through his role as narrator, especially in the final scenes of *I clowns* and *Fellini's Roma*.[12] Moreover, Encolpio's apparent growth in *Fellini-Satyricon* can be traced to those moments at which *he* emerges as narrator – able to tell rather than merely suffer his own tale.[13] And Toby's post facto introduction to his story offers cause for some optimism about his survival of the abyss and what that might mean.[14]

Nonetheless, there also appears to be some ambivalence. Fellini's attempts to make documentaries about the clowns and Rome (to represent them, in other words) fail, as does Guido's attempt to film his own problems in *8½*. Moreover, there is a strong sense that the representer needs to free himself from representation. At the end of *8½* Guido disappears, and is momentarily supplanted by the boy in white before the boy himself disappears. In the final moments of both *I clowns* and *Fellini's Roma* Fellini himself, as the main character, vanishes. He is replaced by an old clown narrator in the former, and effaced by Anna Magnani and a motorcycle gang in the latter. At the end of 'Toby Dammit,' Toby drives across the abyss and is seen no more (no sound of a car crash, no wreckage, just symbols – a waxen head, blood on a rope). As *Fellini-Satyricon* concludes, Encolpio's live image is transformed into a fresco, and his narrating voice stops speaking in mid-sentence. He too has escaped somewhere beyond the bounds of the film. Even Juliet's development can be seen ultimately as a movement beyond representation(s). Not only does she witness the departure of all her spirits near her film's end, she looks the camera (her principal representer) right in the eye, causing it to pull far back. Then, freed of representation, she walks off.

Well, not quite freed. She is still in the film and has no existence outside it. And therein lies the paradox of Fellini's middle period: to exist in a world of representation, one must remain a representation. To escape is no longer to exist. Somehow, though the representers may disappear or withdraw, the representation (film) gets made – and it is all we ultimately have to deal with. So there is no escape from representation – and this comprises one part of our analysis of Fellini's later work. The other part concerns the retreat from representation itself, away from an 'other' or a world that is represented.

From Representation to Signification

First there is *Amarcord*, a film that emphasizes the mere mechanisms of representation by asserting 'I remember' but providing no 'I' who remembers, thus defeating reference. Instead of a unified subject, we have a jumble of narrators, from the verbally inept Giudizio who is unable to articulate anything, to the voluble 'avvocato' who articulates nothing with great eloquence and abundant factual detail. Since there is no 'I' who remembers, the title bespeaks only a generalized state of mind: an inability to go forward, an ability only to recall (to retreat inside one's own representations) rather than live. (In introducing *Amarcord*, Fellini has said: 'Perhaps because I no longer succeed in growing, I no longer succeed in distinguishing past, present, and future' (Tassone 269).

Moreover, the lack of a creative or differentiated voice is reflected in the characters' reliance on social representations. The characters become narrated as it were by ritual: the burning of the witch of winter, the celebration of the founding of Rome, funerals, the entropic wedding that brings the film to a close. ('The gathering of April 21st, just like the passing of the Rex, the burning of the great bonfire at the beginning, and so on, are always occasions of total stupidity ... Since no character has a real sense of individual responsibility ... no one has the strength not to take part in the ritual' (Riva 22).

Worse still, the characters become narrated by fascism and the cultural imperialism of America (movies, the Rex). The conformist world of the town defeats real community; the compensatory fantasies from outside are isolating and unfulfilling. Life turns more and more in on itself (recall the fog sequence and the snow tunnels that separate Titta from Gradisca). The process of representation becomes (as 'I remember' suggests), a process of self-enclosure. ('[A] title I wanted to give it was *Il borgo*, in the sense of a medieval enclosure, a lack of information, a lack of contact with ... the new' (Riva 24–5).) The final enclosure becomes the story itself.

The process of narrative self-enclosure becomes even more extreme in *Fellini's Casanova*. Here we have Fellini offering *his* representations of the autobiographical posturings of a flatterer. This film is all surface, no depth, all pose. Put another way, it is maximum signification and minimum reference. (Note for instance the garbage-bag sea. The absurdity of the signifier draws attention to the process of signification, itself absurd, while undermining any sense of a referent – in this case a 'real' sea.)

In this respect, *Casanova* is a stunning example of Jean Baudrillard's simulacrum. It is a film constructed entirely on the basis of absence, in which representation itself is representation only of absence. Moreover it is a film, as Fellini himself has said, in which there is no history, no real Casanova, just a narrative invention who in effect conquered all the women of Europe without leaving his study (Tassone, 'Casanova' 28–30). Through the effacement of referents – to again invoke Baudrillard – the map (artwork) does not merely replace the territory, it generates it. Fellini's movement to representation-as-absence (another way of describing the movement from representation to signification) is perhaps the crucial shift in the course of his recent films.

Initially, this shift might not seem to characterize Fellini's next movie, *The Orchestra Rehearsal*. The quiet and inexplicable disappearance of the documentary television crew toward the end of the film seems to eliminate mediation and promise the return of something more 'real.' (At the end of *Fellini's Roma*, this kind of promise seems in fact to be fulfilled with the disappearance of the documentary camera.) However, by the time the media leave, they have helped define the musicians entirely in terms of orchestral roles, and thereby broken down any potential for expression outside the signifying structure of the orchestra. Moreover, the orchestra itself is blatantly allegorical – signifying 'conformist/authoritarian society' – and this gives meaning to the musicians' actions only in terms of an abstract system of relationships. The film ends (and can only end) with characters locked into master/slave positions. Moreover, the orchestra ends up imprisoned within the abstract signifying system of a single piece of music, which it rehearses over and over – lacking any purpose, it seems, other than repetition, and lacking any audience or point of reference beyond the act of repetition itself.

In *The Orchestra Rehearsal* it is obvious – as it was in *Amarcord* – that the movement from representation to signification in Fellini's work is accompanied by a shift in focus from individual self-expression to the operation of cultural codes. The representer is indeed effaced, and 'artists' become mere products of cultural signification.

Having made that point, I now come to the one film from this period that seems to defy it: *City of Women*. Here we have what seems to be a highly personal dream vision operating on the margins of social determination. Moreover, *City of Women* seems a throwback to an earlier period in which (self) representation through psychosymbolic activity was a liberating process (see Burke, 'Fellini's Art of Affirmation.') However, we also have a film which seems to suggest that all such growth, *because* it is psychosymbolic, representational, and self-referential, is an illusion. In this sense, *City of Women* seems to be an unmasking of an earlier Fellini, and an implicit critique of the kind of manipulation Guido exercised in turning recalcitrant people from real life – like Luisa – into compliant, imaginative 'spirits.' *City of Women*, in short, is a highly ambivalent film. It encourages at least two readings, and in so doing helps illuminate the role of representation both at this point in Fellini's work and in his earlier films.

On first reading, *City of Women* seems to trace the transformation of Snaporaz from a lecherous middle-aged adolescent who is interested in women only for their bodies, into a figure who sees them more and more in symbolic or spiritual terms: as embodiments of the 'Other,' the Unknown, Potential Transformation. In seeing them this way, Snaporaz risks himself ever more completely, subjecting himself to criticism and self-abasement. He finally confronts the inflated 'Ideal Woman' of his dreams, only to have her shot down by another aspect of himself, the 'grounded' terrorist with the heart of gold. As this happens and he plummets toward earth, he confronts the greatest risk of all, death. Simultaneously, for the first time since much earlier in the film, he faces images of real women, whom he asks in terror: 'Who are you?' When he awakens from his dream and mysteriously encounters several of his dream women (along with his wife) in his train compartment, he is able to accept the mystery, accept the women as both 'real' and 'other,' and return to his dream and the possible terrors it might still hold. Gone is all the aggression he manifested in the film's opening sequence.

This is classic Fellinian symbology cum individuation – promoting an affirmative vision that can easily be buttressed by quotations from Fellini's *Film Quarterly* interview with Gideon Bachman, which was published at the time *City of Women* was released. However, there are plenty of things that impel one to read this work otherwise – as a film about the *representation* of growth rather than its achievement, a film, in short, about male fantasies of self-development.

For one thing, the film as dream is virtually all representation. Women barely exist outside Snaporaz's envisionment of them. (In keeping with this, Woman as Other, the Unknown, and Potential Transformation can be seen merely as self-serving male projections rather than as valid manifestations of women.) Moreover, the film and Snaporaz's dreaming imagination show little tolerance for realistic women or for actual engagement with women. We move from the relatively 'normal' Signora toward increasingly alien figures: the feminist conventioneers, the motorcycle mama, and teenage druggies. As Snaporaz retreats ever further from normal women and potentially normal relations, he enters the pathetic macho world of Katzone, an alter ego who must protect Snaporaz after his devastation in the world 'outside.' Katzone clearly lives in the realm of representation rather than reality. He has his pornographic gallery, his statue of 'Mama,' and his absurd romantic notions of love. (He apparently abandons the one woman he is associated with in this sequence, while also renouncing *all* women.)

Snaporaz himself is more interested in Katzone's sexual equipment than in his own wife Elena, whom he encounters at Katzone's. And in fact he ignores Elena until she drops off to sleep and he can enter his 'city of women': a uterine chute that relates him to women doubly as his own representations – that is, as *memories* within his *dream*. (In line

with women elsewhere in the film, Elena has become alien and grotesque by her final appearance at Katzone's, during which she is wearing a cosmetic mask and singing opera.)

The women in Snaporaz's uterine flashbacks undergo yet another
process of de-realization; they also become increasingly associated with
roles, and thus with cultural determination. Snaporaz moves from
warm personal contact with Rosina, to the distanced observation of live
performers (motorcycle daredevils), to an extensive movie sequence
that culminates with the Mae West figure. It is she who triggers fanny
fetishism, which leads finally to the whore with the enormous ass. By
the end of this sequence women have become only the distortions of a
repressive society – representations not of Snaporaz's paranoid imagination but rather, now, of a culture in which women exist only through
the conjunction of cinematic and psychological projection.

The last major woman figure Snaporaz encounters in his dream is,
of course, the inflated Madonna/soubrette, Saint/Whore: a cultural
cliché if ever there was one. And her destruction, and replacement
with reasonably realistic images of women, terrify Snaporaz. He is so
far into distortive representation that he cannot handle a move back
toward the real. Accordingly, when he wakes up he is unable to relate
to the women in the compartment, the only women in the entire film
who are not purely dream representations.[15] Instead he pulls his coat
around him and settles back to the dream.

Seen in this context, the light at the end of the tunnel provided by
Fellini as the credits conclude is not a hint of Snaporaz's growth, but
rather just another cultural representation – a tritely symbolic happy
ending that substitutes for something more substantive.

It seems to me, in this second reading, that once we have reached the
Madonna/soubrette figure and the 'light at the end of the tunnel' ending, we have left reference and representation behind for pure sign-
play. Moreover, sign-play seems to proliferate elsewhere in the film's
structure, repeatedly turning representation into signification. To the
extent that his dream is a closed system – especially in light of recent
psychoanalytic theorizing that the unconscious is structured like a
language – Snaporaz's experience throughout the film becomes merely
a play of signification without reference 'outside.' (Snaporaz's return
to sleep and dream implies real fear of any 'real' or 'other.') Moreover,
as Fellini indicated in the Bachman interview, the web of association
works in the film so that dream = film = women: women are projections just as movies and dreams are, and in fact all three are inter-

changeable. Yet again there can be no actual women 'represented' – they are merely one term within a chain of significations. Finally, the film is established from the beginning as part of another signifying system: that of 'Marcello/Fellini films.' As the credits begin, a woman's giggling voice says 'Marcello again? Please maestro.' The film, in short, is an in-joke, ultimately only about itself, its maker, and its star as signifiers of fictionality. More precisely, Marcello does not exist as a referent ('real' figure) or even as a sign (referring to a 'real' Marcello). He functions purely as a signifier of his capacity to endlessly (re)signify – by appearing over and over again in Fellini films. In effect, there is an instantaneous collapse of referent into sign and signified into signifier. This kind of implosion not only exemplifies, par excellence, the postmodern play of meaning-minus-reference, but also indicates a radical shift from the earlier 'representational' Fellini films – 8½ and *Juliet of the Spirits* – that *City of Women* initially seems to emulate.

Fellini's work after *City of Women* remains insistently caught up in signifying systems. *And the Ship Sails On* is structured not as dream but as a movie-within-a-movie. It begins as a silent film, complete with the sound of a projector. It ends as a sepia-tinted scratched film, the sound of the projector again audible, and with an iris in to a cartoon conclusion: the film's narrator and a rhinoceros adrift in a lifeboat. Not only does it foreground its self-signification as film-within-film, it emphasizes its status as arbitrary narrative. The viewer is placed at the mercy of an absurd journalist/narrator who does vaudeville hat tricks in front of the camera, quickly gets lost amidst the shuffle of events in the ship's dining room, and concludes his role as narrator by positing four possible scenarios for the film's most crucial event – the sinking of the ship itself – from which he and we are absent. Most important, all this takes place as an effacement of history and politics. The film's events mimic the assassination of Archduke Ferdinand, the outbreak of the First World War, and the sinking of the *Lusitania*. But the mimicry (like *Casanova*'s garbage-bag sea) is so absurd that the original is in effect denied. We have a process of substitution or doubling that destroys reference or at best presents it under erasure.

In *Ginger and Fred*, we are again presented with a world of doubling, repetition, and effacement. Amelia and Pippo, who once made a modest name for themselves by imitating Ginger Rogers and Fred Astaire, are asked to appear on television to imitate their former imitations. When Amelia arrives in Rome for the show, she finds it populated with look-alikes: (Clark Gable among others), and is herself mistaken for a

'Bette Davis' double. Many of the look-alikes ('Proust' and 'Kafka,' for instance) are supposed to resemble people whom most of the film's television audience have probably never seen. The look-alikes thus serve as the originals.

During the film's Christmas TV spectacular, almost everything that might once have had status as an originating or foundational value – religion, love, heroism – is levelled as mere spectacle. Through re-enactment, all 'origin'-ality is lost. What remains are hollow 'resurrection effects,' to use another term from Baudrillard. This is especially apt, given the 'second coming' motif and its debasement in late Fellini.

Ginger and Fred captures an oft-noted tendency of television (and for that matter computer) technology: instead of reproducing reality photographically – hence referring to an original – it simulates the real electronically. In so doing, it effaces the real by turning it into sign system: 'It is no longer a question of imitation, nor of reduplication, nor even of parody. It is rather a question of substituting signs of the real for the real itself, that is, an operation to deter every real process by its operational double' (Baudrillard 4). Then, in a dramatic reversal, television becomes the 'model' of the real, and 'simulation is no longer that of a referential being or substance. It is the generation by models of a real without origin or reality: a hyperreal' (2).[16] In *Ginger and Fred*, this process is linked to the kind of cultural coding and definition-by-role that we saw in *The Orchestra Rehearsal*. Characters end up becoming what television makes them. By film's end, Amelia and Pippo have succeeded only as TV performers (their attempts to spark a renewed relationship are feeble and ineffectual). Moreover, their success is dictated by a media world that wants no part of them once they have completed their dance. At the train station they return to reality and to a moment of potential closeness, only to be reinstituted in their TV roles by autograph seekers. Accordingly, their farewell turns into a recreated piece of business from their televised Ginger and Fred routine: now an imitation of an imitation of an imitation.

The film's final comment on the relationship between TV and the real comes not with the theatrical separation of Ginger and Fred but with the final images: a medium close-up of a TV that instead of representing the world to its viewers, merely tells them about the necessary equipment and strategies for picking up its broadcast signals. Like all other forms of communication in late Fellini, TV proves to be ultimately only about itself. Unable to refer, it can only signify its will to ceaselessly signify.

Fellini's penultimate film, *Intervista*, returns to film as a principal subject for exploration. Made partly in celebration of Cinecittà's fiftieth anniversary, *Intervista* builds on the film studio's history as a principal source of Italian cultural signification for much of the twentieth century and uses it as a point of departure for exploring processes of cinematic sign production. More than that, it ultimately suggests that Fellini himself is nothing more nor less than a series of significations produced at and by Cinecittà.

Intervista is a film about a Japanese film crew making a documentary about Fellini who is making a film based on fiction: Kafka's *Amerika*. Like *City of Women* it focuses on prior Fellini figures (here Anita Ekberg as well as Marcello Mastroianni). It also doubles back on prior Fellini texts (especially *La dolce vita*). A 'flashback' to the Trevi Fountain scene from *La dolce vita* as Fellini, Marcello, and others (including the Japanese crew) are in Ekberg's house suggests that memory itself is no more than prior filmic projection, mechanically and socially produced. (Actually, the Trevi scene is mysteriously conjured up by Marcello, dressed as Mandrake the Magician; this eliminates Fellini – the author/subject – as a source of memory.) At the same time, the centrality of Fellini's earlier work to *Intervista* indicates that Fellini's filmmaking is now merely re-signification. Moreover, it is not creation in any sense, so much as a 'seeing between' ('inter-viewing') of prior significations and codes. (The fact that the film's title lacks a subject – it is a noun rather than a verb – again eliminates agency, and specifically Fellini, from the act of signifying.)

The construction of meaning out of pre-existing codes implies the kind of infinite repeatability we begin to see in all of Fellini's post-representational work. *Intervista*, like *Ginger and Fred*, presents a world in which virtually everything is reproduction. There is the reconstruction of Cinecittà circa 1940, the adaptation of *Amerika*, the projection of scenes from *La dolce vita*. There is also the endless reproduction of Fellini himself, suggesting that he too has become merely a series of codes. Most obviously, he casts an actor (Sergio Rubini) to play himself as a young man, and Marcello Mastroianni – his fictional stand-in since the 1950s – becomes an important personage. In fact, Fellini's mode of filmmaking has become so codified that his assistant Maurizio Mein can do much of his work for him, including finding actors for his films. At one point Maurizio even coaches potential actresses in Fellinian mannerisms, so acting too has become predictably Fellini-esque. This implies the ultimate repeatability, and reproducibility, of the Fellini canon itself (i.e., 'Fellini film' after 'Fellini film'). It becomes clear that Fellini can absent himself from Cinecittà and the process of constructing a Fellini film will go on without him.

Intervista's parodic turn to the Fellinian 'self' and corpus as pure products of Cinecittà and signification may make it the most pointedly 'semiotic' of Fellini's post-representational films.

Fellini's final film, *The Voice of the Moon* (1990), seems initially to return to a more conventional narrative of character and identity reminiscent of his early work. The protagonist, Ivo, recently released from an insane asylum, even seems to offer the kind of 'wise fool' authenticity of a Gelsomina (*La strada*). However, it is precisely on the terrain of character and identity that postmodern reproduction and signification become most apparent. To begin with, Ivo is called 'Pinocchino' by his grandmother, suggesting that he is merely a copy of Pinocchio (and of course a puppet instead of a self-actualizing individual). His principal activity in the film – obsessing over the town beauty Aldina – is articulated largely through citation: he relies on the words of Leopardi to articulate his 'love.' His courtship is enacted in terms of Cinderella, as he steals Aldina's slipper and later tries it on a variety of women. His ultimate conflation of Aldina and the moon reproduces one of the most characteristic clichés of romantic poetry (and one present in the words of Leopardi). The film itself, in rendering/parodying Ivo's experiences, 'reproduces' Méliès's famous early film *Voyage to the Moon* in tone if not in imagery.

Reproduction extends to the world of religion. The local priest Don Antonio has amassed such a large collection of identical madonnas that a heckler is prompted to comment sardonically: 'Is this not a ... compelling demonstration that the Madonna can be considered a race?' The absence of uniqueness and originality implied here is further suggested when Aldina's slipper fits virtually all the women on whom Ivo tries it.

The most extensive analysis of reproduction – and one that clearly sees it as a deconstruction of identity and individuality – is supplied by Gonnella, another recently released inmate, who reads all human activity, including that of his son, as role playing or the enactment of, as he puts it, 'archetypes':[17]

Gonnella: They train so that each one interprets his part perfectly. Did you see the doctor? Did you notice his suit? Indeed the typical suit of a doctor. To be more authentic than that is not possible. Yet it's faked, all faked.

Ivo: But your son ...?

Gonnella: Ah, that is the capstone. We are in the realm of great art. No one could take it any further. The archetype of the son, the platonic ideal ... It's all a fiction, only a representation, all faked.

Gonnella furnishes a perfect description of Baudrillardian copies derived from models rather than originals – exactly what the Madonna has become for the local prelate.

Ultimately, and Gonella's words clearly reflect this, *The Voice of the Moon* is about the endless displacement of identity in a process that is itself a form of reproduction: Ivo first hears voices from wells (the inner self already reproduced and 'evacuated'). He then vainly projects his dreams and self onto Aldina. When she and the moon become interchangeable signifiers, he projects his wounded and rejected identity onto the latter in a vision in which the moon is captured, televised, and 'assassinated.' Ultimately, Aldina, moon, and television become interchangeable: all satellites/sites of projection, possession, and lunacy. In the penultimate scene, the moon takes on Aldina's voice and face and addresses Ivo, offering advice until 'she' has to interrupt herself to announce '*Pubblicità*' ('time for a commercial').

The Voice of the Moon seems initially not to be a film about media and reproduction or simulation, and in this respect seems to differ from Fellini's preceding three movies; yet it ends up in the same place conceptually. Since postmodern selves are endlessly evacuated and projected – or in electronic terms, endlessly dissassembled, reassembled, and transmitted – identity equates with and in fact becomes becomes television, and the latter becomes the inevitable signifier of a world where the self is pure simulation. (The turn to the 'self' as the ultimate site of floating signification does, of course, link *The Voice of the Moon* to *Intervista* and to the latter's treatment of Fellini himself, while also recalling virtually all of Fellini's work from at least *Fellini's Casanova* – and possibly even *8½* – onward.)

In this essay I have argued that representation in Fellini's work begins as a relative non-issue, turns into a seemingly liberating but problematic possibility, and ends up as the vanishing point in a world of signification. In so doing, I have touched only briefly on the workings of individual films. Moreover, I have sketched out only an overall trajectory, and have not indicated the extent to which Fellini's work becomes a detailed examination of the conditions of meaning and being in postmodernity. His seeming abandonment of representation for a world of unanchored signification is not (as some of the above suggests) a neutral process. It constitutes a 'politics of signification' that in turn is a sustained critique of postmodernity and a recognition, perhaps even a plea, that, in the age of the simulacrum, we still live in and through, not merely in renunciation of, reference and representation (see Burke, *Fellini's Films* 312–20).

Notes

1 Crucial aspects of the issue of representation are usefully covered in the Introduction to Arac. See Wallis for a far more detailed discussion.

2 See especially Krauss's chapters on photography. For an interesting discussion of the problematized return of the referent in postmodernism, see Elder.

3 See Gidal, *Materialist Film*; LeGrice; and Sitney. For a response to these, see Penley.

4 See Bondanella, *Federico Fellini*; Lawton, 'Italian Neorealism'; and the 'War Trilogy' chapters (on *Open City, Paisan,* and *Germany, Year Zero*) in Brunette.

5 See Bondanella, *Federico Fellini* 60–6 and *Italian Cinema* 74–141; Overbey; and Marcus.

6 For a discussion of the limitations of the protagonist of 'The Matrimonial Agency' and Marcello in *La dolce vita*, see Burke, *Federico Fellini* 31–6 and 85–96.

7 Zavattini was a scriptwriter (not a major director) whose writings earned him the role of principal spokesperson for neorealism.

8 *The White Sheik* is seemingly self-reflexive since a strong analogy is implied between the *fotoromanzi* and Fellini's own medium of movies. However, the *fotoromanzi* remain only a part of the film's larger analysis of conformity – of the characters' submission to authoritarian illusion (embodied finally by Catholicism). Fellini's use of the *fotoromanzi* never becomes the basis for a thoroughgoing critique of representation. The implication is more that people can lose themselves in things such as *fotoromanzi* and movies, than that these forms of representation are problematic in and of themselves.

9 In contrast to Cabiria and Guido, Marcello in *La dolce vita* can envision nothing. As a reporter he remains tied to the real world. As a result, he remains incapable of (self)transformation.

   Lest I provide too simplistic a picture of 'middle' Fellini, I should note that in 'The Temptations of Dr Antonio,' which Fellini made between

Nights of Cabiria and *8½*, the protagonist is done in by his own representations. So imagining rather than living life gets Antonio in trouble rather than liberating him.

10 Of course, as I suggested earlier, Fellini's early films are also partly about art or its close kin, spectacle. Nonetheless, the examination of art and spectacle is only part of other issues: alienation and self-delusion, loss of consciousness, authority, conformity. In the later films, art and spectacle tend to become the issue within which all other issues are subsumed.

11 Those terms and the affirmative nature of the films of this period can, of course, be critiqued as romantic and transcendental, especially from a post-structuralist point of view. Moreover, my discussion of Fellini's more recent work is meant to suggest, within that work, an implicit if not explicit renunciation of earlier romanticism and transcendentalism.

12 For considerations of these two films as 'positive,' see Prats; Burke, 'The Three-Phase Process'; and Foreman, 'Fellini's Cinematic City.'

13 For discussion of Encolpio's character development in *Fellini-Satyricon*, see Snyder; Robinson. I have actually come to question whether Fellini's film seeks to represent or merely parody such growth. See Burke, *Fellini's Films*, 168–72.

14 For a discussion of Toby's point of view and possible survival, see Foreman, 'The Poor Player Struts Again.'

15 Of course the fact that they pre-existed in Snaporaz's dream means that these women too have not escaped representation.

16 Baudrillard's words in this and the preceding quotation are not directly related to television. However, they are entirely consistent with his vision of a contemporary world that has, to a large extent, become a video simulation.

17 The use of the term 'archetype' seems a knowing 'postmodernization' of Carl Jung, who was a principal influence on Fellini during the period in which he was making films about meaningful individuality – the very opposite of postmodern simulation.

References

Arac, Jonathan, ed. *Postmodernism and Politics*. Minneapolis: U of Minnesota P, 1986.

Armes, Roy. *Third World Film Making and the West*. Berkeley: U of California P, 1987.

Bachman, Gideon. 'Federico Fellini: "The Cinema Seen as a Woman ..."' *Film Quarterly* 34.2 (1980–1): 2–9.

Baudrillard, Jean. *Simulations*. Trans. Paul Foss, Paul Patton, and Philip Beitchman. New York: Semiotext(e), 1983.

Bazin, André. 'Cabiria: The Voyage to the End of Neorealism.' *What Is Cinema?* Vol. 2. Trans. and ed. Hugh Gray. Berkeley: U of California P, 1971. 83–92.

– 'The Crisis of Neorealism.' La strada, *Federico Fellini, Director*. Ed. Peter Bondanella and Manuela Gieri. New Brunswick: Rutgers UP, 1987. 199–220.

Bondanella, Peter. 'Early Fellini: *Variety Lights, The White Sheik*, and *I Vitelloni*.' Bondanella, ed., *Fellini* 220–39.

– ed. *Federico Fellini: Essays in Criticism*. New York: Oxford UP. 1978.

– *Italian Cinema: From Neorealism to the Present*. New York: Ungar, 1983.

Bordwell, David, Janet Staiger, and Kristin Thompson. *The Classical Hollywood Cinema: Film Style and Mode of Production to 1960*. New York: Columbia UP, 1985.

Brunette, Peter. *Roberto Rossellini*. New York: Oxford UP, 1987.

Brunsden, Charlotte. *Films for Women*. London: British Film Institute, 1986.

Burke, Frank. *Federico Fellini*: Variety Lights *to* La dolce vita. Boston: G.K. Hall, 1984.

– *Fellini's Films: From Postwar to Postmodern*. New York: Twayne, 1996.

– 'Fellini's Art of Affirmation: *Nights of Cabiria, City of Women*, and Some Aesthetic Implications.' *Canadian Journal of Political and Social Theory* 6.1 (1982): 138–53.

– 'The Three-Phase Process and the White Clown-Auguste Relationship in Fellini's *The Clowns*.' *1977 Film Studies Annual. Part 1. Explorations in National Cinemas*. Ed. Ben Lawton. Pleasantville, NY: Redgrave, 1977 124–42.

Cha, Theresa Hak Kyung, ed. *Apparatus: Cinematographic Apparatus: Selected Writings*. New York: Tanam, 1980.

Dayan, Daniel. 'The Tutor-Code of Classical Cinema. *Film Quarterly* 28.1 (1974). Rpt in *Movies and Methods, An Anthology*. Vol 1. Ed. Bill Nichols. Berkeley: U of California P, 1976. 439–51.

de Lauretis, Teresa. *Alice Doesn't: Feminism, Semiotics, Cinema*. Bloomington: Indiana UP, 1984.

– *Technologies of Gender: Essays on Theory. Film, and Fiction*. Bloomington: Indiana UP, 1987.

de Lauretis, Teresa, and Stephen Heath, eds. *The Cinematic Apparatus*. London: Macmillan, 1980.

Elder, R. Bruce. 'Image: Representation and Object – The Photographic Image in Canadian Avant-Garde Film.' *Take Two: A Tribute to Film in Canada*. Ed Seth Feldman. Toronto: Irwin, 1984. 246–63.

Eco, Umberto. 'The Multiplication of the Media.' *Faith in Fakes*. Tr. William Weaver. London: Secker & Warburg, 1986.

Foreman. Walter C., Jr. 'Fellini's Cinematic City: *Roma* and Myths of Foundation.' *Forum Italicum* 14.2 (1980): 78–98.

– 'The Poor Player Struts Again: Fellini's *Toby Dammit* and the End of the Actor.' *1977 Film Studies Annual. Part 1, Explorations in National Cinemas*. Ed. Ben Lawton. Pleasantville, NY: Redgrave, 1977. 111–21.

Gidal, Peter. *Materialist Film*. London: Routledge, 1988.

– ed. *Structural Film Anthology*. London: British Film Institute, 1976.

Heath, Stephen. *Questions of Cinema*. Bloomington: Indiana UP, 1981.

Jameson, Fredric. 'Postmodernism or the Cultural Logic of Late Capitalism.' *New German Critique* 146 (1984): 53–93.

Kaplan, E. Ann. *Women and Film: Both Sides of the Camera*. London: Methuen, 1983.

Kolker, Robert Phillip. *The Altering Eye: Contemporary International Cinema* New York: Oxford UP, 1983.

Krauss, Rosalind E. *The Originality of the Avant-Garde and Other Modernist Myths*. Cambridge, Mass.: MIT P, 1985.

Kuhn, Annette. *Women's Pictures: Feminism and Cinema*. London: Routledge, 1982.

Lawton, Ben. 'Italian Neorealism: A Mirror Construction of Reality(?)' *Film Criticism* 3.2 (1979): 8–23.

– ed. *1977 Film Studies Annual. Part 1. Explorations in National Cinemas*. Pleasantville, NY: Redgrave, 1977.

LeGrice, Malcolm. *Abstract Film and Beyond*. London: Studio Vista, 1977.

Marcus, Millicent. *Italian Film in the Light of Neorealism*. Princeton: Princeton UP, 1986.

Nichols, Bill, ed. *Movies and Methods, An Anthology*. 2 vols. Berkeley: U of California P, 1976, 1985.

Overbey, David, ed. *Springtime in Italy: A Reader in Neorealism*. Hamden, CT: Archon, 1979.

Penley, Constance, 'The Avant-Garde and Its Imaginary.' *Camera Obscura* 2 (Fall, 1977). Rpt in *Movies and Methods, An Anthology*. Vol 2. Ed. Bill Nichols. Berkeley: U of California P, 1985. 577–602.

Prats, A.J. *The Autonomous Image: Cinematic Narration and Humanism*. Lexington: U of Kentucky P, 1981.

Riva, Valerio. '*Amarcord*: The Fascism within Us: An Interview with Valerio Riva.' *Federico Fellini: Essays in Criticism*. Ed. Peter Bondanella. 20–6.

Robinson, W.R. 'The Visual Powers Denied and Coupled: *Hamlet* and *Fellini-Satyricon* as Narratives of Seeing.' *Shakespeare's More Than Words Can Witness: Essays on Visual and Nonverbal Enactment in the Plays*. Ed Sidney Homan. Lewisburg, PA: Bucknell UP, 1980. 177–206.

Rosen, Philip, ed. *Narrative, Apparatus, Ideology: A Film Theory Reader*. New York: Columbia UP, 1986.

Sitney, P. Adams. *The Visionary Cinema: The American Avant-Garde*. 2nd ed. New York: Oxford UP, 1979.

Snyder, Stephen. 'Color, Growth, and Evolution in *Fellini Satyricon*.' *Federico Fellini: Essays in Criticism*. Ed. Peter Bondanella. 168–87.

Steven, Peter, ed. *Jump Cut: Hollywood, Politics and Counter-Cinema*. Toronto: Between-the-Lines, 1985.

Tassone, Aldo. '*Casanova*: An Interview with Aldo Tassone.' *Federico Fellini: Essays in Criticism*. Ed. Peter Bondanella. 27–35.

– 'From Romagna to Rome: The Voyage of a Visionary Chronicler (*Roma* and *Amarcord*).' *Federico Fellini: Essays in Criticism*. Ed. Peter Bondanella. 261–88.

Wallis, Brian, ed. *Art After Modernism: Rethinking Representation*. New York/Boston. The New Museum of Contemporary Art in association with David A. Godine, 1984.

Wollen, Peter. *Readings and Writings: Semiotic Counter-Strategies*. London Verso, 1982.

2

Subtle Wasted Traces: Fellini and the Circus

HELEN STODDART

The Cinema is very much like the circus.[1]

The cinema is also circus, carnival, funfair, a game for acrobats.[2]

[The cinema] is an art form and at the same time a circus, a funfair, a voyage aboard a kind of 'Ship of Fools,' an adventure, an illusion, a mirage. It is an art form which has nothing to do with other arts, least of all with literature.[3]

The special characteristic of the circus is that one is creating and living at the same time, without having to keep inside fixed bounds, as one has to do with painting and with literature – one is constantly involved in action. It's an entertainment that's got force, courage – and I think the cinema is just the same.[4]

Even until very recently, critical assessments of Fellini's films have been couched in terms of old-style auteur criticism. Fellini's status as a remarkable '"artist" of the cinema whose "personal" cinema contains a strong autobiographical element'[5] and whose preoccupations are consistently 'expressed' in his films is confirmed through readings that search out the traces of a distinct narrative and visual 'manner' across his work and through elevating comparisons to 'a short story writer or a lyric poet.'[6] However, in beginning this discussion with these quotations from him about the circus and the cinema, I do not wish to consolidate this approach. On the contrary – I want to demonstrate that these much-cited auteurial statements about the connection between the two art forms voice a desire for their impossible convergence, a desire played out in several of his films but also inevitably frustrated.

The circus is not just another of Fellini-the-auteur's 'personal obses-sions.' Rather, his cinematic renderings of the circus point up a failure, or at least a gap, between his reported declarations about the relation-ship between the two forms and what is possible. This is because, most especially in *I clowns*, Fellini's films demonstrate a more complex and subtle understanding of the difficulties of translating a live art into a mechanically reproduced one than is evident in the much-cited state-ments above. At stake in this argument is not only the validity of approaches to Fellini's work that have insistently depended on situ-ating him as an auteur, but also the broader issue of the cinema's relationship to forms of live art – particularly the circus.

Returning now to the four quotations with which I began, I want to interrogate them for evidence of how Fellini claims to regard what he sees as the close relationship between circus and cinema. He begins with a loose analogy – 'the cinema *is very much like* the circus.' We might indeed concur with this, and be inclined to compile a list of overlapping possibilities and characteristics. Yet in his next two state-ments he places the two forms in a relationship of semi-convergence. Fellini claims that the cinema is a unique art form but that it is also capable not just of resembling but of *being* another ('The cinema *is also* circus'). Finally, he identifies a common essence within each, that of 'creating and living at the same time'; this not only allows him to cele-brate what he sees as the dual superiority that these two share over all other art forms from which they are decidedly distinct, but also leads him to deliver the claim that they are 'just the *same.*'

It is acceptable to think that the cinema in some ways resembles or 'is very much like' the circus, and I will suggest here what those resem-blances might be, especially insofar as they relate to four of Fellini's films, *La strada* (1954), *8½* (1963), *Giulietta degli spiriti* (1965), and *I clowns* (1970). However, while several auteur-based critics cited above have taken their cue from these quotations, none has gone any further than demonstrating that the circus has thematic significance in Fellini films. Consequently, all have neglected to examine the cultural and for-mal relationships of the two forms of entertainment. Presuming that the cinema is quite definitely *not* the circus and that when Fellini's films contain a circus *topos* they do not *become* the circus but merely represent it, we can still pose a number of productive questions, the answers to which may have significance beyond Fellini's films. Given that the circus is not the cinema, why would Fellini want to believe it is? What happens to this desire for convergence in the films themselves? What is at stake in this connection, both for Fellini's films and by extension for other kinds of cinema?

All of this is not to say that it is not important to examine how the circus figures in Fellini's films. Indisputably, it is a pervasive theme from his first solo feature film, *Lo sciecco bianco* (1952), during which Ivan Cavalli is entertained in a market square by a fire eater at the lowest moment of his apparently hopeless search for his wife, to *Intervista*, in which Marcello Mastroianni closely resembles a ringmaster in the guise of Mandrake the Magician (1987). Circus figures are also present in unrealized projects such as *The Actor*.[7] Yet beyond this, the mobilization of the circus as a metaphor, and more plainly as a dramatic context, bears on the formal and cultural questions I would like to address. For example, in *La strada* the dominant metaphor of the film seems to be 'the road of life,' but that metaphor is complicated by all three of the circus players who dominate the film's drama (*Il matto*, Gelsomina, and Zampanò), whose acts don't reflect the linear progression implied by the image of the road, so much as an insistent circularity of movement, especially during performance. Their psychic development is fuelled by returns to familiar physical environments along what becomes a kind of circular road.[8] Most obviously, Zampanò begins at the edge of the sea, where he buys Gelsomina from her mother, and ends up prostrating himself through grief and guilt on the beach. Bazin argues that after the deaths of Gelsomina and the Fool, Zampanò acquires a soul, thereby completing a circle that demonstrates the 'interdependence of salvation.'[9] For Bazin then, the circus is an interesting metaphor within the film insofar as it offers Fellini the opportunity to dramatize characters who possess 'an aura of the marvellous' within a world that Bazin elevates to the grand level of the 'quasi-Shakespearean.'[10] However, while Bazin is interested in the circus to the extent that it provides a means of securing Fellini's status a serious auteur – itself a move within the larger project of securing the status of film as a serious art form – he remains uninterested in the specificity of the metaphor. This is something I would like to explore.

There is an important distinction between Fellini's use of the circus as metaphor and those figures in *La strada* whom Fellini allows to *become* the circus. Zampanò is part of the general metaphor that encourages us to compare the journey of life with a travelling show. Yet though he puts on his own small show early in the film, it is as though he doesn't really belong to the greater world of the circus and cannot participate in its ethos. In fact, he is quickly ejected from the circus troupe he joins partway through the film. However, while he and others *perform* circus acts, thus implying a distance between character and routine, Gelsomina *is* the circus, or rather she is a fantasy of what the circus might be. In this sense she is very much like Chaplin's tramp. Naomi Ritter has already noted the resemblance between the two in style and appearance.[11] However, I would argue that the connection is less casual than this, especially when one thinks of Chaplin's *The Circus* (1928), in which the tramp unwittingly becomes part of the clowns' performance when he strays into the circus ring while attempting to escape from the police. His impromptu antics generate far more excitement and laughter than the professional clowns could ever have hoped to do, and he is promptly hired by the manager. However, both Gelsomina and the tramp are natural clowns or life's clowns, and because of this, training and the introduction of 'technique' or routine only serve to corrupt their facility for entertaining. Both fail miserably under these regimes, and while this may be funny in both cases, it is only Gelsomina's suffering as a result of her apparent incompetence that jarringly interrupts the comedy. So here Fellini is consolidating what Slavoj Žižek has identified as Chaplin's 'wild theory of comedy,' based on the blindness of an intradiegetic audience to the scene in front of them. In *The Circus*, Žižek claims, 'the audience laughs and applauds, mistaking his [Chaplin's] desperate struggle for survival for a comedian's virtuosity – the origin of comedy is to be sought precisely in such cruel blindness, unaware[ness] of the tragic reality of a situation.'[12] The same blindness is also present in the scene following Zampanò's cruelty to Gelsomina when they perform for an audience in a public square. Žižek's account of Chaplin's construction of dramatic irony is pertinent here because it draws attention to a multiplication of audience points of view available in the cinema but not in the circus. The cinema spectators move between Gelsomina's, the audience's, and their own removed point-of-view shots and are able to place the spectacle within the context of a narrative – something circus spectators can never do.

In *8½*, after Guido is presented with at least the possibility of shooting himself in the head to evade critical ridicule and accusation, he is led by Maurice the magician to the circus ring, where the circus band of clowns is playing. Guido ushers in all the major figures from his life, who are also the figures who constitute *8½*. As I suggested earlier in relation to *La strada*, it is simpler to construct visual spectacle in the circus than in the cinema. This is mainly because in the circus, characters rarely betray any interiority (i.e., they are pure spectacle) and the relations of looking are more direct (i.e., the spectator has only one point of view and the performer may return his or her gaze). Thus, when Guido turns his world into a circus, that world achieves an order and a structure that he was unable to lend it as a filmmaker. Yet he has done so on film – and in a film in which the distinction between life and performance has been nearly impossible to make and in which distinctions between subjective vision and external reality are constantly undermined or blurred. Consquently, the circus is inevitably framed as an impossible and fantastic world.

In *Giulietta degli spiriti*, it is Fanny the circus dancer – with whom Giulietta's grandfather absconds – who brings the circus into the film, though this function is also shared by Iris and Suzy, since they are all played by the same actress and carry some of the same meanings for Giulietta. Like *Il matto*, Fanny first appears on a circus contraption (*Il matto* on the high wire and Fanny on a trapeze swing) suspended in the air, though at this stage Fanny exists only as an internal diegetic image in Giulietta's head and in this sense is a uniquely cinematic figure from the outset. Shortly after this, as Giulietta retells some significant incidents from her youth, we see how Fanny's trapeze may be counterpoised with the blazing grill to which Giulietta is tied as she plays the part of a religious martyr who is hoisted up to the sky, apparently toward God. The two images could not be more different: Fanny is literally alive and kicking as she guides the flower-draped trapeze backward and forward, laughing and showily dressed; Giulietta is utterly passive, tied down, draped rather than clothed, suffering martyrdom, moved by religious authorities, and surrounded by deadly flames rather than colourful flowers. Her grandfather proves to be the intermediary figure between the two, and it is he who becomes Fanny's lover. Fanny then becomes the symbol of everything that the circus stands for in the film – life, pleasure, autonomy, physical and sexual freedom – and it is her grandfather (or rather Giulietta's memory of him) that finally leads her to symbolically and psychologically liberate herself from the martyrdom that has dominated her life since childhood. She mentally replays the scene of her liberation from the grill, but this time it is Giulietta who is in the active role of (self-) liberator as she takes over from her grandfather. Suzy is also connected to this repertoire of airborne creatures, through the butterfly on her back, her indoor chute, and her outdoor treehouse. Giulietta cannot become

Suzy, just as she does not belong in the circus; yet her encounters with these figures are the most significant in the film, since it is through them that she is able to return to her life anew.

In each of these three cases, then, the circus at times is much more than a metaphor for something else; it enters the film in the form of an impossible figure or a fantasy: Gelsomina, the Fool, the ring of life, Fanny the circus dancer. All these figures provide instruction, inspiration, solace, and an impetus for positive change, yet with this also inevitably comes a sense of loss and sadness, in itself an acknowledgment of the fact that they are indeed fantastic figures. Each is an unearthly form through whom and from whom the protagonists move on. This fantastic status is also signalled through the fact that each is also connected to childhood states and dramas: Gelsomina's naïveté, sexual innocence, and physical androgyny; Giulietta's childhood trip to the circus; and Guido's circus ring at the centre of which is himself as a young boy. The circus is tied up with a nostalgia for childhood,[13] which always fuels action in the present for an adult self – it is a fantasy that enters the real and is involved in reconstituting social relationships. At the same time, the function and meaning of all three instances is dependent on their cinematic constitution. As such, while thematically they may point to the connections between the circus and 'creating and living,' finally they do more to undermine than to illustrate Fellini's assertion that the cinema and the circus are 'just the same.'

It is also evident that there is always a particular kind of ambivalence (fantastic but influential, life-giving but lost, and so on) about Fellini's use of circus figures. This ambivalence not only structures other aspects of these films but, in doing so, leads us to an investigation of the presence of the carnivalesque within them. For this exercise it is useful to consider Bakhtin.[14] For Bakhtin there is necessarily an ambivalence and dualism in all carnival acts. Just as 'crowning already contains the idea of immanent de-crowning'[15] and all symbols are 'two-leveled,' so carnival expressions such as laughter are also ambivalent. This is because carnival rituals – especially those which mobilize ritual laughter – '[deal] with the very process of change, with *crisis* itself.' In 'funeral laughter,' Bahktin writes, 'ridicule was fused with rejoicing,'[16] and this is exactly the confusion of emotion embodied in the clowns' frantic but exhilarating funeral in the last scenes of *I clowns*. The laughter here links death with rebirth, yet the two are never separable, just as Fellini's circus figures are always both temporary and eternal, past and present, fantastic and real. All of them also provide ways of accommodating crisis, change, and renewal.

The circus as discussed above becomes like, or rather overlaps with, the carnival in the sense that it becomes 'the place for working out, in a concretely sensuous, half-real and half-play-acted form, a *new mode of inter-relationship between* individuals, counterpoised to the all-powerful socio-hierarchical relationships of non-carnival life.'[17] In the course of this 'working out,' the carnivalistic impulse 'brings together, unifies, weds, and combines the sacred and the profane, the lofty with the low, the great with the insignificant, the wise with the stupid.'[18] It is precisely these dualities of carnival that are at work in Guido's circus ring; they are perhaps typified in his gesture of kissing the Cardinal's ring before he joins the circle. This gesture is potentially one of mockery – of erasing and possibly ridiculing the Cardinal's social superiority. Yet at the same time, it signals Guido's acceptance into the newly established community, as well as familiarity among individuals.

The cultural significance of Fellini's circuses comes into slightly sharper focus when we pursue the contextual connections with Bakhtin a little further. In his account of Bakhtin's *Rabelais and His World*,[19] Simon Dentith writes: 'The whole book is best read as a coded attack on the cultural situation of Russia in the 1930s under Stalin – or, to use a more Bakhtinian vocabulary, the book is to be read as a hidden polemic against the regime's cultural politics ... The regime's grip on cultural policy tightened significantly after 1934 when "socialist realism" was officially promulgated as the only permissible aesthetic for the novel; much of Bakhtin's account of grotesque realism may be seen as an implicit rejoinder to this.'[20] In the context of all this, Fellini's position as a filmmaker is complicated. In his films he confronted the humourless and rigid tyranny of fascism and at the same time rebelled against the dominant but confining aesthetic of social realism (neorealism). However, in Fellini's case the former was not responsible for promoting the latter; neorealism was of course part of a leftist reaction against Italian cinema under fascism, which had been dominated by inane middle-class studio comedies and propaganda.[21] Yet because neorealism was unpopular with the Christian Democratic government, and especially with one of its key figures, Giulio Andreotti, and because it was later attacked by the communist film professor Umberto Barbaro, it fell between two stools.[22] In this light, we can approach neorealism as a popular but by no means universal or hegemonically enforced aesthetic.[23] In his championing of *La strada*, André Bazin draws attention to Fellini's problematic relationship with (and Roberto Rossellini's falling afoul of) the 'critical guardians of neo-realist orthodoxy,' an orthodoxy that was defined and policed by Marxist *Cinema nuovo* critics such as Chiarini and Aristarco and that, according to Bazin, can now be labelled 'socialist realism.'[24] If *La strada* marked the limits of unacceptability in neorealism for the Marxists with its 'neorealism of the person,' it is easy to see how Fellini's later films such as *8½* and *Giulietta degli spiriti* would have strongly offended Bazin, who contended that 'nothing is ever revealed to us from the interior of the character.'[25]

So both Fellini and Bakhtin, as filmmaker and critical theorist respectively, can be seen as embracing in different ways carnivalesque conventions and rituals in their work as a response – if only indirectly – to a confining and politicized aesthetic that has been labelled 'socialist realism.' For both men, it could be argued, it becomes important to look to the past to rejuvenate and, in doing so, venerate a longstanding popular and festive practice that, as an anti-authoritarian form, has long been marginalized or transformed. Bakhtin discovers the medieval carnival, and contends that many of its anti-authoritarian features survived the bourgeoisification of literature and were transposed into the writing of Dostoevsky and Rabelais. Fellini's work reflects this same popular legacy and also another, connected one – the *commedia dell'arte*. This form of popular theatre, which dates back to the sixteenth century and was performed mainly in marketplaces and public squares (key settings in so many Fellini films), was in the same way as the carnival 'progressively monopolised by well-to-do "society"'[26] during the eighteenth century. Bakhtin finds a continuity between the carnival (as the carnivalesque) and Dostoevsky and Rabelais; Fellini establishes a continuity with *commedia dell'arte* in his work through the figure of the clown.[27]

In the circus clown Fellini finds not only the legacy of a popular and satirical dramatic form, but also a potentially anti-authoritarian figure. Clowns, he believes, are both 'solemn' and authoritarian as well as 'the first and most ancient anti-establishment figure(s).' 'It's a pity,' he laments, 'that they are destined to disappear under the feet of technological progress.'[28] Fellini concedes the duality and ambiguity of the clown in this statement and then goes on to express a kind of Utopian nostalgia for clowning – a nostalgia that has very specific implications for his own form of cinematic art, which of course is part of the detrimental 'technological progress' to which he refers.[29] These tensions come into focus most explicitly in *I clowns*, in which the clowns' ambiguities, and the kinds of tensions these may cause with the filmic form through which they are represented and reproduced, constitute the drama of the film.

In the opening sequences of the film, in which Fellini remembers his first encounter with the circus, he dramatizes the dual potential of the clown. The violent energy of the show makes the young Fellini feel frightened and endangered[30] as well as fascinated; here it is well worth noting that the circus is set up in the shadow of the local mental asylum with its barred, prisonlike windows. This connection is reinforced later when we are offered a flashback in which the Fratellini Brothers are forced by hard times to play in trenches and in insane asylums run by nuns. As the tent is erected next to Fellini's house, hellish groaning noises accompany its movement upwards. The circus, and especially the clowns, mirror the loss of order and limitation that defines the mental asylum's inhabitants; yet in Fellini's terms the circus has licence not to have to 'keep inside fixed bounds' and in fact to celebrate those same deficiencies for which the asylum patients have been confined. The clowns *perform* the insanity that those in the asylum *experience*; the potency of their performance may indeed then lie, as Fellini claims, in their 'creating and living at the same time' in their performance. This may explain why, while the performance is unremarkable to those already in the asylum (because it is more life than art), the spectacular immediacy of this performance is too much for young Fellini. No longer able to differentiate between reality and performance, he is taken away in tears. This of course raises the following question: What happens to the clowns' performance when it is committed to film, if it is indeed the case that its force is derived from its potential to cross the limits that mark performance off from life? This issue was also implicit in my earlier account of the circus figures in *La strada*, *8½*, and *Giulietta degli spiriti*, who go beyond representing or performing the circus to *becoming it*.

The subsequent sequence in *I clowns* however, within which Fellini provides examples of the 'other strange and troubled characters' in his childhood of whom the circus performers remind him, functions to qualify this question. Three of the characters who appear could be labelled Auguste clowns (Big John the tramp, the midget nun, the diminutive drunken husband), and the other three (the stationmaster, the injured war veteran, and the military officer) are white clowns. However, the military officer, brought in by the self-important stationmaster to enforce decorum on the train full of schoolboys, is also exceptional among these. His deathly white complexion and blackened eyes mark him out as an authoritarian white clown. Yet there is nothing about his interaction with either the stationmaster or the young boys that could generate laughter. Rather, his presence commands a fearful silence and a wave of fascist salutes. Again, this seems to suggest that although Fellini has himself characterized Hitler and Mussolini as white and Auguste clowns respectively, these characterizations are merely *metaphorical* accounts of the two figures; whereas, as the appearance of the fascist demonstrates, there are some forms of authority in the real world that cannot easily be mocked or undermined through laughter.[31] There is, then, a limit to the extent to which circus paradigms can be mapped onto or equated with lived experience, and a limit also to their potential to exert cultural or political influence.

So perhaps it is not so much the characteristics and dramatic or political potential of the clown for which Fellini is nostalgic, since these are not qualities he presents in an especially unproblematic or Utopian light. Rather, the clown in this film represents to Fellini a form of *entertainment* (as opposed to art) that he feels is lost to him, and that draws attention to the painful limitations of his own art form, the cinema. I am thinking especially of the implications to be drawn from two scenes in the film that involve the failure of film technology to capture and reproduce a clown act. The first of these occurs on Fellini's visit to the Fratellini family, when Pierre Fratellini decides to show him some rare documentary film footage of the Fratellinis' performance in 1924. The projector, which Pierre explains is 'old like me,' breaks down twice. On the second occasion the film burns up on screen before anyone gets a chance to see anything. The second scene takes place in some French television studios, where Fellini has booked himself in for a special screening of some footage of a performance by the French clowns Rhum and Pipo. As the camera captures the grey, soulless building in which the film is housed, Fellini's voice-over describes how a 'vast funereal atmosphere underlies our search for a lost world.' The assistants there are hostile and ignorant (he is addressed as Mr Bellini); to them the films are merely catalogue numbers, for which they display no feeling. Rhum appears halfway through the film, which lasts only about thirty seconds. Again, Fellini's voice-over accompanying the image conveys his anticlimactic emotions: 'We felt disappointed, as if an undertaking had failed, as if our journey had led us nowhere.

Maybe the clown really is dead.' This conclusion is a premature answer to the questioning discourse with which Fellini had initially framed his quest to find the clowns: 'Where are the clowns of my childhood? Where are they today: that terrifying comic violence, that noisy exhilaration? Can the circus still entertain? The world which it belonged to no longer exists. Theatres transformed into runways. Glowing ingenuous sets, the childish naïveté of the public; they no longer exist. What remains of the old circuses? Subtle wasted traces.' It is not just that the film and the film equipment in these instances are old. There is evidence in these scenes of a more fundamental incompatibility between the circus and the film apparatus that attempts to capture it.

At the heart of Fellini's enterprise in *I clowns* is the recovery of the circus as a live art form – a recovery both driven and facilitated by the process of making a film. Yet the two dramas I've described above illustrate film's inability to capture the life and essence of the circus, which when reproduced on film only appears as 'subtle, wasted traces.' It is as though Fellini becomes caught up in what Noël Burch has described – in reference to early cinema – as the 'pursuit of a class phantasy, ultimately that of a culture: to conclude the conquest of nature by triumphing over death through a substitute for life itself.'[32] He is referring here to the nineteenth-century middle-class fantasy that the cinema would become the ultimate form of representation – that it would not merely scientifically reproduce a 'reality' before a spectator, but would be devoted to 'restoring "beauty" to photography' in pursuit of what he refers to as the bourgeoisie's 'Frankenstein ideology,' within which men would attain immortality by recreating life through the cinematic apparatus and thus symbolically abolish death, the 'supreme phantasm.'[33] When Fellini describes the cinema and the circus as having a common facility for 'creating and living at the same time,' he is attempting to transpose the immediacy and live presence that defines the circus onto the cinema. Yet what the filmic reconstructions of the clowns clearly demonstrate is the impossibility of this: on film the clowns are, at best, two-dimensional traces of a live performance. This leads Fellini to lament and confirm the clowns' disappearance, knowing he will never have the power to recover them.

In this respect, his encounters with these early films confirm the correlations that Siegfried Kracauer, Susan Sontag, Roland Barthes, and Walter Benjamin have established between photographic/film reproduction and the reduction of 'aura' or 'authenticity' in art. Kracauer asserts that photographic images 'by their sheer accumulation attempt to banish ... the recollection of death.' Nonetheless, what they reproduce in their images is 'not the person who appears in his or her photograph, but the sum of what can be deducted from him or her.'[34] Thus the figure in the photographic image stands as a disavowal of death and, since it constitutes only a series of traces of the life represented, also confirms the disappearance of both the moment and the person as they are represented. Likewise, when Susan Sontag claims that photography is 'the inventory of mortality,'[35] she echoes Kracauer to the extent that she has also identified this implication of the photographic image in the evocation of death. However, she also acknowledges the 'posthumous irony' that accompanies the act of viewing old photographs in her suggestion that the viewer's witnessing of the presence of the figures ('people being so irrefutably there') in the picture is at the same time always informed by the inescapable knowledge of the history that has since overtaken the figures represented.

In much the same terms, Roland Barthes picks up on this inevitable and painful interruption of history within the contemplation of old photographs during his account, in *Camera Lucida*, of his discovery, following her death, of photographs of his mother.[36] With one important exception,[37] he laments the pictures' failure to satisfy him either as 'photographic performance(s)' or as 'a living resurrection of the beloved face.'[38] Like Sontag's subjects, Barthes's mother appears in her photographs to be 'caught in a history (of tastes fashions fabrics)' that leaves him 'distracted' from her toward the 'accessories which have perished.'[39] Thus, as he claims later in his essay, the effect of a photograph is 'not to restore what has been abolished (by time, by distance),' since, like Sontag, he accepts that history always acts as a 'division.' Rather, a photograph works to 'attest that what I see has indeed existed' and as a 'certificate of presence,' but, crucially, presence in the past.[40] However, it is also important to acknowledge the distinction that Barthes draws between photography and film in this respect: 'Because the photograph, taken in flux, is impelled, ceaselessly drawn toward other views; in the cinema, no doubt, there is always a photographic referent, but this referent shifts, it does not make a claim in favour of its reality, it does not protest its former existence; it does not cling to me; it is not a *specter*. Like the real world the filmic world is sustained by the presumption that, as Husserl says, the experience will constantly continue to flow by in the same constitutive style.'[41]

In contrast, for Barthes, the power and meaning of still photographs cannot reach from the past into the present except through a form of haunting, because they are always circumscribed by death. Yet unlike stills, in motion pictures each image offers the next so that an expectancy of the future is somehow built into its impellent dynamic. This distinction is interesting in terms of *I clowns* because of the way Fellini appears to be discontented with the still photographs and memories he has of the clowns, and thus seeks to supplement – and perhaps to make complete through the addition of film – the archive/family film and his own.

Fellini, then, is engaged in constructing a cinema of his own that in Barthes's terms not only 'resurrects' the clowns and their particular comic tradition but also gives them life in the present. Walter Benjamin's account of the representational problems involved in recording images/figures/events is especially pertinent to this project, since he is most interested in the specific capacity of film to wither 'tradition':

> One might subsume the eliminated element in the term 'aura' and go on to say: that which withers in the age of mechanical reproduction is the aura of the work of art ... The technique of reproduction detaches the reproduced object from the domain of tradition. By making many reproductions it substitutes a plurality of copies for a unique existence. And in permitting the reproduction to meet the beholder or listener in his own particular situation, it reactivates the object reproduced. These two processes lead to a tremendous shattering of tradition which is the obverse of the contemporary crisis and renewal of mankind. Both processes are intimately connected with the contemporary mass movements. Their most powerful agent is the film.[42]

Not only is the art object removed from tradition once it is involved in the processes of mechanical reproduction such as film, but, Benjamin claims, this process 'emancipates the work of art from its parasitical dependence on ritual.'[43]

When Fellini mourns the disappearance of the clown 'under the feet of technological progress,' he must of course acknowledge his own complicity in this, since it is the mass media of cinema and television that have superseded the circus in popularity and dominance. In trying to recover the clown on film, *I clowns* may succeed insofar as it is a documentary history of significant clowns; but, as I suggested earlier, the film also dramatizes its own painful but fundamental incompatibility with the dynamics of clowning. As a (pseudo-) documentary, the film describes and records clowning as a tradition, tracing its roots through various significant contributions to the Pierrot and Auguste figures. Yet paradoxically *I clowns*, which sets out to recover a tradition, ends by confirming its disappearance, since film (in Benjamin's terms) by its very nature, removes the unique art object, the one-off performance, 'from the domain of tradition' by reproducing and multiplying it. The photographic image by its very nature seems to banish death by preserving the image of an object forever; yet at the same time, the reproduced image becomes a haunting trace of a now irrecoverable dead moment. This situation is exacerbated through the clowns since, culturally, clowning is not only a popular tradition into which the film attempts to breathe new life, but also one that insistently revolves around rituals (which are by definition live), albeit carnivalesque ones, through which mechanical reproduction, according to Benjamin, has apparently wrested art from a 'parasitical dependence.'

It is no coincidence, then, that the ritual chosen for the spectacular finale in *I clowns*, in which Fellini attempts to make the cinema finally do justice to the clowns' talent and energy, is a funeral. The funeral that Fellini presents is both ambivalent and carnivalesque. Aesthetically it offers the film's most dizzying, mobile, and colourful cinematography. Dramatically it provides the most diverse and entertaining range of clown acts and characters seen so far. Yet it is, above all, a funeral for clowns, and the laughter that is reborn in their chaotic and obscene performances is inevitably dualistically attached to an acknowledgment that the entire tradition has died. This is underlined by a couple of the aging, out-of-breath clowns, who discharge themselves from the increasingly frenetic circular procession, and by the film crew's final pronouncement, 'Turn it off. It's over,' over the image of the last clown we see in the film (played by an actor who had earlier appeared as a long-deceased clown). This indicates that the live performance is over, but perhaps also that the clown tradition is over. Now the clowns have been committed to film, and so, like Guillon's partner Fru-Fru, they can be summoned up again; but as this final scene suggests, the figure that appears magically from nowhere and similarly disappears into thin air is a 'wasted trace,' an imaginary, ghostlike figure called back from the dead.

An examination of Fellini's most notable circus films, then, reveals the circus figures within them to be involved in more ambiguous and more critically challenging dramas than much previous criticism has been able to uncover. Fellini's assertion that the cinema could *be* the circus may reflect a 'great European art' director's desire that his highly personal cinematic vision be an influential one, since the circus in his films is valued for its ability to cross boundaries that confine other forms of art and entertainment and, in crossing those boundaries, enter life and transform individual lives. Nonetheless, all of Fellini's circus figures are involved in an impossible relationship with the objects of their influence – an impossibility often signalled by their cinematic constitution, which formally places them at one remove from the circus. The ambiguous quality of the circus in terms of its narrative figures encourages a reading of their carnivalistic potential; yet whereas Bakhtin was concerned with art that dramatized social change and crisis, Fellini is concerned more narrowly with particular lives. The more telling connection between Fellini and Bakhtin lies in their mutual embracing of long-standing but vanishing popular cultural forms, the circus and the carnival respectively. This may suggest a nostalgic desire in each. In Fellini's case, however, the desire to revitalize and preserve the live performance of the circus clowns is a profoundly revealing one for film criticism, since it dramatizes an irreconcilable disjuncture between circus and film aesthetics (as live and mechanical arts), and in doing so operates as a register of the fundamental ambivalence of the film image itself, which both reinvents life and marks its passing.

Notes

1 *Entretiens avec Federico Fellini: Les cahiers R.T.B. series Télécinéma*, 1962, reprinted in Suzanne Budgen, *Fellini* (London: British Film Institute Education, 1966) 52.

2 Costanzo Costantini, ed., Sohrab Sorooshian, trans. *Fellini on Fellini* (London: Faber and Faber, 1994) 30.

3 Costantini 176.

4 Budgen 90.

5 Pam Cook, 'Authorship and Cinema,' in *The Cinema Book* (London: B.F.I. Publishing, 1986) 118.

6 John C. Stubbs, 'The Fellini Manner: Open Form and Visual Excess,' *Cinema Journal* 32.4 (Summer 1993): 51. See also the following examples, which accept as real the truth of such declarations from Fellini regarding the relationship between circus and cinema: Budgen 52; Donald P. Costello, *Fellini's Road* (Notre Dame and London: U of Notre Dame P, 1983) 146; and Naomi

Ritter, *Art as Spectacle: Images of the Entertainer Since Romanticism* (Columbia and London: U of Missouri P, 1989) 276.

7 For an outline of this project see Lietta Tornbuoni, ed., *Federico Fellini* (New York: Rizzoli International Publications, 1995) 23–55.

8 Ritter points to the resonance of the chain with which Zampanò encircles his chest and sees it as a metaphor for his learning to 'burst the circle of his animal self' (301). While it is certainly an important image of circularity in the film, this would seem an odd reading, since it is his 'animal self' that struggles against the chain. It is part of Zampanò's reformation that he accepts the image of the chain and that he can indeed be part of a series of connections between people rather than a destroyer of them.

9 André Bazin, '*La strada*,' trans. Joseph E. Cunneen, *Cross-Currents* 6.3 (1956), reprinted in Peter Bondanella, ed., *Federico Fellini: Essays in Criticism* (Oxford: Oxford UP, 1978) 58.

10 Bazin 58.

11 Ritter 295.

12 Slavoj Žižek, *Enjoy Your Symptom! Jacques Lacan in Hollywood and Out* (London: Routledge, 1992) 4.

13 Ritter similarly identifies in Fellini's use of the circus a 'nostalgia for innocence,' which he projects onto 'various clown figures' (312).

14 Such a reference, however, must be qualified by two of Bakhtin's own acknowledgments: first, that 'Carnival itself ... is not, of course, a literary phenomenon. It is *syncretic pageantry* of a ritualistic sort,' and second, that 'carnival knows no footlights' (Mikhail Bakhtin, *Problems of Dostoevsky's Poetics* [Manchester: Manchester UP, 1984] 122). Thus, we need to hold on to the distinction in Bakhtin between *carnival* and *carnivalized* or *carnivalesque* forms – those which in Bakhtin's terms may have been 'transposed' into art, though he is concerned only with literature. Yet despite these clearly stated distinctions, there do indeed seem to be similarities between Bakhtin's desire for literature to become carnival and Fellini's for film to become circus.

15 Bakhtin 124.

16 Bakhtin 127.

17 Bakhtin 123.

18 Bakhtin 123.

19 Mikhail Bakhtin, *Rabelais and His World*, trans. Helene Iswolsky (Cambridge & London: MIT UP, 1968).

20 Simon Dentith, *Bakhtinian Thought: An Introductory Reader* (London: Routledge, 1995) 71.

21 See Frank Burke, *Federico Fellini*: Variety Lights *to* La Dolce Vita (Boston: Twayne Publishing, 1984) 1–2.

22 For a more detailed discussion of these debates see Mira Liehm, *Passion and Defiance: Film in Italy From 1942 to the Present* (Berkeley and Los Angeles: U of California P, 1984) 99–102.

23 'Throughout the political upheaval, the explosion of neo-realism, and the aesthetic revolution, the Italian cinema did not once cease to pursue what was at that time condemned with particular savagery by the critics, namely the big spectacular, mythology, opera, melodrama' (Pierre Leprohon, *The Italian Cinema* [London: Secker & Warburg, 1972] 96).

24 Bazin 56.

25 Liehm 57–8.

26 John Rudlin, *Commedia dell'Arte: An Actor's Handbook* (London: Routledge, 1994) 4.

27 Like Fellini in *I clowns*, André Gide visited the Cirque Medrano in Paris, but unlike Fellini he did get to see the Fratellini Brothers perform live. He was so impressed that he urged them not to 'hesitate to remain simply clowns, the heirs to the divine commedia dell'arte' (André Gide, quoted in Rudlin 181).

28 Quoted in Costantini 74.

29 Bakhtin too has been charged with providing a utopian account of carnival. See Peter Stallybrass and Allon White, *The Politics and Poetics of Transgression* (London: Methuen, 1986).

30 For a psychological interpretation of this split see Frank Burke, 'The Three-Phase Clown Process and the White Clown–Auguste Relationship in Fellini's *The Clowns*,' *1977 Film Studies Annual: Part 1: Explorations in National Cinemas* (Pleasantville, NY: Redgrave, 1977) 125–6.

31 *Fellini on Fellini*, ed. Anna Keel and Christian Strich, trans. Isabel Quigley (New York: Delacourte/Seymour Lawrence, 1976) 130.

32 Noël Burch, 'Charles Baudelaire v. Dr Frankenstein,' *Afterimage* 8/9 (Spring 1981): 6.

33 Burch 21.

34 Siegfried Kracauer, 'Photography' (1927), trans. Thomas Y. Levin, reprinted in *Critical Inquiry* 3 (Spring 1993): 432.

35 Susan Sontag, 'Melancholy Objects,' *On Photography* (Harmondsworth: Penguin Books, 1979) 70.

36 Roland Barthes, *Camera Lucida* (London: Flamingo, 1984) 63–71.

37 Barthes borrows Proust's words to describe how the 'Winter Garden Photograph' allows him to experience 'for the first time, an involuntary and complete memory' of his mother and thereby to achieve for himself, at least 'utopically,' what he describes as 'the impossible science of the unique being' (70–1).

38 Barthes 64.
39 Barthes 64.
40 Barthes 82, 87.
41 Barthes 89–90.
42 Walter Benjamin, 'The Work of Art in the Age of Mechanical Reproduction' (1935), reprinted in Gerald Mast and Marshall Cohen, eds., *Film Theory and Criticism* (Oxford: Oxford UP, 1982) 852.
43 Benjamin 854.

3

Fellini and Lacan:
The Hollow Phallus, the Male Womb,
and the Retying of the Umbilical

WILLIAM VAN WATSON

In the early years of the last century, Sigmund Freud formulated his theories regarding human sexuality. Later generations have faulted the Freudian Oedipal paradigm for both its male specificity and its hetero-centricity. During the middle years of the last century, French psycho-analyst Jacques Lacan extended the Freudian Oedipal paradigm into the field of semiotics, the study of sign systems. Lacan describes an originary situation of illusory undifferentiated wholeness or plenitude based on mother–infant symbiosis. The phallus intrudes into this situa-tion, diacritically splitting wholeness into differentiated elements and the ungendered symbiosis of the mother–infant unit into 'sexed partial beings' (311). Semiotically the phallus functions as 'signifier of signifi-ers' or 'symbol of symbology,' as the differentiation it provokes divides the sign into signifier and signified, giving birth to semiosis itself. Sex-ually and culturally, this phallus-signifier can conflate confusingly with the penis, as Lacanian theory collapses into the male-specificity of Freudian tradition. For Lacan, like Freud, gender divides into genital-ized groups of haves and have-nots, possessors-of-the-phallus and those without. In each case, however, both are marked with lack, and thus desire, because of their positioning vis-à-vis the lost plenitude of the originary mother–infant symbiotic state.

Lacan thus theorizes a parallel between semiosis and psychosexual-ity. Applied to the semiotic realm, the apparition of the phallus de-notes the 'Law of the Father,' ordering, structuring, and subjecting to ratiocination the now differentiated elements of the previously mias-mic chaos of undifferentiated plenitude by enabling the evolution of knowledge, science, and systems of power, and also the language(s) to express them. Language and Logos attempt to compensate for the loss of plenitude and its resulting sense of lack. Such lack provokes desire, as Lacan notes: 'The phallus is the privileged signifier of that mark in which *the role of logos is joined with the advent of desire'* (287, emphasis mine). Insofar as such ratiocination is phallically determined and constructed, the convoluted term 'phallogocentrism' can be used, indicating the male bias of the authority and organization of semiotic-cultural systems. Such phallogocentric male bias extends into the ostensibly irrational realm of religion insofar as religion is also a semiotic-cultural phenomenon. John 1:1 makes this phallo-semiotic-authoritarian connection glaringly apparent: 'In the beginning was the Word, and the Word was with God and the Word was God.' In monotheistic religious systems such as the Judeo-Christian, the concept 'God' functions as Lacanian phallus. However spiritually absurd it may be to assign God a gender, the pronoun 'He' defines ultimate authority as male. John's equation of God with 'the Word' identifies Him as provider of meaning, source of semiosis, and lawgiver. Lacan writes: 'It is in the *name of the father* that we must recognize the support of the [S]ymbolic function which, from the dawn of history, has identified his person with the figure of the law' (67).

Lacan divides the human condition, culture, and semiosis into three orders: the Imaginary, the Symbolic, and the Real.[1] The Imaginary Order derives from the relatively alienated sense perceptions of vision and hearing, as opposed to the more immediate senses of touch, taste, and smell. Kaja Silverman succinctly characterizes the Lacanian Imaginary as 'a spectrum of images which precedes the acquisition of language in the experience of the child, and which continues to coexist with it afterward' (21). As its name indicates, the Imaginary Order corresponds roughly to the common term 'imagination.' The Imaginary Order privileges fantasies and dreams, which are themselves primarily visual and secondarily aural, and only rarely (if ever) allied to the tactile, gustatory, and olfactory. Lacan asserts that 'no [I]maginary formation is specific' (191). To render an Imaginary formation specific is to fix it within semiosis, to denote its meaning and move it out of the Imaginary and into the Symbolic Order. It is the Symbolic Order that makes sense of the sensory by developing languages both verbal and non-verbal, in what is generally termed 'culture,' which is policeable by the intellect. Freud valued the imagination and dreams as tools to unlock the unconscious; for him, the craft of interpretation was basically one of translating the perceptual Imaginary Order into the conceptual Symbolic Order. As an implicit critic of Freud and Lacan,

Fellini in *Roma* (1972) shows an inverse process when the phallic drill intrudes into the womb of the ancient Roman catacombs. The immediate result is not a Symbolic ordering (although this eventually occurs with the construction of the Roman subway), but rather an erasure of the Imaginary, as visually represented in the ancient Roman frescoes, which rapidly fade away from exposure. For Lacan, translation of the Imaginary into the Symbolic involves subjecting the former to the male bias of the phallogocentric, but for Fellini, the aggressiveness of this male bias threatens to destroy the Imaginary itself.

Lacan's Real Order is known only indirectly through the Imaginary as interpreted within the Symbolic, the Symbolic Order resulting from and mediating between the contact of the Imaginary with the Real. According to Lacan, direct encounter with the Real Order, un-negotiated by the Symbolic Order through the Imaginary, results in trauma. The Real Order is the most abstract yet at the same time the most concrete of the three orders. Its concreteness lies in its immediacy of taste, touch, and smell, while its abstraction lies in its position outside Symbolization in ultra-conscious experiences such as death, abjection, terror, ecstasy, orgasm, love, and other states of ultimate meaning. From within the confines of the visual-aural medium of the cinema, Fellini daringly attempts to leapfrog the Symbolic Order and make direct Imaginary contact with the Real. Fellini's filmography embodies the concreteness of the Real in its overtly metacinematic nature, its emphasis on the physical means and method of cinematic production, and its celebration of its own artifice; while in its attempts to convey meaning beyond signification his cinema also aspires to the abstraction of the Real. Lacan notes: 'The Real seems to include the domain of the inexpressible, of what cannot be [S]ymbolized, and to be the Order where the subject meets with death and inexpressible enjoyment' (164). The concreteness of the Real lies in precisely those sensory perceptions that appertain to the period of mother–infant symbiosis, so that this 'death and inexpressible enjoyment' bespeak an annihilation of the subject in predifferentiated plenitude.[2] In Fellini, as in Lacan, 'death [of the subject] and inexpressible enjoyment' are most often combined in the fullness of the maternal. For Lacan, 'the subject is constituted by the Symbolic Order,' so that the plenitude of the mother threatens an erasure of the differentiated subject born of the apparition of the phallus (106). Fellini demonstrates this dynamic by repeatedly surrendering his male subjects to the siege of maternal plenitude in the form of the overwhelming breasts and buttocks of his female characters.

E. Ann Kaplan notes: 'If Lacan did not actually use the term the "social imaginary," this is implied by his general discussion of the imaginary/symbolic polarity in the sense that every child moves through the *same* [I]maginary and enters the *same* [S]ymbolic' (49, emphasis mine). Despite Kaplan, Lacan's 'general' discussion of the symbolic does not posit it as universally homogeneous. The Symbolic evolves over time and varies from society to society, even as the languages, sciences, and systems of political, social, and sexual order that comprise it evolve and vary. Ethnosemioticians have theorized that sign systems function in different ways within different cultures as those cultures assume distinctly different relationships between the signifier and the signified. Anglo-American culture has tended to ascribe a more direct and reliable relationship between even the most abstract signifier and the signified; in contrast, Luigi Barzini discerns a more dubious relationship in Italian culture between these two parts of the sign: 'Nothing is ever what it looks like, and one can never trust appearances; everything then takes on a double outline ... In fact, the thing and its representation often coincide exactly. They may also coincide approximately, or may not coincide at all. There is no sure way of telling' (85).

The more literal and literate American cinema has a long tradition of fostering directors such as Dorothy Arzner, Preston Sturges, Billy Wilder, John Huston, Mike Nichols, and Woody Allen, all of whom began their careers as screenwriters or in the theatre and then forged filmographies based on repartee. Such cinema visually degenerates into 'talking head pictures,' that place the medium in subservience to the actors' performances. Fellini interpreted this subjugation of the cinema's visual nature to the word in specifically cultural terms: 'Anglo-Saxons are demented on the subject. Absolutely crazy' (in Alpert 234). Italian culture is distrustful of the Anglo-American literal–literate semiotic tradition, and perceives the relationship between signifier and signified as dangerously arbitrary. In its compensatory attempt to fix this relationship, Italian culture, with its rich tradition in the visual arts and operatic spectacle, its dominance in design, and its demonstrativeness, has come to orient itself strongly toward the external.[3] From an Anglo-American perspective, Italian culture can appear as an exercise in semiotic overdetermination. Tadeusz Kowzan notes: 'Spectacle transforms natural signs into artificial ones' (in Keir 60). As spectacular Italian artifice attempts to compensate for the semiotically arbitrary, this symptomatic overloading of the signifier perpetually sabotages its relationship to the signified even as it attempts to fix it. The precarious relationship between signifier and signified remains a fixture of Italian culture, and 'natural signs' remain at a remove. Fellini's cinema embodies this Italian semiotic sensibility. Frank Burke sees Fellini's career as a progression from realism to representation to signification, as the connection between signifier and signified within the sign becomes progressively strained. However, the spectacularity to which Kowzan refers has 'strained' the semiotic connection in Fellini's cinema since its beginnings. *Variety Lights* (1950) deals with theatre, *The White Sheik* (1952) with photoromances, and *I vitelloni* (1953) with performances of masculinity. All three films expose the hollowness of the show.

Fellini's cinema exhibits not only an Italian semiotic sensibility, but also a mutation of the Lacanian paradigm that is distinctly his own. Fellini's name has been virtually synonymous with auteurist cinema, and many critics have scrutinized his content and style to define his cinematic signature and thumbprint. However, unlike more traditional auteurist critics, I am concerned not only with *what* the Fellinian signs are and *what* they communicate, but also with *how* they communicate. Kaplan makes assertions about the sameness of a 'social' Imaginary; in contrast, Lacan himself conceded that his theories should be modified to accommodate the case histories of individuals.[4] Three characteristics distinguish Fellini's semiotic sensibility from the broader contours of the Lacanian paradigm: the hollow phallus, the male womb, and the retying of the umbilical. Cultural character and personal biography are not mutually exclusive categories in determining a semiotic sensibility, and Fellini's case offers an interesting intersection of the two. Fellini's father, Urbano Fellini, was a travelling grocery wholesaler whose job meant that Fellini saw little of him while growing up. In *La dolce vita* (1960) and *8½* (1963), the first two feature-length films he conceived and produced after his father's death in 1956, Fellini laments that they never had an intimate relationship. The relative absence of Urbano Fellini diminished the Lacanian Law of the Father in the Fellini household, leaving the apparition of the phallus weakened, hollow. Insofar as the more conceptually verbal Symbolic is the province of the Law of the Father, Fellini's cinema prefers the perceptually visual Imaginary. In contrast to his more literal–literate Anglo-American counterparts, Fellini began as a cartoonist and used his lifelong habitual doodling on tablecloths and napkins as the point of inspiration for many of his films. As he described his cinema, 'It has to do with images and only with images' (Angelucci and Betti 95). Fellini discarded Gore Vidal's screenplay for *Fellini's Casanova*, asserting his preference for the visual Imaginary over the verbal Symbolic: 'Literary interpretations of events have nothing to do with the cinematic interpretation of those same events. They are two completely different modes of expression' (*Comments* 28). Literature works within the conceptual Symbolic, whereas film plays on the perceptual Imaginary; however, both allow but do not require the reader or filmgoer to translate the work into the opposing Order. Fellini himself sometimes played at such translation, creating jokes in the process. *The Voice of the Moon* (1990) interpolates Nestore's verbal conceits and metaphors into outrageous visual images. However, Fellini disdained as reductive the reverse process of translating the Imaginary into the Symbolic. A self-proclaimed 'conscious mystifier,' '[he] would disclaim any intention to create meaning' (Alpert 292).

Film theorist Christian Metz has applied Lacanian thought specifically to the cinematic apparatus: 'What is characteristic of the cinema is not the [I]maginary that it may happen to represent, but the [I]maginary that it is from the start' (249). In other words, insofar as cinema may optionally represent something else, as signifier of a signified it functions on the level of the semiotic Symbolic. However, for both Metz and Fellini this is of secondary importance compared to the fact that its ontological identity lies within the perceptual and sensorial level of the Imaginary. *The White Sheik*, *8½*, 'The Temptations of Dr Antonio' (1962), and *Juliet of the Spirits* (1965) all vacillate uneasily between the dreamlike Imaginary and the 'official' reality of the Symbolic Order, while in *The Voice of the Moon* the very viability of the Symbolic Order is called into question. *The White Sheik* provides a rationale for the dominance of the Imaginary in Fellini, as Wanda temporarily adopts the dictum that would become the hallmark of his cinema: 'The real life is that of dreams.' A partial insomniac who slept only a few hours a night, Fellini valued his dreams as a source of inspiration. Edward Murray specifically defines Fellini's 'inspiration' as 'the artist's ability to make direct contact between the conscious and unconscious mind' (20). Such 'direct contact' bespeaks the artist's ability to counter the threatened erasure of the Imaginary by the Symbolic, as illustrated in the subway drilling sequence in *Roma* (1972). Both *Nights of Cabiria* (1956) and *8½* examine methods for overcoming such Symbolic erasure and maintaining direct Imaginary contact: Cabiria succumbs to a hypnotist, and Maya's abilities as a seer are presented as genuine.[5] Fellini's pursuit of the irrational and unconscious led to his cultivating parapsychologists, magicians, palm readers, astrologists, and mediums, but mostly it encouraged his intellectual interest in the theories and writings of Carl Jung. Fellini's career-long predilection for Jung constitutes a tacit rejection of Freud, whose phallogocentrism would have 'interpreted' Fellini's dreams, fixing them in the Symbolic. In Jung's concept of the archetype, Fellini perceived an umbilical connection between the Lacanian Symbolic, Real, and Imaginary Orders: 'What I admire most about Jung is that he found a meeting place between science and magic, between reason and fantasy' (in Alpert 170). Jung thus validated Fellini's own belief in 'no dividing line between imagination and reality' (*Fellini on Fellini* 150).

Fellini disdained intellectual Symbolic interpretation as limiting: 'Our rational point of view acts like a prison' (in Alpert 179). Italo Calvino notes that 'the intellectual for Fellini is always a desperate man' (in Fellini, *Quattro* xxii). In *La dolce vita* Fellini uses Steiner's suicide to indict rational, intellectual phallogocentrism as delusional in its attempts to make sense of the sensory. Steiner seeks refuge in the Imaginary Order from the overdetermined Symbolic Order of his own intellectualism by recording and listening to natural sounds. He also seeks refuge in a church, the province wherein the Real Order of faith rules over the Symbolic Order of reason. There, in a display of the sensory over the intellectual, he plays the organ. When the critic Daumier in *8½* claims, 'We intellectuals must remain lucid until the end,' Guido provides this end by fantasizing him hooded and hanged. Fellini also undermines Daumier's attempts at deploying the Symbolic Order to police reality by naming the character after a nineteenth-century French cartoonist, whose work (like Fellini's) functioned mainly within the visual Imaginary. In *Fellini-Satyricon* (1969), Eumolpus's intellectualism proves equally impotent, as his poetic verbiage goes ignored at Trimalchio's feast. In *Fellini's Casanova* (1976), Casanova's pretensions to intellectual pursuits in engineering and literature – his ordering of the world according to Symbolic principles – lies outside the interest of both his contemporaries and the film itself. Despite their intellectual pretentiousness, both Eumolpus and Casanova leave a legacy only of the flesh. Eumolpus's heirs consume his corpse, and Casanova becomes equated in popular consciousness with prodigious copulation. Eumolpus's and Casanova's aspirations to Symbolic mastery degenerate into the concreteness of the Real, as the first is ingested and the latter metaphorically excreted via his portrait in feces.

Lacan claims that 'the moment in which desire becomes human is also that in which the child is born into language' (103). Casanova's obsessive attempt to police the significance of his life through his incessant voice-over narration and hollow platitudinizing functions as Symbolic compensation for a demonstrated lack of mother love. In *Fellini's Casanova* and elsewhere, Fellini frustrates language not only by asserting the pictorial Imaginary, but also by turning the verbiage against itself. The Duke of Parma's banquet in *Fellini's Casanova*, the orgy at Suzy's in *Juliet of the Spirits*, the ocean crossing in *And the Ship Sails On* (1983), and the parties in *La dolce vita* all feature international guest lists that provide Fellini with ample opportunity for polyglot delirium, as specific languages blur into one another and degenerate into pure sound. As the Symbolic Order proliferates, Fellini creates Babel. He most thoroughly confounds this verbal Symbolic Order in *Fellini-Satyricon*, using not only extant languages but also ancient and invented ones, resulting in 'a twelvefold phonic ... arrhythmia' (Angelucci and Betti 36). Fellini also undermined the intellectual policing function of language through his production practices. Throughout his career he was notorious for having his actors count nonsensically, inserting actual dialogue only during the postdubbing process. In *Fellini-Satyricon* he further aborted 'birth into language' by purposefully tampering with the synchronization. Also, the opening image of the film pays visual homage to verbal sabotage by debasing written communication into decor in the form of the graffiti covering the walls of the Roman baths.[6]

As Fellini undermines language, he also undermines the patriarchal authority that Lacan saw creating it. From Zampanò's introduction to his performance in *La strada* (1954), to the fascist rhetoric in *Amarcord* (1973), to the emcee's introduction of Amelia and Pippo in *Ginger and Fred* (1985), Fellini exposes language as the rote packaging of patriarchal self-interest. Even as the patriarchal apparition of the phallus provokes Lacan's verbal Symbolic Order, the apparition of the hollow phallus in Fellini provokes a dysfunctional Symbolic Order. Val's insistence in *Juliet of the Spirits* that Olaf use the formal noun 'Troia' to refer to ancient Troy, rather than the informal noun 'troia' to call her a slut (in Italian), provides just one example. Verbal language degenerates into the nonsense words of Bhisma in *Juliet of the Spirits*, and of Snaporaz in *City of Women* (1980), and into a student's inevitable mispronunciation of a Greek word into a raspberry in *Amarcord*. Language in 'Toby Dammit' (1968) descends from the pinnacle of Shakespearean verse early in the film to Toby's final primal screams. Language fails

Gelsomina altogether in *La strada* when her Real emotions regarding the death of the Fool outstrip her limited linguistic ability to negotiate them, leaving her a Symbolic mute with only the Imaginary voice of the trumpet to express herself.

As auteur-itarian 'Maestro' on the set of his films, Fellini sabotaged the patriarchal verbal and also suffered from such sabotage. Because of his chronic inability to assign names to his characters, he often resorted to naming characters after the actors who played them. In *Juliet of the Spirits* he exorcises this difficulty, having guests assign a blindfolded woman at Suzy's orgy a multiplicity of names in a futile effort to fix her identity. *8½* further demonstrates the hollowness of the phallus in Fellini's psychosemiotic sensibility when Guido fails to split the sign into signifier and signified and accidentally tells the screen image of the actress auditioning to play his wife, rather than his wife, that he loves her. When Guido claims, 'I don't have anything to say, but I want to say it just the same,' he is lamenting his incapacity to name a signi-fied and simultaneously expressing his desire to play with signifiers. In contrast to the semiotic anxiety of *8½*, *Intervista* (1987) revels in semiotic delirium. Fellini places Marcello Mastroianni (who served as cinematic signifier of Fellini in *La dolce vita*, *8½*, and *City of Women*), the actor Sergio Rubini (who serves as signifier of young Fellini in *Inter-vista*), and himself (as self-signifier and trebled signified) all together in the same car! Still more deliriously, *Ginger and Fred* populates the screen with a parade of signifier-lookalikes who bring into question the authenticity of any originary signified.

Narrativity constitutes an extension of the Law of the Father from the atomized writing of a name to the more global writing of a story. A potent Law of the Father results in rigorously structured narrative, such as the tight plotting found in the work of Alfred Hitchcock, a director very much concerned with the Law of the Father as mani-fested both in the forensic policing of society and in the rational polic-ing of psychopathology. In contrast, the hollow phallus in Fellini results in loose plotting and the virtual breakdown of narrative and narrativity. In preparing for *Fellini-Satyricon*, Fellini praised the narra-tive lapses of the original: 'I reread Petronius and was fascinated by ... the blanks between one episode and the next ... that business of frag-ments really fascinated me' (Bondanella and Degli-Esposti 284). Fellini accentuated this open plotting, as his film rearranged and embroidered Petronius's text. Fellini was bisecting his plots as early as *The White Sheik* (1952), in that particular case between the newlyweds Ivan and

Wanda, as Ivan's futile scripting of their honeymoon itinerary gets discarded. The dual focus of *The White Sheik* splinters into the escapades of five friends in *I vitelloni* (1953) and the five swindles in *Il bidone* (1955). *La strada* was the beginning of Fellini's foray into the picaresque structure that carried him through *La dolce vita, 8½, Juliet of the Spirits, Fellini-Satyricon, Fellini's Casanova, City of Women,* and *The Voice of the Moon.* Each of these films recounts the exploits of a single character through a variety of episodes having no cause-and-effect relationship. *Amarcord* and *And the Ship Sails On* further develop a picaresque structure by following a group protagonist rather than an individual. In the metacinematic *8½* the very topic of narrative structure becomes a polemical issue as producers,' critics,' and actresses' demands for a script find Fellini-Guido altogether without a narrative. Daumier demands 'unassailable logic' in Guido's script and criticizes this quintessential Fellini scenario for being 'a gratuitous series of episodes.'[7]

Cause-and-effect narrativity depends on temporal differentiation and sequencing. As a Symbolic and therefore phallogocentric ordering of time, chronology also falls victim to Fellini's hollow phallus. *8½, Juliet of the Spirits, Fellini's Roma,* and *Intervista* all revel in blurring chronology. Fellini vaunted: 'I no longer succeed in distinguishing past, present and future' (in Burke 34). Freud stipulated that there was no chronological time in the unconscious; in this vein, Fellini's disdain for chronology further prioritizes the unconscious and its visual Imaginary. Freed of chronological sequencing, *Roma* and *Intervista* provide the flimsiest rationales for the succession of images Fellini feels like presenting to his audience. These films are 'held together only by the fact that they all ultimately originate from the director's fertile *imagination*' (Bondanella 193, emphasis mine).

Whether in terms of narrativity, sequentiality, or chronology, Fellini discards linearity. Camille Paglia describes 'linearity [as] a phallic track of mind piercing through the entanglements of nature' (1991: 59). Fellini's addition of the maze sequence to Petronius's *Satyricon* metaphorically celebrates the frustration of the linearly phallic by such entanglements. In *Amarcord*, entanglements are more specifically associated with nature, as Fellini abandons linear narrative in favour of the cycle of seasons. In the traffic jam sequences at the Colosseum in both *Roma* and 'Toby Dammit,' circularity visually entangles phallic linearity; in *City of Women*, Snaporaz fails to pierce through the circle of women skating around him. Obsessively reappearing in *La strada, 8½, Juliet of the Spirits,* and *I clowns*, the circus as *leitmotif* of Fellini's cinema epitomizes the director's predilection for circularity over linearity. In *Fellini's Casanova*, by setting the protagonist's first sexual escapade in a circular space, Fellini turns the encounter into a circus, thereby undermining Casanova's vaunted phallic ability to 'pierce through.'

Fellini frustrates phallic linearity not only in his narrative structure and use of *mise-en-scène*, but also in his use of the cinematic apparatus. For example, the introduction to Zampanò's performance of strength in *La strada* provides the camera with an opportunity to perform a circular tracking movement; so does the ascent by Silvia and Marcello of St Peter's dome in *La dolce vita*. In *Roma* the *circonvallazione* of Rome's inefficient freeway system completely derails the on-screen Fellini from the phallic goal-orientation of his tracking shots. As his camera fails to penetrate the city, the piercing forward movement of the tracking shot repeatedly gives way to a sideways wandering pan. Such panning shots are a hallmark of Fellini's cinema and of *Roma*, in particular; the camera grazes on the images set before it much as his characters graze on the banquets in the film. In all his films, his seemingly restless camera wanders among his actors and *mises-en-scène*, first framing one actor, then picking up another and following him or her until it encounters a third, and so on. The effect, far from phallically linear, is at best a zigzag. His camera often tracks an actor or object that stops, leaving the camera to continue on, revealing its prior goal orientation as nothing more than a temporary diversion. Such detailed movements recall F.W. Murnau's 'unchained' camera (i.e., his subjective moving camera), except that often there is no subject in these Fellinian sequences. The subject has been mislaid in the 'inexpressible enjoyment' of the Imaginary (m)other of Fellini's cinematic world. As Fellini discards cause-and-effect, he liberates his camera from the tidy shot–countershot formations that express it. His preference for the unconscious and the primacy of autonomous visual images allows him to employ the associative editing that is typical of surrealism, instead of the more pedestrian continuity editing of realism.

Fellini's filmography further exhibits the symptoms of the hollow phallus in terms of subject construction, particularly of the father, the lover, the military authority, and the religious figure. In *La dolce vita* Marcello refers to Steiner's home as a 'refuge,' but Steiner's mentoring ultimately provides Marcello with only a blind alley of escape from his existential purposelessness. Steiner not only commits suicide but also abdicates the paternal role by murdering his two children. Marcello's father abruptly aborts his paternal visit to Marcello, absenting himself from the narrative in a manner reminiscent of Fellini's own absent father. In *8½* the patriarch degenerates into a corpse; Guido's father appears only as a ghost to lead his son to his tomb. In *Amarcord* Titta's father-as-phallus is literally 'hollowed out' by the fascists who punish him by force-feeding him castor oil. As a result he is infantilized, and robbed of the power and control usually associated with patriarchy. As authoritarians and nurturers, directors and conductors also perform a paternal role in Fellini's cinema, but the directors in *The White Sheik*, *8½*, *Orchestra Rehearsal* (1979) and *Intervista* prove themselves uniformly incapable of having authority over – or nurturing – anything.

These director characters exhibit male performance anxiety within the realm of photoromance, film, and music; however, Fellini more often examines such anxiety in specifically sexual terms. *The White Sheik* presents an early Fellinian critique of the hollow phallus in the guise of the hypermasculine lover who proves to be more adulterous than adventurous. The sheik's incompetent seamanship (semenship?) leaves Wanda stranded with him at sea – an incident that exposes her to a beating from his wife. *I vitelloni* exposes the hypermasculine lover as an overgrown baby, *La strada* as an animal, and *Nights of Cabiria* as a cinematic myth – a view Fellini would also take with the Lex Barker character in *La dolce vita*.[8] Fellini devotes the entirety of *Fellini's Casanova* to debunking the literary myth of its pallid Latin lover protagonist. In *Ginger and Fred* the Latin lover Mastroianni suffers from incontinence and is incapable of controlling his genitalia for purposes of elimination, let alone copulation. In *Intervista* the magic wand recreates Mastroianni's bygone virility, but only by virtue of Fellini's cinematic magic, not the wand's own. This phallus functions solely on the level of the Imaginary, conjuring up the famous images of the Trevi Fountain sequence from *La dolce vita*, now rendered poignant by their contrast with the present Real-ity of the two stars. Apart from this rare and complex moment, Fellini leaves phallic symbols to their own hollowness. *I clowns* reduces phallic symbols to toys: toy cannons, toy guns, toy hammers, and even a toy bazooka. In *Fellini's Casanova*, Casanova's wooden bird, whose pistonlike movement accompanies him in his escapades, by extension reduces Casanova himself to a copulation toy. The greatest accumulation of such objects is in *City of Women* – Katzone's array of obelisks, armless Venuses, bull drawings, penis-shaped lights, and slides of exaggerated costume phalluses from ancient comedy all serve as pointless overcompensation at the level of the signifier for the missing signified of his own virility.[9]

The Lichas sequence in *Fellini-Satyricon* simultaneously undermines both the myth of the hypermasculine lover and the phallocentric authority of the military. Having physically subdued Encolpius, Lichas makes a sham of patriarchy by dressing as a bride and marrying his captured lover. Fellini compounds Lichas's symbolic castration with a form of displaced anatomical castration, showing him decapitated, rather than drowned as he is in Petronius. As Caesar's envoy, Lichas's self-emasculation reflects back on the emperor, who is played by a woman, Tanya Lopert. After she impales herself, a circle of soldiers plunge their weapons into her back in an orgy of displaced sodomy. In *Fellini's Roma*, Caesar's demolished statue earns the name 'halfhead' and is used for target practice by pigeons. Fellini compounds this humiliation by recreating the ancient military leader's assassination as tawdry theatrical spectacle – the signifier again hollowing out the signified.

Fellini more fully addresses the phallocratic political sphere as it manifests itself in fascism. An ambitious bald fat guy, Benito Mussolini, mythologized himself as embodying both political power and erotic potency. Fellini punctures this myth on both counts. In an allusion to Mussolini's draining of the marshes, *Roma* ironically credits the Duce with a glorious victory over the flies; *Amarcord* makes a farce out of Mussolini's bellicose posturings as Titta and his friends report on nonexistent military victories in order to get out of school. Fellini lampoons Mussolini as hollow phallus in the sexual sphere during the visit of the Federale in *Amarcord*, when a fascist comments: 'Yeah, well, all I can say is Mussolini's really got a pair of those you-know-whats.' He accompanies his statement with a spherical curving of his hands, so that the Duce's testicles are effectively represented by a spatial vacuum – hollow phallus here as hollow testicles. This undermines both Mussolini's vaunted potency and his notorious policies regarding fertility. The sequence climaxes in yet another sham marriage, as Titta's least prepossessing schoolmate, Ciccio, weds his heartthrob Aldina. An oversized, two-dimensional floral head of Mussolini officiates over the ceremony, incongruously addressing the flaccidly corpulent Ciccio as 'valiant warrior.' The sequence reads as Ciccio's wish fulfilment, since only in Mussolini's Italy could such an unlikely candidate be considered a valiant warrior and win such a woman.

In *Fellini-Satyricon*, when Vernacchio cuts off an actor's hand during a theatrical entertainment only to present its fraudulent reattachment as a miracle of Caesar, the ascription of the unworked miracle to the emperor taints him with the maimed actor's symbolic castration. The film thus indicts phallocratic authority as it extends beyond the military and the political to the religious realm. Moving from ancient to modern, various characters and sequences in *Il bidone, La dolce vita, 8½, Amarcord,* and *City of Women* allow Fellini to expose the phallocratic hollowness of Catholicism, but nowhere is the signified of spirituality more hollowed out by the signifiers of institutionalized religion than in the clerical fashion show in *Fellini's Roma.*[10] The scene opens with the dusting off of the portraits of dead cardinals that populate the walls of Princess Domitilla's palace. The visiting cardinal himself looks more dead than alive, as Fellini's uncharacteristically dim chiaroscuro overtly highlights his similarity to his framed predecessors. Lights, catwalk, runway music, applause, commentary by an emcee, and even a showstopping finale serve to contaminate the Catholic Church with the syntax of the fashion show; this permits Fellini to reveal their shared function as an exercise in spectacularity. The entire scene belies one character's assertion that 'the world must learn to follow the Church and not the other way around.' From the nuns' swaying hips to the priests on rollerskates, the spectacularity of bejewelled ecclesiastical garments escalates to Fellini's quintessential visual representation of the hollow phallus within the religious realm. Vestments made of mirrors and electric lights move on their own volition without anyone inside. Here the signifier has totally usurped the signified, leaving an empty Symbolic (phallo)centre and revelling in an Imaginary display. The Church as bride of Christ then takes to the runway as bride of death, accompanied by Fellini's wind-in-a-vacuum sound, which is indicative (as always) of the existential void of the hollow phallus, which needs to be filled with signification. The pious sobriety of the audience gives way to hyperbolic (religious?) ecstasy upon the apotheosis of the final, showstopping papal vestment. The sunbeams emanating from his mitre, the oversized robes of white, silver, and gold, and the theatrical presentation replete with lowered proscenium arches, all dwarf the feeble death mask of the 'Pope,' who is himself, of course, only a model. Fellini's Imaginary Order triumphs.

As phallicism proves hollow in Fellini, originary mother–infant symbiosis reasserts itself, often in the guise of what Camille Paglia has termed the Great Mother, a figure she describes in terms of 'gigantism' and 'double-sexed primal power' (41–2). For Fellini, maternal gigantism often manifests itself in the well-endowed bodies of his actresses, both epitomized and parodied in *Amarcord* by the tobacconist whose breasts suffocate an overwhelmed Titta. Mammiferous hyperbole conflates the feminine with the bovine in *Fellini's Roma* when dead cows littering the freeway discourage the director's attempts to penetrate 'mother' Rome, and in *Ginger and Fred* when a buxom Alpine woman accompanies a cow with eighteen udders in the television line-up. In characterizing the Great Mother, Paglia has described 'sex as ... a kind of drain of male energy by female fullness' (1991: 13). Suzanne Budgen's comments on *La dolce vita* corroborate Paglia's: '[Silvia] exhausts everyone else but is herself constantly renewed. When she goes off dejectedly with Marcello, she is miraculously invigorated ... though Marcello already looks as if he could drop from exhaustion' (37).

Projected images in *Fellini's Casanova* and *City of Women* portray female genitalia as the *vagina dentata*. Budgen describes Silvia in *La dolce vita*: 'The first thing she does is eat, with bared fangs, as if she could devour anything in sight' (37). To allude to the *vagina dentata*, Fellini sometimes deploys an archetypal conflation of the feminine with the feline. *La dolce vita* finds Ekberg with a kitten on her head, and in an uncharacteristic use of his medium in *I clowns* Fellini intercuts zooms on her with zooms on roaring tigers as she tells him she wants to buy a panther. Fellini inappropriately costumes Sandra Milo in fur for the summer season in *8½*, and in *Juliet of the Spirits* Juliet names the lost cat 'Suzy' after Milo's character even before meeting her libidinous neighbour. Elsewhere, Fellini supplies his *vagina dentata* with canine teeth, as vicious dogs guard both Ekberg's home in *Intervista* and Suzy's in *Juliet of the Spirits*. The petit-bourgeois Gradisca in *Amarcord*, the degenerate Saraghina in *8½*, and other variations of this *vagina dentata* figure inevitably bear their teeth, lick their lips, and stick out their tongues as a form of shorthand to identify their archetypal provenance. In this manner Fellini exploits the essential complexity of the mouth as a sexual organ, a castrated orifice with blood-filled lips, a phallus with rigidifying tongue, and a castration device with teeth. Such emphasis on the ambiguity of the mouth marks these examplars of the *vagina dentata* with the 'double sexed primal power' of the Great Mother. Still other Fellini females achieve 'double sexed primal power' through the appropriation of the phallus, hollow though it may be in the case of the single-sexed Fellini male. *City of Women* functions as Fellini's key study of the phallic female; it includes a fishwife selling eels, a goddess-diva with Neptune's phallic trident and a serpent on her thigh, a female Mars at the hearth who sexually attacks Snaporaz, and finally a woman with a gun who fires at him.

As the Fellini female appropriates the phallus, the Fellini male conversely appropriates the womb. The director, whose infant son and only child Federico died in 1944, has referred to his work as his 'flesh-and-blood progeny.' He has also referred to 'Gelsomina and Cabiria growing inside,' to cinema as 'uterus' and 'enormous placenta,' and to being 'detached from [his] work [as] unnatural, like a mother who does not recognize her own [child]' (Murray 10, 11; Bondanella 296; Bondanella and Degli-Esposti 230; Murray 182). Having claimed, 'I do not miss having children of my own' (Murray 10), he gave two of his films his surname – *Fellini-Satyricon* and *Fellini's Casanova*. From *The White Sheik* to *Intervista*, directors in Fellini's films invariably suffer from hysteria, a term deriving from the Greek word *ustera* and meaning 'womb-madness.' As an account of Fellini–Guido's gestation process, *8½* revels in such hysteria, even as Guido dreams of returning to the womb of his childhood. When Fellini shoots on location in *La strada* and *I clowns* he retreats into the womblike space of a tent. Many of his outdoor scenes, such as the Federale's visit in *Amarcord* and the bulk of *Intervista*, remain safely within the gestational confines of the Cinecittà backlot. Fellini's preference for indoor studio shooting encourages his use of enclosed spaces and male wombs such as the baths in *Fellini-Satyricon*, the air raid shelter in *Amarcord*, and the wooden whale in *Fellini's Casanova*.[11]

As bearer of the male womb, Fellini responds to engulfing amniotic threats by reincorporating them into himself within the Imaginary Order. Fellini resorted to the studio to produce the dense fogs and shrouding mists of *Amarcord*, as becomes clear when he reveals his filmmaking gimmickry in *Intervista*. He eventually inserts the Real Order sea of his early films into the Imaginary Order of his studio-womb. *Amarcord, Fellini-Satyricon, Fellini's Casanova, City of Women,* and *And the Ship Sails On* all feature plastic seas constructed on the sound-stage. His preference for the plastic sea indexes Fellini's ability to gestate signifiers that contain the signified threat of a female sea by nullifying its amniotic liquidity. The luxury liner *Rex*, phallic by virtue of its Latin name, which means 'king,' can thus venture safely into the female sea. Even the sinking of the ship in *And the Ship Sails On* remains safely within the playful control of Fellini's Imaginary placenta. Meanwhile, his male characters often appropriate the (w)hole-ness of the womb through regression. 'I like [Donald] Sutherland because he ... looks unborn,' Fellini explained regarding his casting of *Casanova*. 'I want a character who is still unborn, still in the placenta' (in Alpert 250). Fellini renders the same enwombed effect cinematically in *8½*: 'Whenever the camera does not embody Guido's subjective point of view, it consistently traps Guido within its restrictive frame while other characters are paradoxically able to move easily in and out of the frame' (Bondanella 171). When Snaporaz in *City of Women* slides down 'a uterine chute' (Burke 37), he ends up caged by women and wrapped in darkness; Katzone expresses his return-to-the-womb desires by obsessively kissing the statue of his mother like a lover. Fellini's predilection for dwarves, dispersed throughout his filmography but culminating in *Ginger and Fred*, serves to encode regression within the human body itself rather than in behaviour.

Most often, though, Fellini illustrates regression in terms of anality. *I clowns* describes his favourite 'Auguste [as] a child who dirties his pants.' That film revels in the sort of anally chaotic play that distinguishes much of Fellini's work from the phallic goal-orientation of more traditionally scripted narrative cinema. With flatulence, raspberries, self-soiling, and urination, *Amarcord* celebrates such anally regressive behaviour as a clownish form of Real protest against the fascist control of Mussolini's repressive Symbolic Order.[12] Pippo in *Ginger and Fred* accuses the enfeebled Admiral Aulenti of missing the medal of 'the Grand Umbilical Order of the Sphincter.' For Fellini, anal regression and regression to the womb are equivalent – a conflation actualized in Fellini's fixation on female posteriors.

Fellini's disdain for fixing his Imaginary Signifier with a definitive signified constitutes a form of semiotic regression. In some ways this is similar to the sporadic degeneration of verbal languages into babble in his cinema. Working specifically within the Lacanian tradition, Julia Kristeva offers a concept of subversive poetic language, which she terms the Semiotic Order, antecedent to Lacan's Symbolic. This Semiotic Order of poetic language underlies the Symbolic as an unlimited reservoir of allusion, connotation, paradox, multiple entendre, and diffuse meaning, all of which the Lacanian Symbolic attempts to straightjacket into ratiocination. She describes the exploitation of this poetic language as deriving from the same sort of anal-umbilical regression to the maternal that marks the Fellinian subject: 'Language as Symbolic function constitutes itself at the cost of repressing the instinctual drive and continuous relation to the mother. On the contrary, the unsettled and questionable subject of poetic language (for whom the word is never uniquely sign) maintains itself at the cost of reactivating this repressed, instinctual, maternal element' (*Desire* 136). Fellini gravitates toward this Semiotically poetic. The riderless horse in *Fellini-Satyricon*, the peacock in *Amarcord*, and the rhinoceros in *And the Ship Sails On* can all be poetically interpreted, but their meaning cannot be fixed Symbolically with any accuracy. In *Ginger and Fred*, Pippo poetically describes the signifier of tap dance as having a signified that is 'something more' than can be defined.

Regressing still further to the aural Imaginary, Fellini's cinema encourages allusive poetic interpretation rather than Symbolic fixity in its exploitation of Nino Rota's music. The shared theme of the Fool and Gelsomina in *La strada*, the nightclub trumpet solo in *La dolce vita*, the boys' mimed instrumental play in *Amarcord*, and the horn duet in *I clowns* all invest music with powers beyond ratiocination. In *La strada* music alludes to the spirit, and in the *La dolce vita* sequence it prompts the magically autonomous exit of the balloons, while in *Amarcord* it metacinematically bridges the diegesis of the soundtrack. In *I clowns* music bridges life and death, as Fru-fru 'converses' by trumpet with his deceased partner. Such poetic sequences aspire to ultimate meaning and to address – but not limit – the abstract Real.

French theorist Jacques Derrida lists the themes 'essence, existence, substance, subject, transcendentality, consciousness or conscious, God, man and so forth' as traditional structuring centres of works of art that remain paradoxically beyond the work's parameters (249). Both this litany and its 'beyondness' replicate Lacan's Real Order. As Guido's designated 'salvation' in *8½*, Claudia functions as just such a structuring centre. In accordance with Derrida's concept of the exiled centre, Guido concedes that there is no part for her in the film, and the pervasive silence of her recurrent appearances aurally connotes her beyondness. In *La dolce vita* Paola plays a similar role, extraneous to Marcello's intrigues, yet ostensibly central to the film's meaning. The culminating moment of the film emphasizes her beyondness, when Marcello can neither hear her nor approach her as the amniotic sea both engulfs signification and separates them. Guido, Paola, and Claudia all qualify as androgynes, as those who have not been split into 'sexed partial beings' by the Lacanian apparition of the phallus. As such, they are whole unto themselves and holes for rational Symbolic meaning. Fellinian clowns such as Gelsomina, the Fool, and Cabiria also qualify as androgynes but playfully celebrate their (w)holeness. In contrast to the transcendent Real-ity of the pre-phallic androgyne, the Fellinian hermaphrodite has descended into the post-phallic Symbolic Order. Such figures are not sexless but rather doubly 'sexed,' and as such are doubly 'partial beings.' Budgen describes the hermaphrodite

Bhisma in *Juliet of the Spirits* as a monster 'smouldering away on his feet, with a doctor in constant attendance to keep it artificially alive ... his general appearance ... an offense to either sex' (77). Fellini exposes this doubly fallen androgyne impostor as spiritual charlatan as well. When Ascyltus and Encolpius steal the hermaphrodite in *Fellini-Satyricon*, and when Fausto steals a statue of an androgynous angel in *I vitelloni*, these faux androgynes prove equally ineffectual: the hermaphrodite expires, and the statue cannot even inspire its own purchase. For Fellini, when the transcendent Real Order directly engages the Symbolic, it abdicates its genuineness.

Conversely, signifiers in the Symbolic Order cannot fully or genuinely signify the signifieds of the Real. In *La dolce vita* the statue of Christ cannot fly or achieve transcendence without the aid of a helicopter, and the apparition of the Virgin proves a media sham that, like Christ's flight, is nothing more than a fabrication of modern technology. In *Juliet of the Spirits* Dolores's desire to render God as a sculpture of her bodybuilder lover reduces the spiritual to the libidinal, while Giulietta's school play of saintly martyrdom allows Fellini to expose the huge discrepancy between the theatrical signifiers and their sacred signifieds. *Intervista* seemingly despairs of transcendent signifieds altogether. When Fellini's technicians paint a backdrop of the sky, the excessively long brushsticks, combined with the painters' 'Go fuck yourself' banter, presents the moment as an apparition of the phallus that, by pushing the Imaginary with/into the Symbolic, diminishes the authenticity of its Real signified. It is typical of Fellini's cinema to fault the hollowness of the phallic Symbolic for its impotency to address the Real, but by the conclusion of *Intervista* Fellini uncharacteristically doubts the Real power of his Imaginary as well. When his precious Studio 5 lies shrouded in darkness, he concedes that he cannot offer any Real illumination for such undifferentiated (w)holeness, but only the electric spotlight of his perceptual Imaginary. Fellini's Imagin(ation)ary usually unites such metacinematic artifice to Real meaning at the level of the archetype, but here it despairs of its (vi)ability to do so.

Signs in general may be cultural constructions and need not necessarily have ontological consistency; that being said, one genus of sign does offer a degree of natural connection between the signifier and signified: the icon. The icon-as-signifier at least partially embodies or overlaps its signified, and thus belongs to the group of what Kowzan calls 'natural signs' (in Keir 20). As 'natural sign,' embedded in the

unconscious, prescient with preverbal meaning and poetically inde-
pendent of the strictures of the Symbolic, the icon functions as a
semiotic correlative to the psychoanalytic archetype, the Jungian concept that so influenced Fellini. Since Fellini's hollow phallus fails to
divide the sign fully into signifier and signified, he privileges the icon-
archetype that maintains an umbilical tie between the two. Transitions
in Fellini from one Lacanian order to another are usually accompanied
by umbilical imagery; this argues for a continuity rather than a division between them. In *Juliet of the Spirits*, Giulietta pulls an umbilical
rope from the amniotic water, and as a result reawakens from the
Imaginary Order of her dreams to her Symbolically negotiated quotidian existence. The train tracks in *City of Women* serve as a rigidified
umbilical, especially as Fellini recreates the Freudian paradigm of the
phallic train entering the uterine tunnel. As Snaporaz falls into slum-
ber, his quotidian Symbolic gives free rein to Fellini's Imaginary. The
umbilical tie between the coexistent Imaginary and Symbolic remains
unsevered when Snaporaz reawakens: the train is still on the rails. In
'The Temptations of Dr Antonio' when Ekberg descends from the metacinematic Imaginary perch of her billboard she invades Dr Antonio's
quotidian Symbolic. As hollow phallus and inept authority, Dr Antonio ineffectually attempts to police and control this Symbolic, which
Ekberg's intrusive presence easily converts into a paranoiac Imaginary.
Her return to the billboard may re-establish the tidy division between
the Imaginary and the Symbolic, but Fellini retains an umbilical connection between the two as the doctor, infantile in his underwear, is
lowered by ropes past her mammiferous image.

Maintaining Lacan's parallel between semiosis and psychosexuality,
Fellini's hollow phallus psychosexually fails to sever the umbilical of
mother–infant symbiosis even as it semiotically fails to divide the sign
into signifier and signified. In the harem scene in *8½*, Guido's ostensibly phallic whip functions equally well as an umbilical chord, tying
him to the engulfing women he attempts to control. In *Amarcord*,
Biscein climbs an umbilical rope of tied sheets up the Grand Hotel's
facade to reach 'all the pussy' of an unattended harem. In *Fellini-Satyricon* the old wizard dangles umbilically from the tower out of reach
of his ideal woman, Enotea; in *City of Women* Snaporaz umbilically
hangs from his ideal balloon woman of Madonna-as-whore – an image
that attempts to (re)fuse the male splintering of female wholeness.
Sequences like these repeatedly reveal the phallically isolated male as
umbilically attached to female plenitude. Nevertheless, the umbilical

bond remains precarious, and on other, more rare, occasions it seems broken. *Amarcord*'s title supposedly plays on Romagnolo dialect for the Italian: 'io mi ricordo.' The Latin roots of the Italian verb 'ri*cord*are' (English: 'to remember') etymologically encode both the umbilical *cord* and its function as extension of the mother's heart or '*cuore*' in Italian. Arguably, Fellini's claim that *Amarcord*'s title derives from Romagnolo rather than Italian may constitute another typical evasion on his part, as '*amare*' in Italian means 'to love,' so that the title would roughly translate from Italian as 'to love the umbilical.' In any case, this otherwise giddy film contains one exceptionally simple and poignant moment when Titta acknowledges (t)his severed cord, as he looks silently upon the empty bed of his recently deceased mother. In a less empathetic manner, *Fellini's Casanova* severs (t)his cord with a maternal vengeance, as Casanova's mother rejects him in Dresden, leaving him to the undifferentiated aural chaos of Fellini's wind-in-a-void on the soundtrack. The opening of the film forecasts such defeat, as the workmen fail to extract the giant submerged statue of Venus from the lagoon, despite being umbilically tied to her by ropes and pulleys.

The retied umbilical in Fellini also attempts to reconnect to the abstract Real, which like (w)holeness lies beyond symbolization. Fernando on his swing in *The White Sheik* and Fanny on her trapeze in *Juliet of the Spirits* both dangle as signifiers of a transcendence unattainable to Wanda and Giulietta, respectively. In *La dolce vita* the statue of Christ hangs umbilically, but from the distinctly non-abstract Real above of a helicopter. In the school play in *Juliet of the Spirits* umbilical ropes and pulleys purport to connect a sacredly Real signified to the Symbolic theatrical signifiers of saintly ascension, but Giulietta's grandfather disrupts the sham. Given such limited success in retying the Symbolic and Real orders, Fellini sometimes resorts to deploying umbilical imagery to reach the Real as holeness rather than wholeness, as death rather than transcendence. In *La strada* the Fool's taut umbilical tightrope walk foreshadows his eventual death. In a more macabre manner, 'Toby Dammit' concludes with similar taut umbilical imagery: blood dripping from a strained cord, together with a waxen head, indicates the protagonist's death.

Perhaps the most famous imagery in all of Fellini's filmography, the opening of *8½*, reveals the director's preference for retying the umbilical of the abstract Real to the visual Imaginary rather than to the verbally Symbolic. The sequence begins with a suffocating Guido multiply enwombed *in* his car *in* a traffic jam *in* a tunnel. Guido momentarily assumes the fetal position as he climbs out of his car, furthering the gestational metaphor. Inhabiting the realm of pre-phallic differentiation, the sequence is without dialogue. Guido then flies, such a transcendence of physical laws having been interpreted by Freud as a metaphoric transcendence of libidinal laws, as a desire to maintain orgasm. However, from a psychosemiotic perspective, Guido's flight more fully expresses Fellini's desire to transcend semiotic laws and evade the division of sign into signifier and signified. In accordance with Lacanian paradigms, a man attempts to pull Guido down from such transcendence, to give him birth into language. The man declares to the approaching lawyer, 'I've got him.' The lawyer's presence fits neatly into Lacan's specific ascription of the Symbolic Order of language to the '*Law* of the Father.' For his part, Guido, like Fellini, resists. However, he fails to extricate himself from the umbilical rope, and while the man pulls him down toward the male-identified, and thus phallically Symbolic, land, Guido actually falls toward the undifferentiated plenitude of the female sea.

In the transitional period from modernity to postmodernism, Fellini's semiotic sensibility holds an umbilical position. Fredric Jameson has assessed 'the breakdown between signifiers' as a distinctive trait of postmodern semiosis (116). Fellini's desire to make *Fellini's Casanova* 'an entire film made up of fixed pictures' (in Fava and Viganò 164) bespeaks this breakdown, as narrativity and sequentiality give way in his cinema to the primacy of the individual image, and the connections between these individual images become increasingly more e/allusive. Still, Fellini's insistence that such 'fixed pictures' are iconic and archetypal renders his relationship to postmodern semiosis complex. In 'The Precession of Simulacra,' Jean Baudrillard describes the simulacrum – now considered the quintessential element of postmodernism – as a floating functional association of signifiers that no longer attempt to anchor themselves to any Real signified. For Baudrillard, the primacy of the signifier in postmodern culture hollows out the significance of the signified, like the empty vestment in the clerical fashion show in *Fellini's Roma*. Fellini's instruction to *Roma*'s designer, Danilo Donati, that '*everything has to be invented*' (in Bondanella 200–1) indicates that like a postmodernist, he concedes and revels in the artifice of the signifier. Nevertheless, for Fellini this does not mean that the signifier's relationship to the signified is completely arbitrary. The Fellinian hollow phallus does not fully split the sign into signifier and signified: the Fellinian umbilical reties them as sign, and the Fellinian male womb gives this sign fused birth as archetypal icon. Fellini explains his preference for studio over location shooting and for construction over reproduction, in terms of the archetype: 'Because it is not an asylum, but *the* asylum; not a garden, but *the* garden, not a wheat field, but *the* wheat field' (in Bondanella and Degli-Esposti 238, emphasis mine). Fellini's abdication of representational reality as a neorealist sign of itself thus paradoxically renders his cinema more Real. For him, the signifier of a Jungian archetype remains anchored to the signified of a Platonic idea(l), no matter how far apart they may seem to drift on his plastic sea.

Notes

1 This essay will deploy capital letters to distinguish a specifically Lacanian use of these terms from their more common usage.

2 An infant recognizes her mother and caregivers primarily through taste, touch, and smell, as she cannot focus her eyes for vision until a certain age, and her hearing attaches only limited meaning to certain (usually nonverbal) sounds.

3 Kinesiologists consider the Italian and Greek cultures to be the two most highly gestural on the planet. Neapolitan culture, in particular among Italian regional cultures, serves as an archetypal model of such gesturality. See Argyle, *Bodily Communication*, and Barzini, *The Italians*.

4 In particular, Lacan makes the point in terms of individuals whose parents are social authority figures, so that the 'Name of the Father' or 'Law of the Father' becomes doubled: 'The father's relation to this law must be considered in itself, for one will find in it the reason for that paradox, by which the ravaging effects of the paternal figure are to be observed with particular frequency in cases where the father really has the function of a legislator or, at least, the upper hand ... excluding the Name-of-the-Father from its position in the signifier' (218–19). Such a doubling, I would argue, might result in either a rigid self-righteousness or else in pathological misbehaviour, as in the case of children of the clergy or the military.

5 However, with *Giulietta degli spiriti*, Fellini's camera begins to assume a more sceptical point of view with regard to such parapsychological phenomena, filming from above in a position of superiority and omniscience, in partial conjunction with the maids Teresina and Elisabetta, who voice their own scepticism vis-à-vis supposed parapsychological events.

6 In *Symbolic Exchange and Death*, Jean Baudrillard defines graffiti as '*empty*

signifiers' whose 'message is zero' (79, emphasis his; 83). He asserts that graffiti artists 'derail the common system of designation' (78).

7 *8½* exorcises a dilemma that Fellini himself had faced while making *La dolce vita*. Bondanella recounts: 'When Mastroianni asked to see a script, [Ennio] Flaiano gave him a stack of blank pages that contained only a drawing by Fellini of a man swimming in the sea with a gigantic penis, reaching to the floor, surrounded by mermaids. Too embarrassed to object, Mastroianni agreed to do the film' (143). Again the Fellinian predilection for the visually Imaginary and his inability to commit to the verbally Symbolis assert themselves. Habitually, no more than two copies of a script could be found on a Fellini set at any given time. Rather than being subject(ed) to the limitations of the phallopatriarchal Word, Fellini extolled liberty: 'I love to improvise' (in Alpert 165).

8 Silvia's boyfriend, Robert, is a discarded ex-Tarzan figure who spends his time doodling on restaurant tables and passively watching as one man after another dances with his girlfriend. Lex Barker, who plays Robert, had, in fact, played the Tarzan role in various films. From *La dolce vita*'s modern mythic Tarzan, Fellini moved on to satirize the ancient mythic Hercules in the hypermasculine figure at the opening of 'The Temptations of Dr Antonio,' who complains that his damsel in distress distresses him since she 'weighs a ton.'

9 His name 'Katzone' sounds like 'cazzone,' meaning 'big cock' in Italian, and was translated as 'Zuberkock' for 'super cock' in certain foreign versions of the film. In either case, Fellini concerns himself with the sensorial Imaginary, the sound of the name, rather than the conceptual Symbolic, the spelling of the name, which only misleads.

10 Swindlers dressed as priests in *Il bidone* invite the inverse inference that priests are swindlers. In *Amarcord* the priest exploits the confessional to swindle the local boys out of their sexual fantasies for his own use, as the semiotically subversive Fellini conflates the literal and metaphoric meanings of the term 'vicarious.' In *City of Women* such vicariously shared fantasies culminate in the potentially pederastic image of priests and boys masturbating together in bed in front of the Imaginary Signifier of the movie screen. After young Guido's encounter with Saraghina at the beach in *8½*, Fellini speeds up the priest giving chase, presenting the clergy, with sacrilegious delight, as Keystone kops. His repeated use of the zoom to express the priest's opprobrium furthers his comic subversion of their self-righteous verbally Symbolic denial of the sexually Real. The adult Guido–Fellini himself spins the actor-signifier auditioning for the role of the cardinal-signified on a turntable, thus confounding the linear with the

circular, the semiotic Symbolic with the anarchic Imaginary, and the sacred centre with the spiralling silly.

11 The female has also traditionally been ascribed the role of homemaker and nurturer, but in Fellini, more often than not, the domus, be it Zampanò's trailer in *La strada*, Steiner's apartment in *La dolce vita*, or Titta's house in *Amarcord*, appears primarily as a male-identified space, while males, from the Duke of Parma and Lord Talou in *Fellini's Casanova* to Trimalchio in *Fellini-Satyricon*, are more likely to serve as hosts and provide food.

12 One of Fellini's most ideologically complex works, *Amarcord* simultaneously associates infantile regression with both the cause of fascism and rebellion against it. When fascist officers forcefully regress Titta's father with castor oil, they effectively appropriate the terms of such anal resistance, interpolating it within their phallic order, and creating an uncharacteristically dark sequence in an otherwise ebullient film.

References

Alpert, Hollis. *Fellini: A Life*. New York: Paragon House, 1988.

Angelucci, Gianfranco, and Liliana Betti, eds. *Il Film 'Amarcord' di Federico Fellini*. Bologna: Cappelli Editore, 1974.

Argyle, Michael. *Bodily Communication*. London: Methuen, 1975.

Barzini, Luigi. *The Italians*. New York: Atheneum, 1964.

Baudrillard, Jean. 'The Ecstasy of Communication.' *The Anti-Aesthetic: Essays in Postmodern Culture*. Ed. Hal Foster. Port Townsend: Bay Press, 1983. 126–34.

– 'The Precession of Simulacra.' *Art after Modernism: Rethinking Representation*. Ed. Brian Wallis and Marcia Tucker. Boston: David Godine, 1988. 253–81.

– *Symbolic Exchange and Death*. London: Sage, 1993.

Betti, Liliana. *Fellini*. Trans. Joachim Neugroschel. Boston: Little, Brown, 1979.

Bondanella, Peter. *The Cinema of Federico Fellini*. Princeton: Princeton UP, 1992.

Bondanella, Peter, and Cristina Degli-Esposti, eds. *Federico Fellini: Essays in Criticism*. New York: Oxford UP, 1978.

Budgen, Suzanne. *Fellini*. London: British Film Institute, 1966.

Burke, Frank. 'Federico Fellini: From Representation to Signification.' *Romance Language Annual*. Vol. 1. West Lafayette: Purdue Research Foundation, 1990. 34–40.

Deely, John, Brooke Williams, and Felicia Kruse, eds. *Frontiers in Semiotics*. Bloomington: Indiana UP, 1986.

Derrida, Jacques. 'Structure, Sign and Play in the Human Sciences.' *The Languages of Criticism and the Sciences of Man: The Structuralist Controversy*.

Ed. Richard Macksey and Eugenio Donato. Baltimore: Johns Hopkins UP, 1972. 247–65.

Fava, Guido G., and Aldo Viganò. *The Films of Federico Fellini*. New York: Citadel Press, 1990.

Fellini, Federico. *Comments on Film*. Ed. Giovanni Grazzini. Trans. Joseph Henry. Fresno: California State UP, 1988.

– *Fellini on Fellini*. Ed. Anna Keel and Christian Strich. Trans. Isabel Quigley. New York: Delacourte/Seymour Lawrence, 1976.

– *Quattro Film*. Turin: Einaudi, 1974.

Freud, Sigmund. *The Interpretation of Dreams*. New York: Basic Books, 1955.

– *Three Case Studies*. New York: Collier Books, 1993

Jameson, Fredric. 'Postmodernism and Consumer Society,' in Hal Foster, ed., *The Anti-Aesthetic: Essays in Postmodern Culture*. Port Townsend Bay Press, 1983. 111–25.

Kaplan, E. Ann. *Rocking around the Clock: MTV, Postmodernism, and Consumer Culture*. New York: Routledge, 1987.

Keir, Elam. *The Semiotics of Theatre and Drama*. London: Methuen, 1980.

Kristeva, Julia. *Desire in Language: A Semiotic Approach to Literature*. Ed. Leon S. Roudiez. Trans. Thomas Gorz, Alice Jardin, and Leon S. Roudiez. New York: Columbia UP, 1980.

– *Powers of Horror: An Essay in Abjection*. Trans. Leon S. Roudiez. New York: Columbia UP, 1982.

Lacan, Jacques. *Écrits. A Selection*. Trans. Alan Sheridan. New York: Norton, 1977.

Metz, Christian. 'The Imaginary Signifier.' Trans. Ben Brewster. *Screen* 16.2 (Summer 1975) 46–76. Excerpted in *Narrative, Apparatus, Ideology: A Film Theory Reader*. Ed. Philip Rosen. New York: Columbia UP, 1986. 244–78.

Murray, Edward. *Fellini the Artist*. New York: Frederick Ungar Publishing, 1976.

Paglia, Camille. *Sexual Personae: Art and Decadence from Nefertiti to Emily Dickinson*. New York: Random House, 1991.

Pecori, Franco. *Federico Fellini*. Florence: La Nuova Italia, 1974.

Saint John et al., *The New Oxford Annotated Bible: Revised Version*. New York: Oxford UP, 1977.

Salachas, Gilbert. *Federico Fellini: An Investigation into His Films and Philosophy*. Trans. Rosalie Siegel. New York: Crown 1969.

Sebeok, Thomas A. *Approaches to Semiotics*. The Hague: Mouton, 1964.

Silverman, Kaja. *The Subject of Semiotics*. New York: Oxford UP, 1983.

Solmi, Angelo. *Fellini*. Trans. Elizabeth Greenwood. London: Merlin Press, 1967.

Solomon, Stanley, ed. *The Classic Cinema: Essays in Criticism*. New York: Harcourt Brace Jovanovich, 1973.

Stubbs, John C. *Federico Fellini: A Guide to References and Resources*. Boston: G.K. Hall, 1978.

Winnet, Irene Portis, and Jean Umiker-Sebeok, eds. *Semiotics of Culture*. New York: Mouton Publishers, 1979.

Witcombe, R.T. *The New Italian Cinema*. New York: Oxford UP, 1982.

4

When in Rome Do As the Romans Do? Federico Fellini's Problematization of Femininity (*The White Sheik*)

VIRGINIA PICCHIETTI

Throughout Federico Fellini's 1952 film *Lo sceicco bianco* (*The White Sheik*), the heroine Wanda engages in performances of femininity that cleverly encapsulate a conventional narrative of womanhood. As both responsible wife and impassioned harem girl she fulfils roles advanced in 1950s Italy as 'natural' and 'instinctive' to women. Her entry into these roles is facilitated by socialization into femininity, which has prepared her to understand the expectations associated with them in social intercourse. The heroine's two roles, however, are typically represented as occupying the opposite ends of the spectrum of sexual identities permissible to women. Wanda's performance thus unmasks a conundrum that reflects women's position in social discourse: as a wife she cannot trespass her wifely identity to become Fatma, the sexualized harem girl, without consequence.

Because femininity as a category of gender encompasses both possibilities, Wanda should in theory be able to inhabit both personas. Her movement between 'Wanda the wife' and 'Fatma' discloses the fact that they are only superficially oppositional; at the same time, it bears witness to the possibility of exploring different facets of femininity, albeit conventional ones. Both roles essentially represent different aspects of one sexual category: femininity. The heroine's unwillingness to inhabit just one reveals to us her own perception of her position within femininity.

Movement between the roles is possible in theory; in practice, it usually provides a crisis, as it ultimately does in the film. Movement is possible only through the subject's interpretation of her position vis-à-vis individual personas, since it entails placing oneself in roles with possibly different codifications and social purposes. As a result, such shifting disrupts both what is expected from Wanda's performances and the relationships built on and arising from the original performances. Even though the two roles are, again, not mutually exclusive (because both are contained in femininity), the heroine's embodiment of the harem girl challenges her viability as wife. This is because each role renders sexuality visible to a different degree and, in the same vein, represents morality differently.

Wanda causes disruption because the personas she embodies are strictly regulated by codifying institutions. In the film these institutions are the Catholic church and the popular *fotoromanzo* (photonovel) industry. These systems set the parameters of her roles: the Catholic church determines their moral currency, while the popular culture industry develops their narrative. Though these institutions seem oppositional at first glance, they are actually complicitous in defining women's identity.[1] The limits they set ensure adherence to specific attributes of femininity: the Catholic church advances the image of the virginal wife as the epitome of feminine virtue; the *fotoromanzo* industry at the centre of the film advances fantasy and desire, contained within a fantastical world built on male desire, as parts of a feminine potentiality. The fictive plots of both the *fotoromanzi* and the Catholic institution of marriage promote the idea that happiness, love, and social acceptance can only be achieved by following strict patterns of gender. In both the institution of marriage and the *fotoromanzi* – which were staples of Italian popular culture and the offspring of classic genres such as the romance and the gothic – a happy ending is determined by the heroine's adherence to the rules of a heterosexual union.[2] The *fotoromanzi* create neat, closed, static worlds in which acts of gender are performed 'daily and incessantly'[3] to construct and perpetuate a standard narrative of womanhood.[4] Both institutions tell Wanda what she can safely embrace as her social purpose: in the guise of wife she can assume the attributes that will create a euphoric, socially rewarding ending to her life narrative; in the guise of Fatma, she can attempt to recreate the romance narrative featured in the *fotoromanzi* she devours every Saturday. But she must keep in mind that this latter persona is antithetical to marriage and will lead to the dysphoric ending of moral ruin.[5]

Wanda's roles are produced as counterparts to the male personas presented by the two cultural systems the film targets. As Ivan's wife, she performs her role against the backdrop of institutionalized Catholic morality, which is upheld – at least superficially – by Ivan and his family. On the other hand, while performing against the backdrop of the *fotoromanzi* as Fatma she must embody the role of sexually knowing or at least willing mistress. The latter role, which the film suggests is 'intrinsic' to womanhood, traditionally ensures an unhappy ending. Wanda refuses to anchor herself to either of these two roles, and instead moves between them. This creates what Marjorie Garber calls 'category crisis.'[6] The crisis generated by Wanda's movement between the roles challenges the notion that they represent two contrasting models of sexuality. The fact that she can (re)present herself as wife and harem girl in social interaction, and that Fellini's film blurs and actually confounds the boundaries between reality (wife) and fiction (harem girl), defies distinctions between them.

Wanda's movement into and out of Fatma territory creates a category crisis by destabilizing the relationships that define her roles. This is confirmed by Ivan's frantic search for her and by the sheik's astonishment at her resistance.[7] Through her marriage, she fulfils Catholic morality; during her honeymoon in Rome she is supposed to be pursuing the pope, its highest symbol. It follows from this that her parallel pursuit of the White Sheik in Rome is also an integral part of her understanding of femininity. This understanding fuels a crisis in her relationships with the men in her life: first she eludes (and deludes) Ivan, and then she rejects (and deludes) the White Sheik.

Wanda's movement and performances make evident to us her conscious desire to maintain a distance between her sense of who she is and the images she projects. Although she does not explicitly articulate this, her actions speak loudly. In her marriage she does at times dress and act the part of the virtuous wife, even while – as becomes clear soon after the film's beginning – her thoughts are elsewhere. Indeed, before marrying she had already planned to pursue the Sheik while on her honeymoon in Rome; clearly, then, she did not perceive an encounter with him as antithetical to her new role. In the romantic scene with the White Sheik, in which she dresses and acts the part of the love-struck Fatma, her thoughts are again elsewhere, on her role as wife. The scenes on the beach between Wanda and the White Sheik brilliantly expose the paradox created when the different possibilities defining femininity in a particular culture are deemed conflictual. Although Wanda is face to face with perfection, as embodied in the White Sheik, she resists being incorporated into the fantasy in which he intends her to be the protagonist. If she did not resist, her performance would jeopardize the dominant moral role of wife. For example, when she finally meets the White

Sheik, she calls him by the actor's name, 'Signor *Rivoli*.' Some time after the Sheik proposes to take her to New York, she reminds him she must return to Rome. When he proposes they go on the boat, she answers reluctantly, noting insightfully, '*Ho una confusione in testa. Che strano, mi sembra di non essere più io*' ('My head is filled with confusion. How strange, I don't feel like myself anymore'). On the boat, she gently fends off his advances, resisting the temptation to participate in the illusion he unremittingly tries to fabricate. Even when she takes part in the adventure, tragically announcing, '*Ci sono cose più grandi, più forti di noi*' ('There are bigger and stronger things than us'), the 'things' to which she alludes are firmly grounded in the reality she has lived up till now: she acknowledges her marriage – '*Non sono libera*' ('I'm not free') – and refuses to call the White Sheik by the name (*sceicco bianco*) that would perpetuate the fantasy.

The tenuousness with which Wanda approaches her characters highlights the problems that arise when feminists attempt to devise theories of the feminine that run counter to prevailing categories such as the ones advanced by the institutions represented in the film. The theories not only attempt to define femininity but also describe how it is performed, and, more significantly, perceived by women. The performance of gender that Wanda undertakes represents an intersection between these differing theories of womanhood. Some feminists view gender performance as a means by which women can enter and play a part in social discourse. It can conceal their lack of a phallus (power and agency in social discourse) behind a (mandated) feminine persona. Psychoanalyst Joan Riviere defines femininity as a masquerade, as something that can be worn and taken off at will for the purpose of surviving and being admitted into social discourse in Western culture. Mary Ann Doane extends Riviere's notion by contending that masquerade creates a distance between the image of woman it presents and the individual's sense of herself – a sort of cultural resistance.[8] Luce Irigaray, for her part, concludes that socialization into femininity forces women to assume a prefabricated image, which they must then present on an already existing social stage (much like a Pirandellian mask), which can be construed as 'a system of values that is not [theirs], and in which [they] can "appear" and circulate only when enveloped in the needs/desires/fantasies of others.'[9] Irigaray's use of the verb 'appear' implies a masquerade: if worn with awareness, the masquerade can ultimately function as a subversive device for preventing the self from vanishing into a role.

For other theorists, the notion that femininity is masquerade is problematic, because it suggests that an essential, originary femaleness
exists. Masquerade implies that although not allowed to surface as
subjectivity, and although remaining suppressed by socialization, this
femaleness can ultimately be reached outside a patriarchal matrix. In
her notion that women are not *born* women but rather *become* women,
Simone de Beauvoir alludes to the impossibility of uncovering an originary essence; in her work on female impersonation, Carole-Anne
Tyler challenges both the notion of masquerade, with its implication
that there is an underlying, reachable essence, and the feminist insistence on its subversive impact. For Tyler, when the theory of masquerade is used as an investigative tool the result is a faulty and incomplete
profile of women's relationship to femininity. Even more importantly,
this approach puts us (in our case, the film's spectators) on the untenable 'metaphysical move to establish an origin' of womanliness.[10]

Wanda's transgressions – first of her wifely role when she becomes
Fatma, and then of the Fatma role when she is once again reintegrated
into her married persona – and the dissatisfaction that is apparent from
her movement in and out of roles, highlight the difficulties inherent in
sociocultural discourses on femininity, and in women's attempts to
represent their own vision of their identities. This vision's syntax is *a
priori* regulated by a specific cultural milieu; even so, Fellini's film
hints that femininity, as a category, is subversive by its very nature. A
reading of the gap that Wanda's transgression creates between her perception of herself and her roles suggests that the film acknowledges a
prelinguistic feminine nature, to which Wanda – through her movement between roles – attempts to return. Poststructuralism has already
proposed that this return is impossible and has even questioned the
viability of considering the prelinguistic self. That being said, the film's
focus on Wanda's inhabitation of feminine roles places the emphasis
on what Tyler identifies as the next step in a theory of femininity,
which is to focus on 'perception as a productive activity' rather than
'productive intentions.'[11] This shift offers us glimpses of women's
desire to resist their prescribed roles. When applied to Wanda, we find
that her perceptions of her two identities – wife and seductress – are
released through a gendered performance that ultimately undermines
the cultural meaning attributed to them.

To regulate gender and to prevent any weakening of its categories,
culture attempts to establish clear distinctions between the personas
that constitute it. One way it does this is by writing personas on the

body. In Fellini's film and Wanda's performance, sexuality is something the spectator *sees*; it is not reflected in what Wanda actually *does*. Put another way, Wanda's assumption of the personas of wife and harem girl is marked by the roles' own particular representations of femininity, rather than by her performance of actions defining the roles. In *La sceicco blanco*, identity is constructed on the body through dress, and dress in turn affects social interaction. We do not see Wanda as a wife *performing* her wifely tasks in the home, any more than we see her *performing* her duties as a harem girl. Rather, her movement between her two identities is made visible through her physicality, despite the fact that the real mark of assimilation is the ability to execute the set of functions attributed to each persona.

Wanda's cross-role movement, visible through change of dress, might be what Garber defines as 'a mechanism of displacement from one blurred boundary to another.'[12] The heroine's assumption of the two *seemingly* binary forms of femininity blurs the distinction between the virginal Wanda and the sexualized Fatma. Her personification of the harem girl highlights the possibility of interpreting female sexuality – always, of course, restricted by culturally available codes. This possibility 'marks the trouble spot, indicating ... a crisis.'[13] When we view all of this through the lens of psychoanalysis, we realize that while Wanda's activity jeopardizes classification and social interaction, even so, it only replicates women's socialization. The hieroglyphics to which Freud refers when discussing female sexuality, and his cryptic question, 'What does a woman want?' reside in the space between Wanda's double-performance.[14] While 'Wanda' and 'Fatma' define her socially as a woman, Wanda is clearly dissatisfied with being confined to either single identity. Her attitude reveals how hard it is to maintain a unidimensional persona that does not explore and exploit the complexities and possibilities, the 'hieroglyphics,' that are inherent to sexuality. Moreover, it reflects the complications that arise when she questions the relationship between how she sees herself and her prescribed roles, between her identity as a woman and femininity.

The scene in which Wanda is actually invested as Fatma reveals how both roles coexist in one gender category and, it follows, the cultural inconsistency of limiting her to one expression of sexuality.[15] Fellini recognizes the importance of Fatma as symbol of Wanda's socialization into femininity, and allows the scene ample cinematic space. This demands close analysis. The scene includes an overseeing paternal figure and an indoctrinating maternal figure, both of whom aid the

fotoromanzo industry in setting Wanda on a path in pursuit of fulfilment of a feminine role. This is really no different from what the
church did on her wedding day. The director on the set of *Incanto blu* is
a patriarch who orchestrates the law of production; in contrast, the
Incanto blu editorial office is run by the maternal Marilena.[16] In female
psychosocial development, it is the mother who ushers the daughter
into prescribed femininity, applying the laws to which the daughter
will later be subject in the paternal Symbolic sphere.[17] Through the
venue of the *fotoromanzo* industry and its promise of desire and its fulfilment, Marilena prepares Wanda to become the object on which the
White Sheik projects his desire.

Using telling pseudo-psychoanalytic language, Marilena proves
instrumental in legitimating Wanda's illusions of feminine desire and
performance; in effect she is playing the mother's traditional role as
indoctrinator. When speaking with Wanda, Marilena faces her directly,
while Wanda faces a wall of stills behind Marilena. The stills thus create a landscape of desire for the daughter, subtitled by the maternal
figure. At the same time, as the maternal figure who ensures her
daughter's socialization (she calls her *bambina*), Marilena directly
places Wanda in an illusory situation vis-à-vis the White Sheik: *'Se tu
fossi in un deserto, di notte, e sapessi che il tuo sceicco é in pericolo, che
diresti?'* ('If you were in a desert at night and you knew your sheik was
in danger, what would you say?'). Finally, as she places Wanda in the
hands of a costumed male actor, she physically propels the daughter
onto the path toward a heterosexual union steeped in romantic con-
vention: *'Va cara, il tuo sceicco ti aspetta'* ('Go my dear, your sheik awaits
you'). Within the culture the film recreates, the encounter with the
White Sheik represents the natural culmination of Wanda's desire as a
woman.

As we have already concluded, the supercharged union with the
White Sheik represents one facet of what socialization into femininity
promises, and it too is the product of a cultural industry that exists to
perpetuate conventional gendered models of behaviour. Once the
manufacture of the Fatma persona is revealed, so too is the irrational
nature of the desire Wanda will play out in this situation. Indeed,
although the fantasy is deemed attainable, the heroine's only real and
realistic choice remains her role as Ivan's wife. Introduced by the fantastic, carnivalesque Rota score, the meeting between Wanda and the
White Sheik takes place in surreal circumstances, with the latter hang-
ing high above trees on a swing that seems to have no attachments,

and then leaping to the ground with great ease. The White Sheik is offered here as the illusory answer to an illusory desire.[18]

Most critical readings of *Lo sceicco bianco* see this episode as symbolic of Wanda's wilful escape from reality into fantasy: Wanda goes to the Incanto blu office and then to Fregene to meet the White Sheik, and accepts the part of Fatma opposite him. Some also stress Wanda's conscious manipulation of the spheres of reality and illusion that make up both the film and Fellini's vision of the world.[19] I suggest instead that Wanda's movement is not between reality and illusion, but simply between roles. This movement excludes her, *a priori*, as architect of the personas she embodies or agent of an escapist journey. Although she is aware of her movement, femininity as a gendered category divests her – again *a priori* – of the ability to determine both the roles she will play out and her own story – an ability constituting subjectivity.[20] It follows that Wanda's entrance into the ready-made fantasy world represented by the White Sheik of the film's title becomes only a logical step in her fulfilment of the social narrative of womanhood. Wanda's quest is not an escape; it merely ushers her into another feminine persona. The 'fantasy' world she enters is only a correlative of the 'real' one and the culmination of her socialization into femininity, represented by her marriage to Ivan.[21]

Wanda's interpretation of the roles reveals that she understands their limitations and is frustrated at the impossibility of inventing them and of finding fulfilment in both. Her interpretation of them, and her movement between them and the unbalance this causes, reveal a cultural uneasiness at a time in postwar Italian society when women were supposed to remain immobile within their roles, while society endeavoured to rebuild itself after the sociopolitical crisis of the Second World War. In a sense, the heroine's growing uneasiness foreshadows the dissatisfaction with which women in the 1960s would approach their traditional roles. As represented in later Fellini films, such as *Le notti di Cabiria* (1956) and *Giulietta degli spiriti* (1965), women's struggles with the shortcomings of their roles, and with the contradictions inherent to femininity that *Lo sceicco bianco* reveals, represent powerful subversions of traditional morality. The heroine of the first film, Cabiria, suffers a struggle similar to Wanda's based on the sexual roles she can fulfil. While a prostitute, she desires the 'normal' life of a married woman. Fulfilling the wifely role would allow her to channel her sexuality from the fringes of society into the mainstream, where it would be socially legitimized. Yet her identity has been delimited by her original role, so after her marriage fails she is forced to resume her work on, and confine her sexuality to society's periphery, rather than participating in society as a single woman. Giulietta, on the other hand, feels stifled by the staid role of bourgeois wife and explores alternatives to her situation. While venturing outside her home she discovers the complexity of sexuality through the colourful characters she meets. In the end she leaves her husband and house and strikes off on her own, happily abandoning the expectations attached to her wifely role. This foreshadows the women's movement that would formally begin just a year later.

In the sociocultural context these films reflect, the expectation placed on women to adhere to strict categories of gender was addressed by the popular literature produced by burgeoning women's groups. This literature often countered the gendered portrayals of the *fotoromanzi*, which overtly linked women's happiness to prescribed performances, and which perpetuated conventional notions of gender and sexuality by featuring traditional stories of love and romance. Alternative publications such as *Noi donne* (*We Women*) – a magazine produced by the recently formed *Unione delle donne italiane* (UDI, Union of Italian Women) – focused on weighty issues such as universal suffrage and equal opportunity. Though committed to advancing women's causes and to presenting articles on significant national and international events, these publications also reflected the sociocultural context in which they were sold. Indeed, to reach its female readers, *Noi donne*, for example, had to also appeal to women's needs within existing roles, and cater to concerns in the private sphere reproduced in the *fotoromanzi*. It prominently featured columns on beauty, fashion, and cooking. These features reflected the emphasis on domesticity of the immediate postwar period.[22] Articles such as '*Le donne italiane hanno votato bene*' ('Italian women have voted well,' 1952) recorded women's progress in the public sphere, while articles such as '*Due novità per essere belle*' ('Two ways to be beautiful,' 1950s) reflected the importance attached to extending performance by offering tips on how to dress and act properly. In the society that *Noi donne* addressed, women were urged to assume a specific feminized persona when entering the public sphere to exercise their newly gained right to vote. Even after gains were made, women's participation in social discourse still entailed personifying the conventional attributes of femininity: beauty, a sweet, submissive disposition, and a shapely body put on display through the proper clothing. That even enlightened literature such as this would champion a performance of gender that perpetuated women's traditional roles speaks to the potency and endurance of categories of gender.

Because Wanda cannot in the end be allowed to fully interpret these gendered roles, she must cooperate in preserving the dichotomy as an act of social self-preservation. Despite her resistance to attempts by Marilena, the *fotoromanzo* crew, and the White Sheik to draw her into the fantasy that would allow her to fulfil the Fatma role, and despite her non-participation in its 'invention,' Wanda resists. Caught, to reiterate, between the euphoric and dysphoric endings of her *seemingly* mutually exclusive roles, and realizing the impossibility of negotiating the interpellation into both roles, Wanda attempts suicide.

Wanda's suicide attempt occupies a problematic space in the heroine's story. On the one hand, it can be described as defiance of the performance of gender. Wanda-Fatma chooses to put an end to the personas she is interpellated to fulfill by performing an ultimate act of resistance, the bodily destruction of both Fatma and Wanda. On the other hand, Wanda-Fatma is divested of agency in the act through the scene's comic overtones. The film itself resists her act of resistance to both roles by enlisting the suicide as a symbolic act. The act thus becomes a failed attempt by Wanda-as-Fatma and, as a consequence, ensures the conventional dysphoric ending to Fatma's story, while it reinstates the socially prescribed euphoric ending once Wanda is returned to her wifely role. By ending her story comically, the film safely contains Fatma within the realm of fantasy, negating this persona's value and legitimacy in social discourse. Wanda's suicide attempt endangers the wifely role and in so doing threatens social order; worth noting in this regard is that the attempt is made in the public sphere when Fatma ventures into Rome. After resisting Fatma, the heroine should naturally have returned as Wanda to her wifely role in Rome. Her reluctance to do so, and her choice to put an end to both Wanda and Fatma, reflects the depth of her resistance to being restored to a one-dimensional role. This is made clear when Wanda states that she has dishonoured her husband's name but immediately adds that real life is the life of dreams.

By introducing Fatma, who personifies her desire, into Rome, the stage on which her marriage is played out, Wanda is revealing the crisis in the neatly defined categories that determine the configurations of social intercourse. When those around her glimpse her suicide act, she is still in her Fatma costume and is thus considered insane, that is, outside the realm of normalcy because outside the parameters of desire and duty prescribed for her primary identity as wife. Her committal to a psychiatric hospital as Fatma results in the public eradication of a role that would lead to moral ruin and would also privilege the fulfilment of a sexual persona outside marriage.

Lo sceicco bianco challenges prescribed feminine roles by exposing the paradoxes inherent in them. That being said, the moral authority the Catholic church represents is sustained through Wanda's suicide attempt and, ultimately, her conflation of her two roles in her attempt to destroy them both. Wanda's act seems an exercise of the agency deprived her in the fabrication of her roles. It seems a final attempt at choosing an ending for her story. Wanda's reintegration into a euphoric narrative is finally complete, however, when she transfers her fantasy from Fatma into her wifely role, from the White Sheik to Ivan, and walks off blissfully to see the pope, symbolic patriarch of Wanda's socially proper performance.[23]

Through the very act of reaffirming one role over another, *Lo sceicco bianco* underscores the performative nature of gender. While it does not offer an alternative ending to the role its heroine embodies, its characterization of Wanda illuminates the quandary inherent to embodying femininity. In the 1950s, when the film was set, organized Italian women's groups such as UDI were just beginning formally to articulate the problems and consequences of women's position in society. But not until the 1960s would these groups begin to offer alternatives to the conventional euphoric ending and make them possible through social, political, and cultural changes. Because it problematizes femininity, *Lo sceicco bianco* stands as an insightful reflection of the dilemma that women faced in the gendered performance advocated by 1950s popular culture. At the same time, it cleverly unravels this performance to expose the contradictions on which it is built. While Wanda is not a proto-feminist character, her movement between roles subtly reveals the wilful interpretation of the self's position in social intercourse. Unfortunately, within the conventional, institutional universe of Fellini's film, her vision must ultimately be confined to the role that guarantees a moral euphoric ending for her to participate as a functioning member.

Notes

1 This parallel is made immediately apparent by the first two opening sequences. These cleverly frame the film when the second is repeated at

the end and provide the context in which Wanda's roles develop. The opening credit sequence features the tattered set of *Incanto blu*, the focus of Wanda's odyssey and later reconstructed with her at its centre. The scene that follows focuses on the Vatican, symbol of the institutional source of the staid world and principles of its characters.

2 *Fotoromanzi* continue to enjoy an audience in Italy. For information on *fotoromanzi*, see J. Risset, *Fellini: 'Le Cheik Blanc': L'annonce faite à Federico* (Paris: Adam Birro, 1990). For information on the relationship between popular literature, such as the Harlequin romance, similar in theme to the *fotoromanzi*, and its female audience, see Tania Modeleski, *Mass-Produced Fantasies for Women* (Hamden: Archon Books, 1982), and J. Radway, *Reading the Romance: Women, Patriarchy, and Popular Literature* (Chapel Hill: U of North Carolina P, 1984).

3 In her analysis of socialized roles, Judith Butler defines gender as 'a corporeal field of cultural play' whose 'legacy [is] sedimented acts' performed constantly. 'Performative Acts of Gender Constitution: An Essay in Phenomenology and Feminist Theory,' *Performing Feminisms: Critical Theory and Theater*, ed. Sue-Ellen Case (Baltimore: The Johns Hopkins UP, 1990) 282, 274.

4 The socialized narrative developed for women has been the topic of many feminist readings of Western culture. In analyses of fictional narratives, these studies gauge the patterns of gender established for heroines – patterns reflected in Wanda's own situation. For example, in *Writing beyond the Ending: Narrative Strategies of Twentieth-Century Women Writers* (Bloomington: Indiana UP, 1985), Rachel Blau DuPlessis concludes that the conventional plot sees the heroine enjoy one of two outcomes for her story. The result of a successful performance of gender, the *euphoric* ending, culminates in the socially mandated heterosexual union of marriage, through which the heroine's fantasies and desires should ultimately be fulfilled. Conversely, the dysphoric ending, the result of the heroine's privileging of her desire, climaxes in death. The start of a project for liberating women from these restrictive patterns, DuPlessis argues, must include looking 'beyond [these] ending[s].'

5 Fellini subjects both Wanda and Ivan equally to the moral laws of marriage. However, even though Ivan lies to Wanda about his purity, having spent the night with a prostitute, his little secret will not undermine his image or the power and position he holds as head of the family. If Wanda, on the other hand, were to act out her desire in a tryst with the White Sheik, her 'impurity' would debase her moral worth and call into question her character in the eyes of her husband and family.

6 Although Garber's definition is applied to cross-gender transvestism (among other categories based on class and race), the theory has implications in our reading of Wanda's relationship to femininity.

7 Within the economy of the film, both Ivan's and Wanda's movements in the public sphere are limited, and the one parallels the other. Ivan's are limited to a pursuit of Wanda and the pope, whereas Wanda's are limited to the pursuit of the conventional weekly *fotoromanzo* fantasy of love with a white knight. Nevertheless, it is made clear that Ivan normally has a 'respectable' career elsewhere. And although his movements are often comical, the fact that he moves freely in the public sphere is not at all unusual, whereas Wanda's venture outside the domestic sphere causes great upheaval and concern.

The film clearly sets up this dichotomy at the beginning. When we first meet the principal characters, Ivan is searching for his wife at the train station. He is a clearly distinct presence among a crowd of people. Wanda, on the other hand, is obscured by those around her – in psychoanalytic terms, a present absence. In this simple introductory sequence, the film firmly establishes Ivan's autonomy by making him the bearer of the look that authorizes Wanda's presence and identity. To underscore this point, the film's script notes: '*Ivan ... tenta di farsi capire ... da qualcuno che sta nello scompartimento*' ('Ivan tries to make himself understood by *someone* on the train'; emphasis mine) (*Lo sceicco bianco* [Milano: Garzanti, 1980] 23–4). Thus, we see and know Wanda *because* of Ivan. At the same time, the film relies on Wanda's femininity – on her status as object – to distinguish her from the rest of the crowd. Once again the film's script underscores her objectification, describing her as '*una giovane ragazza dal volto di bambina*' ('A young woman with the *face of a doll*'; emphasis mine).

8 In her famous analysis of an 'intellectual woman,' Joan Riviere defines masquerade. Briefly, when on the job, this woman would slip into a performance of femininity to undermine her performance as intellectual in the public sphere. Based on this case study, Riviere concludes that 'womanliness ... could be assumed and worn as a mask' ('Womanliness as Masquerade,' *Psychoanalysis and Female Sexuality*, ed. H.R. Rultenbeek [New Haven: College and University Press, 1966] 213). Drawing from Riviere, Doane positions masquerade within the realm of female identity, or non-identity. Masquerade allows women to 'create a distance between oneself and the image,' the 'image' being determined by 'patriarchal positioning' ('Film and Masquerade: Theorizing the Female Spectator,' *Screen* 23.3:82 and 23:4:81). In his own study of masquerade, Stephen Heath, whose analysis parallels that of Luce Irigaray (see body of text and endnote 9), points out

that 'masquerade is the assumption by the woman of "femininity" as the representation of desire, she playing out the economy of the phallus, becoming in a mirroring turn the signifier of the desire of the Other' (*Questions of Cinema* [Bloomington: Indiana UP, 1981] 187). See also C. Johnston, 'Femininity and the Masquerade: Anne of the Indies,' *Jacques Tournier*, ed. C. Johnston and P. Willemen (Edinburgh Film Festival, 1975) 36–44.

9 Luce Irigaray, *This Sex Which Is Not One*, trans. Catherine Porter (Ithaca: Cornell UP, 1985) 134.

10 Simone de Beauvoir, *The Second Sex*, trans. H.M. Parshley (New York: Knopf, 1953); Carole-Anne Tyler, 'Female Impersonation' (diss. Brown University, 1989) 48.

11 Tyler 35.

12 Marjorie Garber, *Vested Interests: Cross-Dressing and Cultural Anxiety* (New York: Routledge, 1992)16.

13 Garber 17.

14 For Freud's definition of women's sexuality, see 'Female Sexuality' and 'Femininity,' *Freud on Women: A Reader*, ed. E. Young-Bruehl (New York: W.W. Norton, 1990) 321–40 and 342–62.

15 Both personas, it can be argued, are based on male desire and adhere to conventional portrayals of women's sexuality in patriarchal culture. I base my argument on the fact that Wanda operates within a specific cultural context that is the reality with which she can work and out of which she can explore and attempt to create an identity.

16 Frank Burke similarly reads the set of the *fotoromanzo* as a family, with the director as patriarch. See *Federico Fellini* (London: Columbus Books, 1984).

17 There is much feminist literature on the role the mother plays in women's early development. See, for example, E. Badinter, *Mother Love: Myth and Reality* (New York: Macmillan, 1981); A. Rich, *Of Woman Born: Motherhood as Experience and Institution* (New York: W.W.Norton, 1986); and L. Muraro, *L'ordine simbolico della madre* (Rome: Editori Riuniti, 1992).

18 The Sheik himself actively participates in the perpetuation of this scenario, declaring, for example: '*Che strano questo nostro incontro. É una ... grande sensazione irreale*' ('Our encounter is so strange. It is a tremendous, unreal sensation'). And later as himself, the actor Fernando Rivoli, he continues the charade by instructing the makeup artist to render Wanda more 'Oriental,' thus furthering the construction of the masquerade.

In his divinelike appearance to Wanda, the White Sheik takes on qualities of the unreal and of perfection. When addressing the nature of the unreal, Hans Robert Jauss argues that in its ability to fascinate, the *irréel* appears more real than reality itself. This is due in part to the fact that while perfection is indeed unreal (*l'irréel de la perfection*), enjoying self-sufficiency and embodying an ideal, it gives the illusion of being real, of being a quality achievable in reality. In this capacity, it surpasses any judgment of credibility (*La perfection, fascination de l'imaginaire,' Poétique* 61 [February 1985]: 4).

19 See Peter Bondanella, *The Cinema of Federico Fellini* (Princeton: Princeton UP, 1992); Burke; L. Chomel, 'Fellini's *The White Sheik*: The Beginning of an Adventure,' *Varieties of Filmic Expression. Proceedings of the 7th Annual Kent St. University International Film Conference*, ed. D. Radcliffe-Umstead, April 11–12, 1989, 119–25; and Risset.

20 My notion of subjectivity is informed by Vegetti Finzi's own definition of subjectivity as the ability to tell and thus shape one's own history and life narrative ('Alla ricerca di una soggettività femminile,' *La ricerca delle donne: Studi femministi in Italia*, ed. M.C. Marcuzzo and A. Rossi-Doria [Torino: Rosenberg è Sellier, 1987] 144).

21 In his reading of the film, John Baxter points out that 'Fellini seemed to be exposing the dangers of a life nourished by fantasies' (*Fellini* [New York: St Martin's Press, 1993] 93). In my own reading, I propose that the film goes beyond this exposition to investigate the actual production of fantasy and its place in women's socialization.

22 Columns focused on the *fai-da-te* (do-it-yourself) culture and featured such titles as 'I vostri uomini ritornano, siate belle per loro' ('Your men are returning, be beautiful for them,' 1946). These columns lasted through the 1960s, disappearing in the 1970s. See the retrospective number of *Noi donne*, February 1993.

23 When Wanda is in the insane asylum still dressed as Fatma, Ivan brings her her 'proper' clothing, thus reintegrating her into the role of wife.

5

Whose *Dolce vita* Is This, Anyway?
The Language of Fellini's Cinema

MARGUERITE R. WALLER

> It is not memory that dominates my films. To say that my films are auto-
> biographical is an overly facile liquidation, a hasty classification. It seems to
> me that I have invented almost everything: childhood, character, nostalgias,
> dreams, memories, for the pleasure of being able to recount them. In the sense
> of the anecdotal, there is nothing autobiographical in my films ... I could easily
> make a film composed of memories and nostalgias on Turkey, a country that I
> do not know at all.
>
> –Fellini, *Panorama*

These comments by Italian film director Federico Fellini concerning the
relationship between his filmmaking and memory call attention to an
issue in the semiotics of cinema that complicates any notion of the
usefulness of film as a locus for certain kinds of historical and cultural
analysis. I will argue that a film like Fellini's 1959 release, *La dolce vita*,
though highly relevant to investigations of autobiographical and historical discourse, makes good on Fellini's suggestion that his project does
not stand in any hierarchical, mimetic relation to memory. Instead, this
film – not unlike the films of the early *Nouvelle Vague* and the writings of
then young theoreticians such as Michel Foucault and Jacques Derrida
– challenges the regime of the written word and its attendant historiog-
raphies, notions of identity, and, inevitably, sexualities.[1]
 To begin, let me urge that the film's title, *La dolce vita*, or 'The Sweet
Life,' can be construed literally as well as ironically. Notwithstanding
the dismay of many high-ranking members of the Italian government
and press, who wanted Fellini to make substantial cuts in the film in
order to mitigate what they took to be its scandalously negative portrait of late-1950s Italian society, the film can be viewed as a positive as

well as a negative exposé (e.g., Liehm 174–7). For a relevant analogue, one might go to the fourteenth-century vernacular Italian poem that offers a scandalously negative portrait of late fourteenth-century Italian society under the ironically literal title *La Commedia – The Comedy*. As many readers have noted, one of the principal issues in Dante's poem is the effect of its new medium, vernacular Italian, on how the world and the self are understood (Waller 58–62, 143). By promoting Italian to the status of a language in its own right, and not simply a degraded form of the hegemonic Latin that was the official language of Church and state throughout Europe, Dante remapped his contemporaries' understanding of both languages. Latin began to lose its privilege and the appearance of universality that went with it. Both languages appeared more obviously to be technologies of signification, equivalent in their contingency and materiality, though endlessly and suggestively different in their grammatical, syntactical, and lexical idiosyncracies.

Fellini's refusal to take memory as the ground of his films, and his disinclination even to call them autobiographical are, in effect, rigorous comments on the nature and status of his cinematic language. Like the *Commedia*, Fellini's film enacts the potentially profound and happy impact of a new medium, a whole new set of signifying possibilities, on the ways of patterning experience – as it is lived and as it is remembered – that have been elaborated through other, older signifying practices. Fellini's love affair with moving pictures can have 'happened,' but it cannot be 'remembered' insofar as it successfully transforms the terms of historical and autobiographical 'knowledge.' It is possible, of course, to constrain the grammar and syntax of a new medium like cinema to fit conventional ideologies and structures of perception rooted in verbal – and especially written – culture. I will say more later about Fellini's brilliant use of the American actor Lex Barker, one of Hollywood's Tarzans, and Anita Ekberg, a late-1950s Hollywood sex symbol, to parody the retrograde cinematic language of the American film industry. But Fellini's abandonment of 'himself' to 'the pleasure of being able to recount' in ways that are fundamentally and innovatively cinematic is a project or a decision or an event – verbal terms are interestingly inappropriate here – that cannot, rigorously speaking, be presented as part of or continuous with the portrayal of life outside filmmaking.[2]

My starting point, therefore, will be a rudimentary discussion of some fundamental but rarely discussed properties of cinematic signification in general. Following this I will look at what might be called the 'poetics' of *La dolce vita* in particular. The fundamental property of moving pictures is – one keeps needing to remind oneself – that they *move*. That is, whether or not the *image* moves, the *film* is always in motion. Each second, twenty-four frames (in current sound film production) move through the pull-down mechanism of the camera or its mirror image, the projector.[3] This constant physical movement of the celluloid itself allows a great many things to happen. One of the most striking, as theoreticians of the kind of editing known in this country as 'montage' have emphasized, is that visual images that are not contiguous with one another geographically or chronologically, and are not shot in the same scale, through the same lens, from the same angle, or in the same light, may become intimately related to one another – much more intimately and dramatically related than images within the same frame. In part this is because the audience is drawn to participate in relating them. For example, in the special case sometimes known as 'separation,' where two people talking to each other are shown alternately in separate framings, the audience will combine the alternating shots to form a mental picture that includes both figures (Sharff 6, 59–65).

This 'picture' need not be visual, though for visually oriented people it often is; rather, it has to do with relating the separate images conceptually. (For example, one figure, shot closer up or from a lower angle than the other, may be read as dominant.) Once this process is set in motion – once the audience has been empowered to create such mental images – the filmmaker is further empowered to play subsequent screen images off against these mental images and to play mental images off against one another. Since the scene constructed in the mind's eye need not resemble any pre-existing or already known physical space, it will itself change dimension and density as tones of voice, lighting, angles, and distances of the camera are varied. In other words, the physical movement of the film may ultimately become translated into a complex variety of conceptual movements. Many filmmakers make it a rule of thumb to end such a sequence with a resolution of some kind – often a shot of the two characters in the same frame. This resolution both lessens the audience's involvement and tends to direct the play of signifiers in the sequence toward a particular conclusion.

In *La dolce vita*, by contrast, separation sequences are lovingly belaboured and often unresolved. The central character, Marcello, a *National Enquirer*–style 'journalist' (played by Marcello Mastroianni), has recurring, inconclusive telephone conversations with his unhappy mistress, Emma. These unresolved sequences, in which the characters are never shown in the same frame, are paradigmatic of the film's refusal to resolve either visually or narratively the sexual and political conflicts it unfolds. Similarly, when a discontented rich woman, Maddalena (played by Anouk Aimée), whose after-hours habits are much the same as Marcello's, proposes marriage to him in the whispering gallery of a fifteenth-century palazzo, the film language even more pointedly diagrams, but refuses facilely to resolve (to 'marry'), the forces at play in the sequence. After whispering her proposal, Maddalena ignores Marcello's answer; instead she responds to the embrace of a man who has joined her at the stone shell that acts as the gallery's natural 'microphone.' Her drift into an embrace with another man in the midst of her extraordinarily dramatic exchange with Marcello suggests that resolution and release are not the natural and inevitable products of the processes set in motion by separation. On the contrary, the curtailment of these processes may always involve the intervention of an arbitrary, and in that sense non-cinematic, requirement that disparate visual and mental elements coalesce in a stable atemporal or extratemporal unity – a unity that film is ill suited to convey because film is always in motion and this motion is always governed by time.

The suggestion raised by the whispering gallery scene is more than borne out by the *tour de force* of the final scene of *La dolce vita*. Here, separation is used to suggest a certain closeness between the two characters, Marcello and a young waitress named Paola whom he encountered earlier in the film, but separation sequences alternate with shots including both figures to suggest a simultaneous distance. The two ways of shooting, in other words, themselves operate in separation to create a kind of 'separation to the second power.' The associations and cross-referencings that become possible as long as these separations are not resolved – and they never are – present themselves as fast and as furiously as we can make them, though the screen images themselves are unusually austere. A few examples of how this scene is working will indicate the difference it makes – especially in how we come to terms with the thematic issues raised in *La dolce vita* – that the processes set in motion by the motion of the film not be curtailed.

Two medium close-ups – one of Marcello and the other of Paola, each seen from the other's point of view – signal that each recognizes and remembers the other from their earlier meeting at a seaside restaurant where Paola works and where Marcello, significantly, went with his typewriter to escape the complaints of his live-in mistress, Emma. Neither shot gives us a clear sense of how far away from each other they actually are. Variations in the screen sizes of their images in subsequent shots indicate instead when something – a reaction or realization – is being underlined or emphasized. Interspersed with sequences of this kind are shots of Marcello and Paola in the same frame, made with a telephoto lens from an oblique angle behind Marcello's back. In these shots both lens and angle horizontalize the relationship between the two figures, while their placement within the same frame interrupts the current of their exchange as it is shot in separation.[4] These visual interruptions are reinforced by, though not necessarily synchronous with, alternations on the soundtrack between moments of deafening wind and wave noise and moments of quiet in which Marcello's words suddenly become clearly audible. Both kinds of interruption – audio and visual – begin to signify, not as naturalistic representations but rather as relevant conceptual cues, when we realize that neither the noise of the wind and waves nor the distance between the two figures can be blamed for Marcello's incomprehension of Paola's hand gestures. He can see her hands perfectly clearly, we realize, and in any case, nothing physical prevents him from walking closer. The obstacle to his deciphering her gestures is not physical but mental (as Paola indicates when she signs that Marcello is being thick in the head). Either he does not remember, or he failed to register in the first place, that she asked him back at the restaurant to teach her how to use a typewriter.

Both the very loud sound and the extreme long shots, then, can be associated with Marcello's inability to make the connection between what Paola asked him earlier and what she is signalling here. Recalling that encounter at the restaurant, we can understand more about why this connection does not get made. (Cinematically, in fact, Marcello's bewilderment may work to stimulate our recollections of the earlier scene.) Marcello's side of the earlier conversation turned on the waitress's purported resemblance to the angels painted by the Renaissance Umbrian artist Raphael. Marcello's elegantly turned compliment, though, betrays a significant pattern in his treatment of both art history and the young woman. Raphael's angels look the way they do in part because the Umbrian physiognomy served as his model. The waitress is Umbrian. Therefore it might have been more appropriate to note that Raphael's angels resemble the Umbrian waitress. By putting the case the other way around, Marcello avoids recognizing that even the most sacred or captivating cultural icons have their local, historical roots. By lending to Raphael's angels the status of a disembodied ideal and by then assimilating Paola into that ideal, Marcello is doing just the opposite of what Fellini's film does: he is flattening her into a static, two-dimensional image (quite literally when he has her pose for him in profile) and detaching that image from the context that presented it to him. He decontextualizes and dehistoricizes both Raphael's art and the young woman in front of him – a dislocated, homesick young woman who needs to acquire an empowering skill, not fatuous compliments, if she is to find a place in modern Italian society different from that of the dependent and battered women who otherwise inhabit Marcello's world. The fact that in this earlier scene Marcello was already seeing Paola not as a signifying being, but only as a sexual and aesthetic object, makes his later 'degeneration' from yellow journalist to completely mercenary publicist seem less a change of direction (as he feels it to be) than an externalization or literalization of what he was, in effect, already doing. Eventually it will become Marcello's, and by extension the Italian mass media's, profession to turn people into commodities and submit them to the 'hasty classification' and 'facile liquidation' from which Fellini distinguishes his own work. The blindness of such a position is deftly figured by Marcello's inability to 'read' the gesturing he can so clearly 'see' in the final scene.

Marcello experiences external forces over which he thinks he has no control and for which he assumes no responsibility. But the film shows us that it is Marcello's own 'noise' and 'distance,' rather than the noise and distance that seem to him to be external conditions, that separate him from Paola. Once we recognize that we do not have to identify with Marcello, but are freed by the cinematic text to make our own connections, many further potent rearrangements of the elements of this and other scenes suggest themselves. Determinations of centre and periphery, foreground and background, actions and setting, may shift dramatically. As the women in the film are emancipated from Marcello's gaze, their actions and words take on new significances in relation to each other. For example, Marcello's phone calls with Emma at the beginning and end of his first meeting with Paola strongly link Emma's unhappiness (precisely what Marcello was trying to get away from by bringing his work to the restaurant) and Paola's situation. This linkage suggests that Emma's needs and anxieties are not necessarily innate, individual, or unilateral, but readable also (or instead) as products of the economic and sexual politics of the world represented by and through Marcello. (This suggestion is confirmed elsewhere when Emma, abandoned by an angry Marcello at the side of the road, is shown contentedly picking flowers.) The situations of the women in the film, every last one of whom is beaten or brutalized in some way, in turn speak eloquently to the malaise from which the men are suffering – a connection that the men, *because* of their malaise, are incapable of making. Marcello and his older existentialist friend, Steiner, fail to recognize their own violence as they reduce the world, including its women and children, to acontextual, two-dimensional images. Consequently, it goes without saying, they also fail to make the connection between that violence and their increasingly virulent social and domestic claustrophobia. To do so they would have to relinquish their privileged (and well-paying) positions as knowers of truth and arbiters of culture – a position that Marcello can still nevertheless sense as being implicated in his behaviour toward Emma when he construes her suicide attempt as an attempt to 'ruin' his journalistic career. Underscoring the point, Marcello's dignification of Steiner's much more horrifying infanticide/suicide constrasts sharply and tellingly with his reading of Emma's overdose.

This thread I have followed from the shot construction and editing of Marcello's second encounter with Paola through some of the film's thematic elements is not intended to be exclusive or exhaustive. My interest lies rather in the way the complicated, multidimensional, multidirectional operation of the film's own movement overwhelms and 'ruins' the two-dimensionalizing – the dehistoricizing and decontextualizing – that many of its characters practise and that most are victimized by. This is the 'sweetness,' so to speak, of the life subjected to the gaze of the moving picture camera. It is a sweetness explicitly, pointedly, and wittily opposed to the fetishized sex and violent action that – as Fellini is neither the first nor the most recent to point out – are the mainstays of commercial Hollywood film. Through his use of the two Hollywood personalities Anita Ekberg and Lex Barker (playing Sylvia Rank and her fiancé Robert), Fellini comments on the anticinematic nature of these pleasures and on the self-destructiveness of a cinema that tries to pander to them. For example, when Sylvia returns to her hotel with Marcello at dawn, and Robert, awakened by the paparazzi stationed around his car, slaps her, she remonstrates tearfully, 'You shouldn't do things like that, especially in front of people.' Her primary concern, in other words, is with the inviolate consistency

of her image (an image, Fellini stresses through her provocative gestures and costuming, precisely of violability and promiscuity). She
must always appear the same, off-screen and on. Neither off-screen nor
on must there be any metamorphic encounter or exchange. To be affi-
anced to Tarzan is fine, but only as long as the two images simply reinforce – not complicate and problematize – each other. A good sex
symbol, it seems, does not in fact really have much to do with sex. The
perfect finishing touch to this deliciously ironic portrait of the fetishized celluloid woman is delivered by Sylvia, when, with her back to
the camera, she expresses her fear of being scratched. Her complaint,
in English, can be heard on the soundtrack: 'I've had enough ... Oh,
these men! They have long nails.'

Analogously, the physically powerful, action-oriented male hero of
Hollywood film – Tarzan, for example – simply repels whatever threatens his inviolable integrity. In the typical American action film there is
very little of the kind of conceptual movement I have been describing.
Conventional American film stops short at spectacle – the spectacle of
larger-than-life, violent, onscreen confrontations that, like the image of
the fetishized woman, evoke involuntary somatic reactions, and perhaps reinforce the conservative dynamics of the unconscious, but go
no farther. Few conceptual problems are presented: the good guy/bad
guy morality and politics of such films leave nothing (which is to say
everything) to be questioned and investigated.[5] Fellini's joke on the
Robert/Lex/Tarzan character is to remove him from his generic context and put him in a far more complex setting where the figures he
happens to slug it out with are a woman and the physically unthreat-
ening Marcello. Robert looks less than heroic slapping Sylvia and
punching out Marcello, even as they look less than romantic being
slapped and punched by Robert. As the three figures are 'translated'
by the film from one genre to another (Marcello's Latin lover persona
having already provided a usefully amusing contrast to Robert's
American macho, and Sylvia's 'sex bomb' image and Robert's attempts
to be a caveman already having proved wildly dissonant), we find ourselves in an interesting position as spectators. This is not the position
of the knower, of one who thinks he sees through the details and con-
fusions to what really is. It is, instead, the position of the mediator
between languages.[6]

The kind of cinematic movement I have been describing creates a
never before seen or experienced time and space – a time and space in
which the fundamental activity is not representation, or even significa-

tion per se, but rather a perpetual production and confrontation of different systems and logics. This movement aspires to produce fragments, 'little ruins,' each suggestive of a whole of which it might be a part (like a figure in a separation sequence), yet each also free to combine and recombine with other similarly suggestive elements to create immense and unexpected new fields of analysis and action. It is about *how* we are empowered to see Rome or Turkey – in the relationships made possible by the production and confrontation of fragments – not, or not merely, *what* can be seen. It disturbs the illusory coherence that we lend to geographical, narrative, or dramatic contiguity when we seek to achieve a sense of cognitive mastery.

The stunning, historically evocative opening shot of the film and the sequences that immediately follow will offer a concluding and generalizing example. A longish, low-angle shot picks up two barely discernible objects in the distant sky to screen right and follows them until they resolve themselves into two helicopters, from one of which dangles an open-armed statue of Christ. This odd combination flies past the ancient Roman aqueduct of San Felice, and is followed by the camera as it recedes screen left, casting a shadow on the wall of a new highrise apartment building that is being constructed in the suburbs of Rome. This opening suggests several ironies. The juxtaposition in the same frame of cultural artifacts from three such different eras, or dimensions, of Roman history is itself striking. We are invited, perhaps, to laugh, and also to ask what these artifacts and the cultures they represent have to do with one another. Though envisioning them simultaneously involves no violation of documentary realism – these alignments *can* happen in Rome – it does violate a habit of chronological compartmentalization, called periodization, that usually keeps helicopters and ancient Romans at a safe distance from each other. Is Christian culture casting a benign benediction on the Imperial Roman culture it has supposedly displaced, or does the Roman construction hugely and immovably remain to dwarf the silly pretensions of its heirs? Does the Christian icon mock the false transcendence of the flying machine? Or has Christianity been reduced to an empty, dead, outward form, taken in tow by a modern, technological society? Who is dependent upon whom here, and what is dependent upon what?

Like the sea monster pulled ashore just before the end of the film, this ensemble of images has no determinable head or tail. Not only are the three cultures thus ironized – like the movie stereotypes, made to appear nonhegemonic with respect to one another – but so is any attempt to depict historical change or cultural difference in terms of stable subjects with stable narratives. Most notably, past and present are not opposed here. All three of the artifacts that we see are equally 'present' physically. Their vertical arrangement, which can, in the first place, be read equally legitimately from bottom to top (ancient to modern) or top to bottom (modern to ancient) or from the middle outward in either direction, is clearly an optical effect created for a moment by the relationship between the camera's placement and the helicopter's trajectory. The sense that however fruitfully allegorical, this visual moment is also highly contingent, is carried through in the framing of the shot that leaves the aqueduct without a ground and the helicopter blade pointing beyond the frame line at the top of the screen. The great stone arches do not signal the origin, nor modern technology the endpoint, of a historical continuum. Either one could as easily be the middle term suspended in a different triad. Most crucially, the very use of three contrasting objects rather than two in the construction of this scene works to challenge the binary logic that so thoroughly informs all the structures of information processing to which I have been alluding.

The shots following this shot begin to fulfil and extend these promises, clarifying the stakes involved in doing so in the particular sociopolitical milieu of Marcello's Rome. Experiencing these shifts – experiencing the radical temporality and contingency of our perceptions from the outside, so to speak – is one of the greatest gifts and political tools film can give us. Though Fellini's film actively denies us the position of cognitive mastery we might think we need – and feel we want – it also shows this position to be conducive to a range of political and psychological ills. Where does this leave the self and auto-biographical/historical knowledge? Although Fellini's intimate relationship with Rome is everywhere evident in the film, it might as well be set in Turkey in the sense that, fulfilling the logic of the medium, it works toward fragmentation and separation, leaving new syntheses and unifications to the spectators to perform. We are empowered to *shift* focuses and perspectives, whether they are trained on Rome or Turkey. In other words, the film's politics need not be confined to its own setting. As well as knowledge about or memory of a particular self in a particular place, the politics of our perceptions of these particularities become readable. What we gain is an experience of the richness of social possibility that is resistant to Marcello's reductiveness or Steiner's despair.

Notes

1 For example, in François Truffaut's *Les quatre cent coups* (*The Four Hundred Blows*), released in 1959, Antoine Doinel's problematic relationship to writing is pervasive, leading to his eventual arrest and incarceration. Jean-Luc Godard's *Alphaville* (1964) globalizes the issue of the imperializing and colonizing uses of writing, a capability that the film represents as vulnerable to poetry and to love. In order to ensure an antipoetic stability of meaning, words for desire have been expurgated from Alphaville's 'dictionary,' a text that all its citizens are required to abide by on pain of death, and women have been reduced to automata-like 'seductresses' whose sexuality is affectless and who lack any semblance of subjectivity.

   In 1967 Jacques Derrida's *De la grammatologie* (*Of Grammatology*) further denaturalized all verbal language, including speech, by questioning the romantic distinction between speech and writing. Foucault, in *Les mots et les choses* (*The Order of Things*), powerfully historicized the entire complex of categories and identities within which the romantic and modernist debates over the origin and nature of language have been staged.

2 A reasonably helpful analogy – one that my reference to Dante may already have suggested – would be the trope of conversion. Another would be the Freudian trope of the psychoanalytical 'cure.' In both cases the self produced by the process of reading or telling of itself in a new way must reach a point of significant discontinuity from the self under spiritual or psychoanalytical analysis in order for the conversion or the cure to have happened.

   But in these two cases, unlike the case of cinema, the physical bodies of actors are not involved in signifying other, earlier incarnations of the self. Also, unlike the case of cinema, language remains the dominant medium, the medium through which alternative modes of visual and somatic signification are made accessible to interpretation. Thus the radical subversion of the ontological integrity or continuity of the self implied from the start of such projects remains, possibly, something of a verbal game. And if the language in which the game is played out is itself the ground of the subjectivity of which we are speaking, as numbers of philosophers and linguists have repeatedly suggested, then these discussions reconstruct and reinforce the 'self' as fast as they can theoretically disassemble it. My sense of these issues is greatly indebted to Bruss.

3 This standard speed for shooting and projecting sound film has as much to do with economics as with physics. During the silent era it was discovered that at least eighteen frames per second were required in order to eliminate 'flicker,' that is, to activate the human eye's 'persistence of vision,' and give

us the illusion that we are seeing moving pictures rather than a succession
of still photographs. Eighteen frames per second became the standard, then,
because it was the least expensive. With the introduction of sound this minimum number had to be increased to twenty-four in order to eliminate audio
distortion. Film can, however, be shot and projected much faster than this.
In several large formats, such as Showscan and Cinemax, the film is shot
and projected at sixty frames per second, the increased speed giving the
image a much higher resolution. (Shooting film more slowly or more
quickly and then projecting it at standard speed results in fast motion or
slow motion, respectively.) Film remains a time-based medium in all these
instances, but as resolution increases, various axioms of film language
change. Among other things, the use of make-up, painted backdrops, and
various lenses becomes problematic. The shot/reverse shot structure of
much Hollywood cinema ceases to work effectively, especially when
increased speed is paired with a larger frame size, increasing the depth of
field and making it difficult or impossible to manipulate background focus.
We have grown accustomed to conflating the properties and possibilities of
film shot at its lowest threshold with those of film per se. The variations that
higher speeds (which use up more film and are therefore more expensive)
introduce remind the film theorist just how arbitrary and contingent these
properties and possibilities are. An awareness of this seems taken for
granted in Fellini's conceptually complex experiments (in *La dolce vita* and
elsewhere) with lenses, aspect ratios, sound perspective, and other technological possibilities in the twenty-four-frame-per-second format.
4 The telephoto lens flattens perspective. It is the lens used, for example, to
create the sense of a figure endlessly running toward the camera without
ever seeming to cover much ground. In telecasts of baseball games, it is the
lens that makes pitcher and batter look much closer together than we know
them to be. The wide-angle lens, by contrast, exaggerates perspective,
making background objects appear farther away from foreground objects
than they would seem either to the human eye, or if looked at through a so-
called 'normal' lens. In this instance, Fellini's use of the telephoto lens in
conjunction with the extra-wide Cinemascope screen serves to separate
Marcello and Paola horizontally, without hierarchizing their relationship as
a more 'normal' foreground, background configuration would. Thus, as in
the phone conversations between Marcello and Emma, formal resolution is
avoided. When the two figures appear within the same frame, they do not
'meet.' Their respective spaces remain heterogeneous in relation to each
other, neither one being subsumed by or subordinated to the other. Thus,
not only do these shots work syntactically to interrupt the current of

exchange set up by the use of separation, but they also work this way com-
positionally.

5 I do not mean here to slight the highly sophisticated and politically significant work that has been accomplished by feminist film theory in the past
fifteen years. Laura Mulvey, Annette Kuhn, Mary Ann Doane, and Teresa
de Lauretis, to mention only four foundational figures in the project of
theorizing the pleasures and dangers of Hollywood cinema, have opened
up a territory in which the role of the visual in the creation and maintain-
ance of sexual and gender oppression has become accessible to analysis.
But in this paper I am interested in a kind of filmmaking that, though very
aware of the ways of seeing and modes of visual representation that
underwrite Hollywood-oriented commercial production, starts with the
assumption – inherited from early Soviet filmmakers – that film is a
medium particularly well suited to disestablishing and transforming those
visual/conceptual/psychological/somatic habits (Eisenstein, Vertov). In
a 1990 double issue of *Camera Obscura* on spectatorship, Giuliana Bruno,
Laura Mulvey, and the editors, Janet Bergstrom and Mary Ann Doane,
among others, begin to raise the question of the relationship between
feminist analysis of the past fifteen years and related issues of subjectivity
having to do with nationality, class, race, age, ethnicity, and so on (Bruno
103; Mulvey 79; Bergstrom and Doane 14).

6 The notions of the spectator as a 'translator,' and of film as a medium more
involved with translation than with reference, were suggested to me by 'Les
figures ou la transformation des formes,' Chapter 2 of Gilles Deleuze's
L'image-mouvement.

References

Bruss, Elizabeth. 'Eye for I: Making and Unmaking Autobiography in Film.'
Autobiography: Essays Theoretical and Critical. Ed. James Olney. Princeton:
Princeton UP, 1980. 297–320.

Camera Obscura 21 (1990).

Dante Alighieri. *The Divine Comedy*. Trans. with commentary, Charles Single-
ton. Princeton: Princeton UP, 1970–5.

De Lauretis, Teresa. *Alice Doesn't: Feminism, Semiotics, Cinema*. Bloomington:
Indiana UP, 1984.

– *Technologies of Gender: Essays on Theory, Film and Fiction*. Bloomington:
Indiana UP, 1987.

Deleuze, Gilles. *Cinema 1, L'image-mouvement*. Paris: Les editions de minuit,

1983. Also available in English translation as *Cinema 1: The Image-Movement*. Trans. Hugh Tomlinson and Barbara Habberjam. Minneapolis: U of Minnesota P, 1986.

Derrida, Jacques. *De la grammatologie*. Paris: Les éditions de minuit, 1967.

Doane, Mary Ann. *The Desire to Desire: The Woman's Film of the 1940's*. Bloomington: Indiana UP, 1987.

– 'Film and the Masquerade – Theorizing the Female Spectator.' Screen 23 (1982): 74–88.

Eisenstein, Sergei. *Film Form: Essays in Film Theory*. Ed. and trans. Jay Leyda. New York: Meridian Books, 1958.

– *The Film Sense*. Ed. and trans. Jay Leyda. New York: Harcourt, Brace, Jovanovich, 1975.

Fellini, Federico. Interview. *Panorama* 18 (14 January 1980).

Foucault, Michel. *Les mots et les choses: Une archeologie des sciences humaines*. Paris: Gallimard, 1966.

Kuhn, Annette. *The Power of the Image: Essays on Representation and Sexuality*. London: Routledge and Kegan Paul, 1985.

– *Women's Pictures: Feminism and Cinema*. London: Routledge and K. Paul, 1982.

Liehm, Mira. *Passion and Defiance: Film in Italy from 1942 to the Present*. Berkeley: U of California P, 1984.

Mulvey, Laura. 'Visual Pleasure and Narrative Cinema.' *Screen* 16 (1975): 6–18. Rpt. in *Visual and Other Pleasures*. Bloomington: Indiana UP, 1989.

Sharff, Stefan. *The Elements of Cinema: Toward a Theory of Cinesthetic Impact*. New York: Columbia UP, 1982.

Vertov, Dziga. *Kino-Eye: The Writings of Dziga Vertov*. Ed. and intro. Annette Michelson. Trans. Kevin O'Brien. Berkeley: U of California P, 1984.

Waller, Marguerite. *Petrarch's Poetics and Literary History*. U of Massachusetts P, 1980.

6

'Toby Dammit,' Intertext, and the End of Humanism

CHRISTOPHER SHARRETT

Federico Fellini has long been identified as a humanist on a journey of self-discovery, pursuing meaning on a perilous 'road'[1] and creating melancholic heroes stifled by introspection in the manner of the Renaissance humanist self or subject.[2] I will argue that while it is indeed difficult (perhaps even pointless) to separate Fellini from an essentially humanist world view, his project since the 1960s entails a negative dialectic involved in a debunking not only of the contemporary milieu and mediascape, but of much cultural tradition and the artist him/herself. As such, his work is implicated in rather than adversarial to the postmodern cultural predicament. While Fellini has little in common with the Frankfurt School's project, he seems to share its impulse toward a consistently negative hermeneutic in the analysis of synthetic postwar transnational culture. Many of Fellini's key films from the 1960s onward show a concern for the limits of representation – particularly its ability to mediate issues of history, culture, and human experience.

Fellini's project while working in this mode is satirical, with a melancholy cynicism. If one reads humanism as the desire to assert the efficacy of individual human action and humane values against dogma, commerce, and functionalism – this indeed seems to describe Fellini's basic impulses – the director's faith in such ideals, teetering in *La dolce vita* (1960), are collapsing by the late 1960s. While Fellini's insistence on negativity is not quite equatable with Adorno's attempt 'to resist the structures of domination and reification that existed in society,' it does embrace a concern to make art a domain where 'consciousness could be critical.'[3] Fellini's works evince skepticism toward the codes and conventions of representational cinema and the adjacent seductions that distort the nature of reality. Like the Marxist side of high modernism, Fellini by the time of 'Toby Dammit' (1968) was confronting a system characterized by impervious totality and a logic of disintegration. This system is also extremely atomized, fragmented, and disjunct, and is so described in Fellini's visual style by the late 1960s, with its distanciation effect. It tracks slowly across faces, interiors, and landscapes that are both familiar and alienating, even grotesque, and that offer a cool but grisly sense of the *Unheimlich* that would come to earmark much postmodern film imagery twenty years later.

Several critics have noted Fellini's prescience in sensing the failure of signification, and have recognized his artistic practice since the late 1960s as essentially postmodern in various important features.[4] In particular, his work suggests an anxiety about the onrushing demise of the humanist subject. But far from shoring up fragments of a dead cultural past against the brutishness of the present in the manner of Eliot,[5] Fellini's later period suggests an increased scepticism toward artistic tradition and representation. This tendency is evident with *8½* (1963) and *Juliet of the Spirits* (1965), works whose essential romanticism barely stayed clear of the deliberate 'flattening of affect' associated with postmodernism. The turning point of his aesthetic is the small film 'Toby Dammit,' part of an anthology based on several stories by Edgar Allan Poe, released by American International Pictures in 1968 as *Spirits of the Dead* (*Histoires Extraordinaires* in Europe, and *Tales of Mystery and Imagination* in Britain).

'Toby Dammit' marks a transition for Fellini toward a kind of 'artificial cinema' fully manifest in *Fellini-Satyricon* (1969) and *Fellini's Casanova* (1976). These works hearken back to Méliès in their utter contrivance. They were shot entirely on sound stages at Cinecittà with sets and special effects noteworthy for their synthetic staginess (the plastic lagoon in *Casanova* is the example *par excellence*). The artifice of late Fellini lacks, of course, the naïveté of Méliès or the adversarial political project of Brecht. It also represents more than a final break with neorealism. Indeed it suggests nothing less than a distrust of representation itself and a nihilistic sence that artistic poetics has been exhausted. These works might be associated with the modernism of Eliot, primarily because they are an assault on the restrictions of capitalist culture from a conservative perspective. They are more properly associated, though, with postmodernism in their anguish (flavoured with nostalgia) over the passing of humanist culture, and in their admission that there is no history outside of representation. Fellini's version of postmodernism, like most others, cannot conceive of an alternative notion of history and human conduct once conservative cultural tradition and representation have been dispensed with. Fellini's postmodern sensibility comes through in various interviews, especially the ones he gave during the production of *Satyricon*, in which he expressed great skepticism over, for example, art's ability to represent history. He emphasized his reliance on the extravagant conventions of popular genres (especially science fiction) and on tropes provoking extreme distanciation, even as he decried the conventions of Hollywood, which represented the past through such forms as the biblical epic.[6]

With 'Toby Dammit,' Fellini shows his deep affection for popular culture (his love of comic books is well known). His appropriation of popular forms in his later work amounts to a critique of the 'grand opera' style that has influenced much postwar Italian cinema. The grandiosity of this style was unappealing to Fellini, who remained distant from overbearing ennui (Visconti), and from operatic approaches to Marxist romance (Bertolucci). *Amarcord* (1973) and *Orchestra Rehearsal* (1979) can be seen as responses to these tendencies; that being said, Fellini's conservative debunking is most obvious in his attitude toward allusion. Fellini's allusionism, unlike that of 'late' postmodernist works such as Quentin Tarantino's *Pulp Fiction* (1994), retains a humanism simply through its consciousness of a wider world, a consciousness informed by more than film-fan consumerism. The implied impossibility of representing this wider world within a commercial culture that erases it gives Fellini's later works a sense of the catastrophic, and consequently retains their connection to humanism.

Much has been written about Fellini's continuity within classical art, his affinities with the Italian Renaissance. Dante has often been cited as an interest of Fellini's and as a source of the frameworks for some of his key films.[7] 'Toby Dammit,' with its many citations of classical art and contemporary cinema, shows him beginning to reject the Eliot-like reactionary position that looks at art as an ennobling, consoling force in a degraded world; instead he finds it now fully complicit with a civilization rapidly eroding the subject. Furthermore, intertextuality – the hallmark of the postmodern moment – is seen in the later films as suggesting not the interdependence of works, or the disappearance of the authorial voice (celebrated by much of postmodernity), but rather the formulaic, mind-deadening mass production of art, the culture industry's resuscitation and reformulation of bankrupt styles and conventions in its constant search for new forms and satisfactions. This outlook is immediately visible in the director's approach to his source material and to his overall project. In *La dolce vita*, a work that amounts to the summary statement on Fellini's humanism, individual icons and images are wrenched out of their signifying context (the statue of Christ dangling from the helicopter in the celebrated opening). This suggests the fragility in the modern context of traditional institutions and the moral concerns they supposedly represent. By the time of 'Toby Dammit' these free-floating signifiers have a different aspect: they represent the domain of intertextuality that we could associate with William Burroughs's 'cut-up' technique, wherein images and ideas no longer have any autonomy, nor can they support authorial intentionality or broad notions of cultural tradition. As offered by writers such as Burroughs, cut-up and montage tend to have a liberating function; this suggests a more cultivated consciousness than that of the author-centred, logocentric mode of representation imposed by dominant culture. Yet for Fellini, the cut-up nature of contemporary consciousness, determined not by any adversarial formations or fringe movements within culture but rather by the dominant society itself, suggests merely the totality of alienation in the final stages of a representational practice imposed by commerce.

Walter Foreman has analysed 'Toby Dammit' as Fellini's meditation on the erasure of the subject through the erasure of the actor: that is, the end of the artist as manipulated figure subscribing to a 'corporate vision' of art.[8] What follows here supports Foreman's remarks, but argues that a fuller account needs to be taken of 'Toby Dammit' as a product of late-1960s international cinema. The style of 'Toby Dammit' is so mannered that the question arises whether what is going on in the world of the film is 'really happening' according to standard narrative rules about which we suspend disbelief, or whether events are merely the projection and fantasy of the protagonist. This work suggests that the director is frustrated with the crisis of representation, and that his ostentatious stylization is an attempt to involve the audience in a meditation on the artist's (increasingly ineffectual) ability to manipulate. Fellini's real frustration (and perhaps ours) centres on the problem that his later films are *seductive*; their peculiar aspect, while often icy and alienating, does not awaken the spectator to the tricks of cinema, so enamoured is s/he of all that is 'Fellini.' This dilemma forms a good part of the horror of 'Toby Dammit.'

Although 'Toby Dammit' is only loosely based on Poe's 'Never Bet the Devil Your Head,' its basic theme and the film's title character are indeed derived from the Poe antitranscendentalist morality tale. Fellini enjoys playing fast and loose with this material in the manner of other Poe 'adaptations.' Like earlier Poe-based films, Fellini's is filled with personal excesses and conceits that foreground the contrivances of Hollywood-style representational art. Like many of his films (*La dolce vita*, *8½*, 1972's *Fellini's Roma*, and 1980's *City of Women*), 'Toby Dammit' is strongly autobiographical, but here autobiography is not associated with a *cri de coeur*, nor does Fellini especially link himself to Poe, the archetypal 'tortured artist.' Fellini creates an authorial *raisonneur* in Toby, but one that is entirely circumscribed by the conventions and demands of the movie industry. Fellini loses himself fully and deliberately in the game of adapting Poe for the commercial cinema, and by so doing banishes humanism from his ongoing autobiographical project.

Spirits of the Dead was marketed in the United States as one of American International's Edgar Allan Poe horror films, a cycle begun by the studio in 1960 with *House of Usher*. James H. Nicholson and Samuel Arkoff produced these pictures, with Roger Corman directing almost all of them. *Spirits of the Dead* was indeed promoted as another film in the Poe cycle; the directorial presences of Roger Vadim (for the *Metzengerstein* sequence), Louis Malle (*William Wilson*), and Fellini received rather little play in advertising copy.[9] Yet Fellini's morbid and garish mise-en-scène became a natural extension of and complement to the Corman/Poe films; Fellini's kinship with Poe, the master of the grotesque and arabesque, is visible in the two artists' devastatingly bleak visions, manifest in Fellini in his refusal to acknowledge any transcendent, redemptive function for representational art. The film is, at root, a genre work, something that Fellini seems to have approached with the derision of one in love with pop culture, and also with skepticism about high culture's continued worth for mediating human experience. The bowdlerization of Poe in the AIP cycle seems convenient to a film artist who is uncomfortable with adaptation. The common wisdom has long held that making a movie of a writer's work is the ultimate validation, but one that simultaneously makes the work unrecognizable and erases the author. As Fellini discovered with *Fellini-Satyricon* (1969) and *Fellini's Casanova*, adaptation also reveals the paucity of the source, the kitschiness of 'big ideas' from literary history. Genre film is a comfortable vehicle for the critical agenda undertaken, as Fellini piles up genre tropes as a way of showing the inherent generic contrivance, the 'trashiness,' that is basic to all such representation.

Several of the Poe films (*The House of Usher*, *The Pit and the Pendulum*) begin with tacky yet unsettling colour washes. 'Toby Dammit' opens in the same way, with a prolonged shot of a bizarre sky – a grey-green, pink-blue melange. The title finally appears, accompanied by Nino Rota's eerie, tinkling piano motif, which serves the same atmospheric function as Les Baxter's *musique concrete*–like sounds in other Poe films. We suddenly find ourselves in the cockpit of a commercial aircraft, looking at the scene from Toby's perspective, approaching a destination much in the way male ingenues approach mansions and crumbling castles in other Poe films. The film embarks on other associations. The cockpit shot is decidedly not *Triumph of the Will*, that kitsch reworking of Romanticism's valorization of the subject. Nor is it Friedrich's *The Wanderer over the Mist*, filled with the sublime *angoisse* that so infuses American and European paeans to the male subject. The sequence becomes an acid reference to the manipulation that is essential to all representation. (How many Second World War films have similar sequences?) And this plane delivers not the unbridled Id as in Riefenstahl, but rather the subject who barely exists, preferring not to evidence himself in the world. In emphasizing the humdrum, boorish (and confrontational) nature of the flight crew and Toby's fear of landing, Fellini is extending Poe's jibe at transcendentalism and merging it with his own project in this film, which is to debunk the 'spiritual' nature of art. The film lampoons the notion of God as ultimate director/manipulator by calling attention to the mythologies of cinema.

We learn that Toby is a fading British stage actor now relegated to genre films. His visit to Rome recalls two mythologies. The first is the traditional Italian Journey that rejuvenates the Western artist as he returns to the font of civilization. Toby's journey is closer to Thomas Mann than to Goethe, although this journey lacks the apocalyptic resonance of *Death in Venice*, in which the explosion of the Romantic self-concept has a tragic and epic force suggestive of *fin de siècle* end of illusion. At the same time, this Italian Journey, like Mann's, is not revivifying: Toby equivocates about making it ('This trip, which had taken me so long to decide upon ...'). Doom envelopes the trip very early, when Toby becomes convinced, as the sunglassed eyes of the ferryman/pilot stare at him/us, that the trip is 'very important,' and he feels an ominous 'invisible web' of the airport pulling his plane 'unresisting toward earth.'

Just as Aschenbach is taken aback by the greeting of the grotesque dandy at the docks of Venice, Toby is appalled by the predatory denizens of the new, Americanized Rome, which seems as impoverished as Mann's (or Visconti's) Venice, incapable of provoking any realization that might stop the compulsive, suicidal downward turn in which the subject is immersed. Also present here is a new myth conjoined to the Italian Journey: that of the expatriate actor, whose Roman exile is for a revivifying purpose, albeit one more narrow, venal, and pathetic than that of eighteenth- and nineteenth-century cultural heroes. Many American and British TV and film actors migrated to Cinecittà in the early 1960s as their careers faded on the home front. Their journey is usually represented with derision, as a site of Hollywood Babylon debasement, and as an image of the throwaway aspect of the actor in the consciousness industry. The situation is neatly capsulized in a song by the late-1970s post-punk group Last Men about the migration of fading character actor Steve Cochran:

Later in the fifties
When things got rough at home
You got that letter from Lex Barker
Saying 'Come to Rome.'[10]

Fellini chronicles the moment well in *La dolce vita*, which features a dissolute and dissipated Lex Barker very much playing himself, (paparazzi giggle, 'To think that he used to play Tarzan'). The *locus classicus* for the narrative of the expatriate actor's Italian Journey is the story of Clint Eastwood, who after the cancellation of his 1950s TV western *Rawhide* was catapulted to international fame as The Man With No Name of the Sergio Leone westerns. The Italian western's centrality to the faded Anglo-American stars enrolled at Cinecittà in the 1960s has pertinence to 'Toby Dammit.'

The Italian western, and then the western itself, became an amalgam genre in the 1960s – an exemplar of intertextuality. Its revisionism questioned not only the fundamental text underneath it – the American civilizing experience – but also a broad philosophical and aesthetic territory. As the western began to fade as a dominant American genre in the wake of the Vietnam war, it became a popular vehicle for dissecting ideologies – rather ironic, since the western had long been closely associated with conservative agendas. *The Good, the Bad and the Ugly* (1967) is a meditation on the death camps and the devastation of two interimperial wars as much as it is about the Civil War as prelude to frontier adverturism (its poster art slogan: 'For three men the Civil War wasn't hell – it was practice!'); *Once Upon a Time in the West* (1968) is an early postmodern work in its broad reflections on the history of the genre. Indeed, many European directors (and their critics) found the archetypal narratives of the western handy for rebuking the ideological assumptions of much cultural tradition: Pasolini's *Teorema* has been referred to, rather ostentatiously, as a reworking of *Shane*.[11] By the early 1970s, films such as Alejandro Jodorowsky's *El Topo* were making indulgent use of the western for some vulgar forays into psychedelic-era spirituality, complete with motley mytho-religious and cinematic allusions. (Indeed, Terence Stamp, who plays Toby, participated in precisely the kind of venture that ensnares his character in the continentalized western *Blue*, released the same year as *Spirits of the Dead* and heavily disparaged by critics.) In 'Toby Dammit' the Italian western is not employed to suggest the opening up of the 'mythic' aspects of the genre to allow it to encompass new intellectual vistas and gain legitimacy; but rather to suggest that such forms merely reflect Europe's desire to compete in the post–Marshall Plan international market and, more cynically, to use the discards (often human) of the American and British media industries.[12] The seduction of this new cinema is that it updates the myth of the reviving Italian Journey, only writ rather large, since the Italian western – an American form with a European *frisson* – became an attempt to validate a genre with the homeopathic magic of European association, a 'high culture' infusion into a business that holds contempt for culture.

Toby is contracted to make the first 'Catholic western,' about the 'return of Christ to earth at frontier's end.' Toby's introduction to the project during his arrival at the airport turns the film into a parodic anti–*8½*. Instead of taking seriously the entrapment and torpor of the artist, the film sends up the conceits of earlier Fellini; it focuses as much on the artist's arrogance, indulgence, and madness as on the commercial circumstances that confound and bedevil him. But the more crucial focus is on the character's artificiality.

Like Guido in *8½*, Toby is delivered into the hands of an avaricious, garrulous production team. At this point Toby makes a silly, vain retreat, Sisyphus-like, riding backwards on an up escalator. The Catholic priest who represents the producer is an image of the church central to Fellini, here only slightly less sardonic than that similar conjunction of secular and religious authority in Pasolini's *Salò* (1975). In this sequence the failure of 'intertext' and of discourse itself is reflected in Toby's suffocation by the priest/producer and his entourage, and by the scheme they offer. Throughout the sequence, Toby speaks very little; he is an actor without a voice. He mumbles, whimpers, and emits groans as he swigs from a whiskey flask, an act so painful it doubles him over. Instead of Toby 'transforming his life into the material of art,'[13] he is the emblem of failed signification. He has 'no voice and no identity.'[14] His voice-over narration at the opening is a reference not so much to the fading authorial consciousness, or to the favourite Fellini conceit of the artist's captivity, as to the emptying out of these conventions. Toby quickly becomes a hyperbolically conventional figure, not only as exile actor/expatriate artist on leave in Italy, but as the perfect AIP wastrel/villain of the Poe series. With his pale face, blond-white hair, hypersensitivity, and Carnaby Street Victorian suit, he is a desiccated image of Swinging London filtered through Vincent Price's Roderick Usher – several layers of simulation focused on the vacuousness of the Misunderstood Artist stereotype.[15] He is Hammer Films's Dracula for a moment, when he swashbuckles with paparazzi, collapsing on the escalator, saying 'I live only during the night' – a statement that precedes some mannered gesticulation as Toby has his first vision of the girl/demon. The vulnerability of this hero/villain depends on the vulgar Freudian approach to Poe associated with Marie Bonaparte – an approach that fascinated Roger Corman and saturated the Poe series.[16] Toby's speechlessness, his 'loss of breath,' tends to lampoon the onrushing psychoanalytic readings of Poe, ferreting out issues of impotence and castration anxiety. The girl/demon with the bouncing ball, the figure of evil appealing to 'the English' (as Toby suggests), is not merely Salomé with the Baptist's head (and all the tired castration reference of that classic image); she is also the far more specific and contemporary moment (especially in reference to the legend of the fading male movie star) of pedophiliac lust entrenched in film cult lore, as the faded, alcoholic star achieves new depths of inversion while losing all contact with the social. But Fellini's allusions are puns that constantly return the narrative to the essential failure of such gestures. *Contra* Toby, this Devil may indeed suggest a Catholic vision that finds in woman the root of all evil and in pedophilic lust a damnation that axiomatically constructs Toby's temptress as Satan. At the same time, the Devil seems just as clearly the production industry that torments the beleaguered and fading artist (again, the relationship to *8½* stands out). This amalgam is so typically Fellini that it becomes its caricature. Fellini consistently links the female temptress to the demands of industry, the imposed compulsion to create, the confrontation with self-doubt. In short, the female is constructed as a curse, as the archetypal drain on the dwindling resources of the male. Yet in 'Toby Dammit,' Fellini seems able for a moment to confront these hysterical notions and to contextualize them within an awareness, if not of male hysteria, then of the need to project the collapsing masculine project onto an Other. Toby's melancholia – often a cartoon of Dürer's classic engraving – is provoked both by the flight of the muse (Toby's better days are behind him, and he cannot articulate) and by the allure of a succubus, both figured as women. The girl/demon possesses something (and the fact that she does suggests her appropriation of phallic power), and so does the mystery woman in the nightclub, and so does the human mannequin in the TV studio. The deliberately 'unreal' aspect of the female figures in the film might suggest the worst possible manifestation of the female as projection of the feeble male ego, except that Fellini draws them so blatantly from a history of such representation (in the case of the demon, the child monsters of horror films are in the background, along with *She Demon*, *Leech Woman*, and *Burn, Witch, Burn*) and from the manifest image of woman in the culture industry (the figures in the studio and nightclub). And the image of the dried up actor tormented by the teen bitch temptress is all tabloid lore: Fatty Arbuckle up on charges; Barrymore and Flynn drunk in L.A. whorehouses; Clift and Dean beaten up in sadomasochistic bars (a gay inflection); and William Holden dead drunk in a hotel, still bedevilled by young female trade.

Toby's impotence, and the vacuity of Toby's story, are underscored by his disembodied aspect. During his ride from the airport we witness not only his frailty but his fragmentation, which corresponds to the world around him. He seems decapitated from the outset,[17] and the images of his disembodied head complement the general sense of disjunction everywhere. The priest/producer depends on a translator, who occasionally misses what is said and doesn't seem overly concerned ('Something about vice, but I didn't quite get the point'); this conveys not only the routine, pointless aspect of discourse, but the disjunction between signifier and signified. The many masklike faces Toby confronts (also our point of view) at the airport and on the road are photographed in Fellini's signature style. Faces are objectified, and gestures are rendered mechanical, and all this suggests the functionalist, affectless aspects of everyday life that approach the 'beyond alienation' status identified with postmodernity. In describing his Catholic western, the priest/producer tells Toby he wishes to make Christ a 'concrete and tangible presence.' The line is another pun that summons up the helicopter-born Christ statue that opens *La dolce vita*, one of many cultural fragments that saturate the Fellini *oeuvre* and raise questions about the legitimacy of the cultural past in the current landscape. Like the huge broken or half-seen heads of *Fellini-Satyricon*, *Fellini's Roma*, *Fellini's Casanova*, and *Amarcord*, Toby's own head suggests the delegitimation of the human being, as an icon from a revered antiquity that was once a real, dynamic presence, and as it now exists in a postmodern cut-up milieu. We see not only Toby's 'floating' head as he moves through the world, but also his fragmented, blown-up, represented head covering the walls of the TV studio during his interview. The camera catches posters of Toby as the discourse again goes nowhere, and is about nothing – the genuine tale told by and to idiots (the Shakespeare ceremony seems to underscore the inadequacy of the Western literary 'canon'; this in turn suggests the failure of the 'universal,' 'timeless' perspective on the function of art in modern circumstances). Toby sighs 'what a shame' to the canned applause of a non-existent studio audience; meanwhile, TV technicians manipulate dials during his what's-your-favourite-colour interview. Toby's fleeting enthralment with the mannequin-like model on a 1950s-style kitchen set in an adjoining studio must be associated with the Dream Girl/'Ruby' sequence at the awards ceremony. What Toby *wants* is associated with what Toby *is* – all is within the realm of simulation and artifice. At the end of the film Toby's decapitated, waxen, and patently artificial head merely underscores what has been stated and reiterated ad nauseum: Toby is a puppet, a functionary within the arena of allusion.

Toby's Catholic western is clearly a consignment to a new inferno, yet knowing this does not ennoble or liberate the seer. The priest/producer's proposed intertext – his idea of fusing 'Carl Dreyer and Pasolini, with a touch of John Ford,' 'to reconcile the biblical countryside and prairie, Pier della Francesca and Fred Zinnemann' – reminds us, especially in retrospect, that such fusion has been the sum and substance of postmodernity. The piling up of signifiers serves merely to create new attractions and commodities – to dehistoricize art, as Fredric Jameson notes,[18] by removing it from all social/political/economic context.

The meddlesome priest's attempt to make spirituality 'concrete' is counterposed to the images seen by Toby from his limo window, and by the images in turn projected on him. Shot through an amber, hazy filter suggesting pollution, the camera shows an open truck with huge,

Francis Bacon–like sides of beef; a road crew paving the highway; mannequin-like fashion models; and other indices of the hyperreal, frenzied cityscape. All of these are offered as possible projections – again in the manner of most Poe characters – and suggest not so much Toby's tormented psyche, but rather the cliché of this trope in the literature of the fantastic. Through the limo window we see Toby's spectral face, which looks separated from his body due to the glare on the glass, onto which is superimposed other images: cartoons, movie posters, advertisements. The film creates a world in which little is 'concrete' and all is within the realm of simulation – specifically, the tired conventions of the horror film for which Fellini is a willing contract employee. Toby offers his hand to a gypsy fortune teller and then withdraws it with a rictus grin: Larry Talbot/Lon Chaney Jr in a wolfman movie, getting the dismal word from Maria Ouspenskaya?

The question of Toby's monstrousness, and of the world around him as his projection, becomes pronounced in the ghostly nightclub award ceremony. The extreme artifice of this set piece makes clear how distant this film is from representation, or rather, how involved it is in perusing representationalism. It can be argued that the Dream Girl who pledges her total love and devotion to Toby as he drifts into a drunken nap – Ray Charles sings 'Ruby' on the soundtrack – is yet another she-devil. This is best demonstrated after Toby's laboured *Macbeth* reading, when he bemoans his lot to the vapour-filled, near-empty club. Toby suddenly berates the woman, who has disappeared. At the start of his harangue, Toby's face forms an evil, half-shadowed Expressionist grin – the perfect horror film mask – as he leaps to the microphone, his huge, soon-to-be-lost head abruptly filling the screen as the camera cuts to the few silhouetted, motionless phantoms who compose the award show audience. His retort, 'Lady, I haven't been waiting for *you*!' is a caricatured Angry Young Man rejection of domesticity, an opting for Hot Rods-to-Hell freedom/self-destruction.

The Ferrari ride itself – Toby has been preoccupied with the car since arriving – is very American. Toby associates this high-performance car with total freedom, obviously, when he tear-asses through the deserted Roman streets. As Frank Burke suggests,[19] this is actually Toby's own Catholic western, but there is less redemptive self-discovery here than a punning re-enactment of the civilizing experience of the West itself. As in Frederick Jackson Turner's observations of the American experience of the West, this is the expenditure of energy along a trajectory until boundaries are confronted, forcing energies into new, often self-destructive directions.[20] Of course, the immediate references of Toby's midnight run are not involved with the western as much as with the hot car/motorcycle films that were AIP's bread and butter in the mid to late 1960s. Toby's run recapitulates the supercharged, suicidal male action/adventure imagery of the period, such as encountered in *Bullitt* with Steve McQueen, and *The Wild Angels* with Peter Fonda (who co-stars in the 'Metzengerstein' segment of *Spirits of the Dead* and whose career was launched by AIP). *The Wild Angels* features the emblematic motorcycle outlaw of the period, whose phallic bike and unleashed horsepower are in vainglorious pursuit of Utopia, which from the out-set seems axiomatically involved in apocalypse and self-destruction. Toby's silent disappearance into the abyss inserts all this into the hor-ror film – with the attendant nightmares of journey, recovery, expan-sionism, and conquest – under all male-oriented adventure genres that found their way from America onto the international market. The jour-neying, compelled hero indeed falls off the edge of the earth, or reaches the boundary of the ocean, only to keep going. Toby's suicidal journey reminds us that, as with *Don Quixote*, the romantic quest, the 'impossible dream,' was already parodical.

The demon woman, the Eve/Pandora/Salomé/Delilah/juvenile-temptress from the annals of filmdom, waits to reaffirm the fantasies that have driven the entire patriarchal civilizing enterprise. Toby moves into a domain of entropy as creative energy – already dissipated and degenerate, based on the abundant evidence of the entire narrative – turns in on itself. The conclusion invites Frankfurt theorization con-cerning the total system of capital: Toby's attempt to transgress bound-aries by insisting that he must 'get across' (finally take part in true discourse?) is less about his suicidal impulses (such seems only the lawful consequence of the cultural system's contradictions) than about the absorption and co-optation of such transgression under such a sys-tem. Fellini's presentation of an obvious stage model of the broken highway emphasizes the banality of Toby's suicide, undercutting the 'grand gesture' aspect of a trope that so typifies notions of tragedy. The image is also representative of Fellini's love of artifice. Such self-consciousness would be central to the plastic lagoons and papier-mâché busts of subsequent projects.

'Toby Dammit' is finally a comedy tinged by the director's sense of anguish over the limits of humanism. Released not long before *Fellini-Satyricon*, 'Toby Dammit' would seem to herald a new direction for this filmmaker, and his triumph at a particular juncture of film history. Yet almost all of his later work is marked by some degree of dissatisfaction, mainly with the ability of his own art to grapple with the issues that concern him. Nowhere is this more evident than in *Fellini's Casanova*, the prerelease interviews for which were peppered with Fellini's contempt for his subject and himself. (The atmosphere for this film was especially poisoned, since Fellini approached *Casanova* as a fall-back project after he failed to realize *Voyage of G. Mastorna*.) While *I clowns* (1970), *Amarcord*, and *Fellini's Roma* continue to show Fellini's humanist commitments, these sentiments are overwhelmed by *Satyricon, Casanova, And the Ship Sails On* (1983), *City of Women, Ginger and Fred* (1985), and *Intervista* (1987), works whose grimness is often less a matter of their scripts than of a style that suggests the director's struggle with representationalism, and a sense that the concerns of traditional representational art are banal. More important, Fellini's specific meditations on subjects such as history (the Enlightenment as the Dark Ages in *Casanova*) are understood in light of the artist's doubts about the worth of and his control over his craft (note the many cinematic allusions in the post-1960s films, such as the 'magic lantern' sequence in *Casanova*). It has been argued that Fellini's preoccupation with artifice is an indulgence and a conceit, given that Fellini isn't much interested in examining the ideological assumptions under representation, but merely wants to complain about the decay of the standing order. (Such charges seem supported when one examines a film like *Orchestra Rehearsal*.) 'Toby Dammit,' which neatly capsulizes (and parodies) all of the central preoccupations of early Fellini while presaging all that Fellini would do in the remainder of his career, is a signal moment for Fellini and for the crisis of modernism. In confronting the limits of art, Fellini intentionally becomes complicit with those limits by making a film that fully accommodates the production industry. He is then able to parody that industry, with a work that savages genre film, AIP, and all the tendencies that have erased humanist concerns in art. In the process, however, he parodies himself, reveals how easily all that is Fellini is subject for caricature, and – perhaps worst of all – replaces imagination with fancy as he indulges the industry he criticizes.

Notes

1 See Donald P. Costello, *Fellini's Road* (Notre Dame: U of Notre Dame P, 1983).

2 Timothy Hyman, '8½ as Anatomy of Melancholy,' in *Federico Fellini: Essays in Criticism*, ed. Peter Bondanella (New York: Oxford UP, 1978) 121–39.

3 Susan Buck-Morss, *The Origin of Negative Dialectics: Theodor W. Adorno, Walter Benjamin, and the Frankfurt Institute* (New York: Free Press, 1977) 189.

4 See Frank Burke, *Fellini's Films: From Postwar to Postmodern* (New York: Twayne, 1996). See also Dale Bradley, 'History of Hysteria: *Fellini's Casanova* meets Baudrillard,' and Frank Burke, 'Fellini: Changing the Subject,' in *Perspectives on Fellini*, ed. Peter Bondanella and Cristina Degli-Esposti (New York: G.K. Hall, 1993) 249–59, 275–92.

5 See Robert Richardson, 'Waste Lands: The Breakdown of Order,' in *Film and Literature* (Bloomington: Indiana UP, 1969).

6 See Dario Zanelli's 'From the Planet Rome,' in *Fellini's Satyricon* (New York: Ballantine Books, 1970) 3–20.

7 See Barbara K. Lewalski, 'Federico Fellini's *Purgatorio*,' in *Federico Fellini: Essays in Criticism*, ed. Peter Bondanella. 113–21.

8 Walter C. Foreman, 'The Poor Player Struts Again: Fellini's "Toby Dammit" and the Death of the Actor,' in *1977 Film Studies Annual. Part 1. Explorations in National Cinemas*, ed. Ben Lawton (Pleasantville: Redgrave, 1977) 111–23.

9 It must be noted that while the film's European release by Cocinor obviously does not contain the AIP imprint and has more art house allure, its relationship to the AIP Poe cycle is still very manifest.

10 Last Men, *Ordeal of Cochran* (ZE Records, 1979).

11 References to *Shane* as a means of illuminating *Teorema* are a commonplace. Raymond Durgnat goes a step farther in discussing Pasolini's film as an 'erotic western' that has roots in *Duel in the Sun*. Durgnat shows greater prescience in associating Teorema with the Italian western, with Pasolini's Stranger an erotic 'Man from Nowhere.' See his *Sexual Alienation in the Cinema: The Dynamic of Sexual Freedom* (London: Studio Vista, 1972) 21–2. It is not incidental that Terence Stamp played the Stranger of Pasolini's film; his role is the inverse of Toby's, and his Italian Journey is involved in a western so degenrefied that its critical respectability is guaranteed. Nevertheless this film *depends* on the western, in the sense that its weightier meanings only become legitimate and comprehensible when filtered through the recognizable and tired conventions of the western. Stamp's situation indeed seems close to Toby's.

12 Examples are plentiful in late-1960s European cinema. Among the most ironic and bizarre is Clint Eastwood's appearance in *The Witches* (1967), an Italian art-house anthology film produced by Dino de Laurentiis, who wanted chiefly to find a vehicle for his wife Silvana Mangano. The film features stories by Pasolini, Visconti, and De Sica. In De Sica's segment, 'A

Night Like Any Other,' Eastwood (who had just finished *The Good, the Bad, and the Ugly,* played a dullard suburban husband incapable of fulfilling his wife's fantasies.

13 Foreman 120

14 Burke, 'Fellini's Film' 148.

15 Both Foreman and Burke ('Fellini's Film') have noted that Stamp was made up by Fellini to resemble Poe.

16 The approach had more than a little impact, even as it was dismissed, on criticism of the AIP/Corman-Poe cycle. See David Pirie, 'Roger Corman's Descent into Maelstrom,' in *Roger Corman: The Millennic Vision,* ed. David Will and Paul Willemen (Edinburgh: Edinburgh Film Festival, 1970). The *locus classicus* is of course Marie Bonaparte, *The Life and Works of Edgar Allan Poe: A Psychoanalytic Interpretation* (London: The Hogarth Press, 1971).

17 A point noted by both Foreman and Burke.

18 See Jameson's 'Postmodernism, or, The Cultural Logic of Late Capitalism,' *New Left Review* 6 (July–August 1984): 53–92.

19 Burke, 'Fellini's Film' 153.

20 Perhaps the most insightful approach to some of the assumptions of Turner's frontier thesis is Brooks Adams, *The Law of Civilization and Decay* (1924; rpt. New York: Knopf, 1959). Adams' synthesis of science, philosophy, and historiography ultimately points to entropy as fundamental to the expenditure of energy underneath the civilizing process.

7

Fellini's *Amarcord*: Variations on the Libidinal Limbo of Adolescence

DOROTHÉE BONNIGAL

It is impertinent to call my films autobiographical. I have invented my own life. I have invented it specifically for the screen ... I lived to discover and create a film director: no more. And I can remember nothing else.

– Fellini, *Fellini on Fellini* 164

Revealing the bond that ties Fellini's lifetime *of* films to his lifetime *in* film, Fellini's own caveat constitutes a paradoxical point of departure when considering *Amarcord* (1973), a film whose premise – as the very title implies (*Amarcord* means 'I remember') – is an act of narrative recollection predicating the substantiality of a recollected object and the existence of a recollecting 'I.' Under such circumstances we could, as Frank Burke does, argue that *Amarcord* is 'a film which emphasizes the mere mechanisms of representation by asserting "I remember" but providing no "I" who remembers – thus defeating reference' ('From Representation to Signification' 36). On this basis, we could read the film in strictly metacinematic terms, namely as a film on the cinematic act and processes of remembrance themselves (Burke's 'mere mechanisms of representation').

The 'actual' or 'tangible' existence of the recollecting 'I' (i.e., Federico Fellini as 'real' person or referent) is problematized by *Amarcord* – and for that matter, by all of Fellini's films – yet we could contend that a remembering 'I' dwells at the heart of Fellini's cinematic and retrospective project. An 'I' whose existence is constituted by the act of representation itself, it relocates Fellini's 'remembrance of things past' within a space charted by Fellini's reinvention of himself through cinema. A cinematic construct that refers to nothing but the process of cinematic

(self-)creation from which it arises, it points to an aesthetic and ontological project that informs Fellini's lifetime filmography.

This project, which is based on a strong assertion of the power of
film, originates in the complexity of Fellini's position in relation to
postmodernity. Indeed, it is in light of and in response to 'the postmodern condition' that Fellini's aesthetic counter-project finds meaning. In
espousing the poststructuralist upheaval of subjective congruity and
referential continuity, the director displays a keen understanding of
the constructedness of the notions of subjectivity and referentiality.
In this sense, Fellini's filmography constitutes a precious and subtle
contribution to 'the poststructuralist project' – to what Spivak, quoting
Derrida, describes as 'the deconstitution of the founding concepts of the
Western historical narrative' (31). Therein lies its visionary compatibility with poststructuralist readings and approaches.[1] Yet Fellini's participation in the poststructuralist project is inseparable from the
simultaneous elaboration of a counter-project characterized by a form
of aesthetic resistance to the restrictive consequences of postmodernity's ontological quandary. Foregrounding the constitutive fictionality
of the artistically created subject, Fellini not only implements poststructuralist conclusions but also enunciates the terms of a newly
found form of authenticity. This new form of authenticity is based on
establishing a crucial link between aesthetic mediation and ontological
substantiality, a link that paradoxically limits ontological authenticity
to the aesthetic sphere. Reinstating the role of the creative imagination
in ontological construction, Fellini carries out and at the same time
goes beyond the poststructuralist project.

In this regard, Frank Burke is right to point out Guido's apparent 'loss
of author-ity and subject-hood' at the end of 8½ ('Changing the Subject'
280–3). But the decentring and splitting of Fellini's alter ego reflects
more than a purely deconstructive impulse and a rejection of individuation. Guido's dissolution and fusion with the body of subjects that surrounds him also marks the constitution of a multilayered subject. In the
aesthetic space charted by the film, a 'substantial subject' arises; at once
indivisible and multiple, self-determined and limitless, it subsumes and
constitutes the creative subject who – inscribed as the origin and the
end, as a part and the whole – encounters the liberation and omnipotence he sought all along. Needless to specify, the 'omnipotence' of this
aesthetically constructed 'subject' is strictly limited to the cinematic
sphere and never claims to exceed the boundaries of the space charted
by Fellini's reinvention of himself through film.[2]

In this sense, Amarcord's overthrow of reference must be regarded as primarily twofold and as informed by a double-subversion of referentiality:

- a *deconstructive* subversion that explodes and undermines the unity and stability of the conventionally unified and stable 'I,'[3] and in doing so disclaims traditionally sanctioned referentiality; *and*
- a *reconstructive* subversion that elaborates a surrogate system of representation – a self-determined referentiality that defeats reference by substituting an idiosyncratically sanctioned referential system for the discarded one.

The cinematic entity embedded in and arising from this idiosyncratically sanctioned referential system could be defined as Fellini's 'hyperself' or, given the link posited earlier between self and film, Fellini's 'hyperfilm.'[4] In her essay on *Ginger and Fred*, Millicent Marcus describes 'hyperfilm' as 'the unitary, on-going creative project that links the artist's biography to his cinematic corpus at a relatively high level of abstraction, where the author's *life in filmmaking* comes to coincide with the *film of his life.*' Given the commensurability of self- and film-making in Fellini's case, I consider the notions of 'hyperself' and 'hyperfilm' somewhat interchangeable, or at least deeply interrelated. 'Hyperself' points to an ontological approach, 'hyperfilm' to an aesthetic or metacinematic one.

In this context, when we view adolescence and maturation as central motifs in Fellini's *Amarcord*, we uncover a complex cinematic dialogue between 'real' life and 'cinematic' life, between history and fiction, and between self and hyperself – a dialogue that conflates personal recollection and political memorandum within metacinematic reflection. Three areas of exploration structure Fellini's lyrical evocation of the passageway to adulthood and map out a web of associations in which the personal, the national, and the cinematic are seamlessly woven. The notion of adolescence unifies the film's triple-focus and establishes an informing parallel among three distinct yet interwoven histories:

- the adolescent years of a *personal* history;
- the Fascist years of a *national* history; *and*
- the juvenile and pubescent stage of an *aesthetic* history.

Consequently, *Amarcord* can equally and simultaneously be characterized as:

- a cinematic reconstruction and recreation (in short, a 'cinematization') of Fellini's adolescent years;
- a powerful representation of fascist Italy – or what we could call, in keeping with Fellini's witty and devastating association, Italy's political puberty; *and*
- a metacinematic reflection on what the director sees as the 'adolescence' of his artistic itinerary – an evocation of the pubescent years of Fellini's 'hyperfilm,' as an analysis of the film's intertextuality reveals.

In this regard, the various levelling devices operating in the film must be read as clear invitations to parallel and interweave the three realms of investigation (personal, political, and aesthetic) that inform Fellini's celebration of a momentous season of life: a time when flowers bud and hormones surge, a time of change and awakening, but also an age of stupidity and ignorance that subjects the world to the supremacy of its sexualized and mystified gaze. The episodes in *Amarcord* are marked by an editing economy that tightens the film's associative structure[5] and drives the narrative at a frantic pace. The curtness of the juxtapositions highlights devastating associations between adolescence and fascism – think, for instance, of the loaded juxtaposition between the notorious masturbation scene and the fascist rally. The result aptly conveys the agitation, fever, and erratic enthusiasm of adolescence. The deft and trim editing, as well as several unifying signifiers (the fog, the smoke,[6] the motorcycle, the music) that mesh the various dimensions of the narrative, contribute to the 'purified smoothness of *Amarcord*,' as Aldo Tassone nicely puts it (284). They establish the sense of homogeneity and self-sufficiency, but also self-enclosure, that characterizes the world of *Amarcord*.

Amarcord's 'purified smoothness' also stems from a structural association between two apparently contradictory impulses. The film's narrative linearity is repeatedly fractured by circular patterns and images that do not, however, threaten the congruity of the whole. *Amarcord* is constructed as a moving spiral that interweaves circular and linear orders,[7] leading the spectator (and the characters) to the end of a season of life – a season that coincides with the end of a retrospective and introspective journey. This structural alliance is signalled in the film's opening sequence, which meshes the linear events of a personal history with a communal celebration of nature's permanent cycle of death and regeneration. The film opens on the circular space delineated by the town's cyclical celebration of the end of winter. The town's inhabitants are gathered on the *piazza* (a circular space that constitutes the town's main square and meeting place) *around* a ritual bonfire (a visually circular configuration). Yet, the individuation of the protagonist, Titta, establishes narrative linearity in very subtle terms: Titta's desire to join the celebration (i.e., the circular and cyclical order) is hampered by paternal authority (an episode that fractures the circular order). As the script specifies: '[Titta], a strapping lad of about fifteen, is carrying a chair with a broken leg high above his head. Just as he is about to *step through the circle* of spectators standing *round* the bonfire, a hand seizes him by one ear' (Fellini and Guerra 10; emphasis mine).

The seasonal framing of the narrative – the film opens and closes on the return of springtime – also marks the fusion of the linear and the circular by allowing the narrative to come full circle at the end. This structural duality signals both progression and paralysis, and allows Fellini to represent adolescence as a seasonal and transitory stage within a larger whole (personal, political, and cinematic), but also, in itself, as a vicious circle of ignorance and confusion that must be thrown open to ensure individual, national and artistic maturation.[8]

All crucially formative stages in the making of the adult self and the evolution of the male subject, the climactic events related in the narrative point to the necessity of growth and change. From the death of the protagonist's mother, in which the confrontation with death and the resolution of the Oedipal complex happen simultaneously, to the final celebration of a marriage, which marks the entrance into the domestic sphere (i.e., the legitimization of sexuality and the accession to social maturity), the film's culminating events coincide with a terminal departure from the space of the small town, a decisive rupture with the *borgo*.[9] This suggests a close correspondence between the end of adolescence and the necessity to break through the enclosure of the small town – a parallel Fellini had already made explicit in *I vitelloni* (1953), which depicts the departure of Moraldo at the film's conclusion, and *Fellini's Roma* (1972), which depicts the arrival of Moraldo/ Fellini in the city. This association between coming of age and migration underlines the transitoriness of adolescence, and endows Fellini's depiction of his adolescent years with the sense of progression already established by the film's structure.

But as the duality of the film's structure implies, this sense of progression is inseparable from a simultaneous sense of paralysis. Fellini's representation equally stresses the enclosure inherent in adolescence. Hence the consistent supremacy of the adolescent system of values throughout the narrative, as the representation of the key adult figures in the film reveals. The ascendancy of authority figures (parents, teachers, and priests) is the repeated object of caricature and debunking, thanks to typical adolescent 'weapons' (flatulence, excrement, and obscenities). This reflects a natural stage in the dynamics of identity formation. Female figures presiding over sexual awakening are inscribed in the film as mere objects of desire. It is significant, in this regard, that the buttocks of Gradisca, Volpina, the tobacconist, the country women, and the town statue should all be equated as interchangeable fetishes for the pubescent heroes.[10] Notable in this context is the absence of an adult outlook presiding over the act of retrospection. The film exuberantly and consistently subjects the world to a pubescent lens, wallowing in the grotesque and in caricature; it simultaneously reflects and relies on the process of sexualization and mystification that characterizes the adolescent gaze.

Peopled and controlled by a bunch of eternal adolescents – from Pataca, coming right out of *I vitelloni*, to crazy Uncle Teo, whose 'voglio una donnaaaaa!' ('I want a woman!') ironically makes him one of the most imperious spokesmen in the film[11] – *Amarcord* luxuriates in a sort of 'arrested development during the phase of adolescence' (Fellini, '*Amarcord*' 20), in which the incursions of the 'adult' world are systematically chastised.[12] Any attempts to escape the film's authoritative/authoritarian points of view usually result in joyously scatological retaliations meant to mortify the 'grown-up' intruder and doom his/her influence to silence and resignation. This is what the town chronicler (referred to as the *avvocato*, i.e., the 'lawyer') comes to understand. Originally a spokesman of the adult world 'continually thwarted by an unseen heckler' (Hay, 'Godfather Fascism' 166), the *avvocato* becomes another agent of mystification as he narrates some of the town's favourite collective fantasies. From Gradisca's legendary 'baptism' to Biscein's one-thousand-and-one concubines (twenty-eight, actually), the *avvocato*'s narration is led to adjust to the film's dominant perspective. In this sense, *Amarcord* can be read as an infinite embedding of adolescent fantasies: it not only recalls adolescent desires but also adopts an adolescent perspective in its representation of them, so that the memories and the act of remembering become indistinguishable, fused in the libidinal limbo that pervades the film.

The supremacy of this mediated and mystified vision allows Fellini to establish a parallel between the film's authoritative perspective and the authoritarian political context.[13] For Fellini, fascism is Italy's *âge bête*,[14] the country's political puberty: 'I consider Fascism as a kind of degeneration to a historical level comparable to the stage of an individual – that of adolescence – which corrupts itself and can proliferate monstrously, without succeeding to evolve and to become adult. Also Fascism and adolescence are certainly representations of our most concealed complexes, expressions of a confused and repressed psychic state which is, therefore, stupidly aggressive' (in Stubbs 40).

This analogy leads Fellini to one of the most compelling representations of Italy's *anni del consenso* ('age of consent'),[15] without locking him into the dry limitations of a political agenda. As Fellini points out, 'Fascism and adolescence continue to be, in a certain measure, permanent historical seasons of our lives: adolescence of our individual lives, Fascism of our national lives' ('Fellini's *Amarcord*' 21). Focusing on 'the emotional, psychological manner of being a Fascist' instead of 'the economic and social causes of Fascism' (20), Fellini surveys and represents Italy's fascist experience from an indigenous perspective, exploring its tangible effects on a small town's collective life. As the director acknowledges, in *Amarcord*, 'Fascism is not viewed, as in most political films that are made today, from ... a judgmental perspective. That is, from the outside. Detached judgments, aseptic diagnoses, complete and definite formulae always seem to me ... a bit inhuman' (20).

This is what the representation of fascist repression best reveals. Turned into a comic story of excrement and humiliation (somewhat reminiscent of an earlier scene of humiliation inflicted by Titta and his cronies on one of their classmates trying to solve a math equation), Fellini's representation of the 'castor oil treatment'[16] captures and caricatures the paternalistic condescension of the fascist leaders, who refer to the subversive faction as a bunch of dissolute teenagers unaware of the 'benefits' of the regime's authority. 'But why? Why? Why don't *they* understand?' dramatically exclaims one of the decadent and deathly-looking fascists during Aurelio's 'purge.' In keeping with the carnivalizing disposition of the adolescent gaze, however, the violence and abuse of fascist repression are dedramatized (the Fascists look like mummified villains of comedy), as Titta's concluding reading of the whole sequence confirms: 'Christ, Dad, what a stink!' (Fellini and Guerra 51). Flatulence, castor oil, excrement: adolescent weapons at the service of an adolescent world. The circumscription of the narrative structure within the vicious (and often hilarious) snare of an adolescent perspective not only connects the personal and political spheres, but equates them in a devastating look at fascist Italy.

In this sense, *Amarcord* elucidates Fellini's relation to politics and ideology throughout his artistic career; it also reopens the debate over Fellini's political engagement as a filmmaker in the aftermath of neo-realism. While *Amarcord* explicitly addresses the political reality of Fascism and 1930s Italy, the modalities of this reconstruction reassert the necessity to escape the judgmental and the militant. A parched and abstract didacticism is seen as another form of paralyzing totalitarianism by the artist. Not limited to the strictly political or ideological markers of fascist dictatorship, *Amarcord* admits other related emblems that, as Hay suggests, 'all loosely interweave to form what can be described as the town's fabric of consensus' ('Godfather Fascism' 167). The political and the historical are thus redefined as intricate webs of cultural, metaphysical, personal, and collective realities. Fascism, the Grand Hotel, the Rex, Hollywood, America, and car races are equally posited as interchangeable elements of one unified reality – a reality that constitutes Fellini's object of inquiry and fantasy.

The desire to *touch* is a recurrent motif in *Amarcord*. We can think of the boys' relentless urge to touch the objects of their desire – an impulse that is usually resolved by their touching themselves! Or Gradisca's desire, during the fascist parade, to 'touch' the fascist *federale*, just as she dreams of becoming one with the 'larger than life' image of Gary Cooper on screen (Hay, Godfather Fascism' 176), while Titta's hand is venturing under her skirt. It is as if the entire *borgo* had arrested its development at the tactile stage. The reiteration of this motif conveys the enclosure and isolation of the world of *Amarcord*, the *borgo*'s entrapment within a vision that leaves the 'real' world and the 'real' self untouchable, as unattainable as the phony glamour of the cardboard ocean liner or the deserted Grand Hotel.

Interestingly, this quest for contact and tangibility in a mist of mystifying mediations is itself inscribed in an introspective and retrospective journey – that is, in Fellini's attempt to touch base with his past through the mediation of the cinematic apparatus. Paradoxically, it is through the foregrounding of the cinematic mediation – through the insistence on the constructedness of the cinematic replication of the past – that Fellini's representation ensures its authenticity. For Fellini, an authentic vision of reality necessarily implies the recognition of an introspective mediation and a full awareness of the mystifications that fundamentally suffuse human perception. As a result, an authentic version of reality refracted through the cinematic medium includes foregrounding the artificiality of cinema's reconstruction of reality. As Fellini recalls: 'In *Amarcord*, I built the sea. And nothing is truer than that sea on the screen. It is the sea I wanted, which the real sea would never have given me' (Fellini, '*Fellini on Fellini*' 165).

At a (meta)cinematic level, *Amarcord* thus establishes the basic fact that a vision which does not avow its constructedness and artificiality is potentially deceiving and manipulative. This admission that the sense of immediacy and truth produced by cinema is fundamentally illusory resonates critically with the political regime it represents as a perpetrator of mystification and as a manipulative system exploiting man's 'most concealed complexes' and 'repressed psychic state.' But it also inscribes Fellini's resistance to the glamorous mystifications of the Hollywood machine[17] by way of an implicit analogy between fascist totalitarianism and Hollywood's supremacy as a cinematic model. Hollywood and fascism are recurrently linked in the libidinal limbo of the film, just as they are consistently parodied and caricatured. As exemplified by the cartoonish ocean liner 'from America' erupting from a plastic sea, the motifs of fascist and Hollywood mythology are equally reappropriated and mimicked, turned into objects of mockery, so as to denounce the oppression of political authoritarianism and suspend the hegemony of Hollywood's artistic totalitarianism. Carnivalized and demystified, fascism's and Hollywood's symbols of inaccessible glamour and idealized selfhood are turned into comic clones, openly counterfeit and phony.[18]

It is interesting to note, in this context, how the fascist censors privileged Hollywood productions during the 1920s and 1930s and how fascist ideology naturally identified with Hollywood 'kitsch.'[19] As Angela Dalle Vacche suggests, in *The Body in the Mirror*, 'Kitsch refers to menial objects raised to the realm of the aesthetic, while high art is lowered through serial reproduction.' Significantly, both Hollywood and fascist 'kitsch' are the results of an attempt to 'project an image of cultural prestige on a national level that bridged the gap between high and popular arts.' 'Kitsch repeated the logic of the spectacles staged by the regime [fascist in Dalle Vacche's argument but, I would argue, capitalist as well] to cover up poverty and abuse, repression and violence. With its aura of prestige, kitsch worked like a therapeutic [or rather compensatory, I would argue] device' for two nations 'haunted by a demoralized self-image' (24), in the aftermath of the First World War in the Italian context, and in the midst of the Great Depression in the American context.

Because it simultaneously carnivalizes fascist and Hollywood kitsch, we can read *Amarcord* as a joyous carnivalization of Hollywood orthodoxy, marking a return to an authentically popular form of entertainment, denouncing and deflating the deceitfulness of a pompous luxury synonymous with bourgeois values. Its chief impulse is to spoof kitsch and glamour through a sassy reappropriation of the classical motifs and genres of Hollywood mythology. But Fellini's film also fully participates in Italian cinema's attempt to exorcise its fascist past in the aftermath of May 1968, as Dalle Vacche insightfully argues. This participation discloses the film's historical and political dimension. Italian cinema in the 1970s was characterized by an obsessive concern with the country's fascist experience. As Dalle Vacche suggests, 'this was a time when the sons interrogated the fathers' (52).[20]

In this sense, and in keeping with the triple-focus of the film, *Amarcord* mirrors the resolution of three embedded Oedipal crises:

- In the personal sphere, the death of Titta's mother at the end of the film furthers the protagonist's progression toward adulthood. 'You're a man, now,' are the last words of Titta's mother to her son.[21]
- In the political sphere, the carnivalization of Father Fascism discredits the dictatorial regime.
- In the aesthetic sphere, the demystification of Father Hollywood compromises the authority of the dominant cinematic model.

While discarding the cinematic and political traditions that affected Fellini's adolescence, this triple resolution resonates critically with Fellini's filmography, introducing, by way of an inscription of the director's two earliest films, *The White Sheik* (1952)[22] and *I vitelloni* (1953), a reflection on the filmmaker's own artistic itinerary and development. The film's intertextuality reflects the modalities of a cinematic retrospection which consists in providing a technically mature sequel to Fellini's earlier treatments of *Amarcord*'s informing themes. The technical mastery that the film displays in its approach to revisited subject matter marks the sole presence of a 'mature' perspective in the film.[23] This metacinematic mode is inseparable from the director's consistent subversion of ideological and cinematic orthodoxies, and denotes a self-critical and self-reflexive tendency – a tendency that, as *8½* epitomizes, signals a rejection of an institutionalized artistic identity and practice and a fear of enclosure within a self-determined orthodoxy.

Amarcord's exploration of the same libidinal stage of development that characterized *I vitelloni*, and its re-examination of the dangers of a mystified and sexualized perspective that constituted the central theme of *The White Sheik*, demonstrate the technical and stylistic progression that Fellini achieved over twenty years of filmmaking. In so doing, *Amarcord* fulfils the wish that Fellini formulated in an interview with Giovanni Grazzini: 'Often in later years while preparing complex and difficult productions like *Satyricon, Roma, Casanova*, I have thought with nostalgia of *The White Sheik*. I would like to make it again, with the *experience* and *detachment* of now and the intention of playing with the story and characters more casually' (Fellini, *Comments* 83, emphasis mine).

While the presence of *The White Sheik* in *Amarcord* can be sensed quite pervasively at a diegetic level, through the film's focus on the distortions that a mystified vision imposes on reality, one sequence is especially reminiscent, both thematically and technically, of Fellini's first film as solo director. Set in the oneiric glamour of the Grand Hotel, this scene relates the adventure which, in the town's collective imagination, gave Gradisca her name. The scene's focal point is Gradisca herself, and the narrative point of view is mainly hers, though the camera does not fail to show us Gradisca in a more 'objective' light, so as to suggest the gap between the character's mystified and mystifying perception and the 'reality' of the situation. This discrepancy is the main source of comic effect in the sequence. The hero of Gradisca's (and the town's) fairy tale is, as it should be, a charming Prince (charming only in Gradisca's eyes, for he has the decadent and deathly appearance of all Fellini's aristocratic characters). Dressed in white, he is an unattainable and surreal apparition in a fantasylike setting of luxury, in which, because of his stony immobility, he looks like another prop of the phony decor. His unreality is confirmed by Gradisca's unsuccessful attempts to get his attention, until, naked in his bed, she finally utters the legendary 'gradisca' (i.e., 'help yourself') as an invitation to enjoy her offered body.

What is especially interesting in this scene – which reminds us of Wanda's first encounter in *The White Sheik* with the film's eponym on his aerial swing – is Fellini's adoption of a device from his 'early days,' namely, an inscription of the photographic snapshot that breaks and freezes the continuity of the cinematic image. Fellini relies here on the same editing technique he used in *The White Sheik's* photo-shoot scene. A succession of still shots are juxtaposed, mirroring the content of the photo-romance in the making. The representation of Gradisca's efforts to seduce relies on a similar dismantling of the cinematic image, in a disjointed series of still images that follow the stages of Gradisca's striptease. Yet in *Amarcord*, Fellini does not rely solely on the editing to arrest the image on the screen. As if they were posing for the camera, the characters themselves strike the pose, introducing a sense of artificial stasis within the moving image. This is what the first image perceived by Gradisca as she enters the Prince's hotel room establishes. Before the apparition of the 'white Prince' we see two *valets de chambre*, both petrified, as it were, by Gradisca's gaze, one of them caught with a leg up in the air – a witty touch that, for the viewer, instantly demystifies the glamour of the scene.

This carnivalized version of Medusa's gaze has more serious aesthetic implications: it literally suggests the petrifying effect of a skewed vision. Significantly, in Fellini's films the representatives of an oppressive or totalitarian order are always characterized by their mummified and embalmed appearances, so as to convey the desiccated fixity and deathly stasis they impose on the individual and the artist – a fixity of meaning and of image that entraps and paralyses. The institutionalized and the authoritarian are always conflated with stasis, death, and entrapment, and as such are systematically rejected. This association of the still shot and stonelike paralysis is established earlier, thanks to the juxtaposition of the class photograph sequence and the physics course, in which, significantly, the topic is 'stones'! Inscribed in each of his films, literally and/or symbolically, this rejection of the embalmed image always marks Fellini's artistic claustrophobia, his fear of a return to Zampanò's circus of mechanical performance from which only death arises.[24]

In this regard, *Amarcord*'s re-exploration of the liminal world of *I vitelloni* and the film's reassertion of the necessity to mature beyond this eternal adolescent stage also exorcise Fellini's fear of creative stagnation. The *vitellone* figure, stuck in the limbo of his ignorance, laziness, and confusion, represents what Fellini could have become without his art and what Fellini's art could have become without its constitutive self-criticism. By looking at the world once again from an adolescent perspective, but with the technical mastery of a mature *auteur*, Fellini is celebrating his own cinematic coming of age, so as to exorcise the lethal threat of enclosure within an aesthetic, ideological, and personal system. Self-critical in this sense, *Amarcord* ultimately expresses Fellini's simultaneous desire for renewal and his rejection of those vicious circles that confound vision and obliterate the artist.[25]

Notes

1 For a poststructuralist reflection on Fellini's work, see Burke, 'Changing the Subject.'

2 On this subject, see my essay, '*Il Casanova di Federico Fellini*: Exorcising the Loss of the Baroque Circle.'

3 As Burke notices, 'instead of a unified subject, we have a jumble of narrators, from the verbally inept Giudizio unable to articulate anything, to the voluble "*avvocato*" who articulates nothing with great eloquence and abundant factual detail' ('From Representation to Signification' 36).

4 I am inspired here by Gérard Genette's terminology. See *Palimpsestes*, in which Genette defines the notion of *hypertextuality* as 'any relation linking a text B (that I will call the *hypertext*) to a preceding text A (that I will, of course, call the hypotext) on to which it stitches itself in a way that differs from mere commentary' (13, translation mine).

5 Aldo Tassone contrasts the economy that presides over the montage in *Amarcord*, with that of *Roma*, in which, he argues, 'Fellini seems to have been preoccupied with the linking of episodes.' He continues: 'One has the impression that the director, having become aware of the fragmentary aspect of *Roma*, tried to remedy the problem by inserting an artificial transition between the tableaux of this many-sided work of art, which is annoying because it is not necessary ... In *Amarcord*, on the contrary, the director has edited the film without restraint in creating a spectacle of unusual proportion' (284). Though Tassone's speculations on Fellini's discomfort with the fragmented form in *Roma* are denied by Fellini's consistent taste for the episodic form and the obliteration of narrative links, his reading of *Amarcord*'s editing points to the homogeneity that characterizes the world of *Amarcord*, both literally as a self-sufficient and self-enclosed world (that of the *borgo*) and artistically within Fellini's creative imagination (*Amarcord* depicts the familiar, the origins, a naturally integrated constituent of Fellini's self). This unity – physical, ideological, psychological, and artistic – is reflected by the structural coherence of the whole (town, era, film); hence the understandable economy presiding over the editing process.

6 The smoke and the fog both signify isolation and confusion. As Millicent Marcus points out, the smoke 'implies the obfuscations of Fascist thought, engulfing an entire population in its cloud of confused and chaotic mis-

belief' ('Fellini's *Amarcord*' 420). And as Bondanella suggests, the fog is an equally 'eloquent concrete metaphor for the obscurantism of the period' (*The Cinema of Federico Fellini* 270). On this point, see also Parshall 26.

7 In this regard, it is interesting to point out the three occurrences of the motorcycle – one of the film's unifying signifiers – during the narrative. The first time, it circles around the piazza, inscribing a circular motion; the second time, it passes back and forth on the pier, inscribing a linear motion; the third time, it drives through the maze of snow erected on the piazza. The figure of the labyrinth symbolizes the complex combination of circularity and linearity that structures the film and out of which one must emerge to mature and escape the liminal and libidinal limbo of adolescence.

8 In this regard, it is interesting to point out that Fellini considered calling his film *Il borgo* 'in the sense of a medieval enclosure, a lack of information, a lack of contact with the unheard of, the new.' However, he continues, 'scribbling little sketches for the title, this word came to me – *Amarcord*; but you have to forget its origin. For, in its mystery, it means only the feeling that characterizes the whole film: a funereal feeling, one of isolation, dream, torpor, and of ignorance' (Fellini, '*Amarcord*' 25).

9 Titta's mother departs from the small town in death, and Gradisca in matrimony, as she follows 'her Gary Cooper' to Battipaglia, a town in the south.

10 This is what the masturbation scene establishes, as the participants enumerate the various objects of their fantasies.

11 On this point, see Parshall 23. I am also thinking here about Fellini's wonderful sketch of crazy Uncle Teo, 'Lo zio matto,' perched on a tree and screaming '*Voglio una donnaaaaa!*' Reproduced in Bondanella, *The Cinema of Federico Fellini* 278.

12 This reading of *Amarcord* is supported by other elements of the narrative, including the fact that, as Bondanella points out, 'Fellini has chosen the village idiot to open the film' (*The Cinema of Federico Fellini* 279) and keeps him as a regular mediator and focalizer throughout the film, together with the mythomaniac Biscein, crazy Uncle Teo, and other clownish eccentrics already introduced at the beginning of *I clowns*. These characters are significantly the most 'natural' and 'normal' inhabitants of the world of *Amarcord* (see in particular Uncle Teo's sequence and Tassone's reading of it as 'a moment of ecstatic identification with nature' [282–3]). On this point see also Burke, 'From Representation to Signification' 36.

13 This particular aspect of the film has already been the object of several comprehensive critical discussions. Consequently, I do not emphasize it in this present essay. On this subject, see in particular Fellini, 'Fellini dit *Amarcord*'

and '*Amarcord*'; Bondanella, *The Cinema of Federico Fellini*; Hay, 'Godfather Fascism'; Keyser; Pashall; and Renzi.

14 *L'âge bête* can be translated as 'the age of stupidity' or the 'wild teens,' but the French expression is more appropriate in this context, because it specifically refers to the adolescent years of emotional and intellectual puberty, when hormones seem to take over and distort the individual's vision and behaviour.

15 I am relying on Renzo De Felice's term and interpretation of fascism in Italy. To De Felice, Italy's 'age of consent' covers the years 1929 to 1936: 'The consensus of these years is a consensus for a certain Italian situation; in part an economic one, in part a social peace ... The country was thinking more about the evils that Fascism had avoided than whether it brought true benefits. The consensus was based on that which Italy did *not* have, on the disadvantages that had been avoided, on the security of life that, for better and for worse, Fascism had guaranteed to Italians' (64–5).

16 The 'castor oil treatment' depicted in the scene was a common practice by which the fascist 'fathers' literally purged their dissident 'children' of their rebellious impulses.

17 Fellini's rejection of the supremacy of the 'classical' form, as it is expounded by the Hollywood model of narrative linearity and 'straightforwardness,' and his opposition to classical narrative cinema's obliteration of 'all traces of the enunciation' (Metz 91), inform his entire film career. In this sense, Fellini's cinema can be regarded as a cinema of resistance, a counter-discourse to cinematic hegemony. For a discussion of classical cinema's tendency to 'masquerade as story,' see Metz.

18 Besides the ocean liner, we can think of the Grand Hotel, another keystone of the Hollywood mythology. Also significant is the literal presence of the movie screen on which a larger-than-life Gary Cooper is projected (in *Beau Geste*, a film released in Italy only after the war, as Kezich points out [428–9]). Bondanella's suggestion that 'such a conscious anachronism plays up the metacinematic intentions of the entire sequence' is very convincing (*The Cinema of Federico Fellini* 274).

19 For an analysis of fascist kitsch, see Angela Dalle Vacche, *The Body in the Mirror* 18–56. It is fascinating to notice that the tropes of modernity, technology, and progress – which ironically connote and enunciate, in the Hollywood system, the standards of American democracy – are paradoxically turned into props of the fascist master narrative; while in the American context they are the favoured props of the capitalist master narrative. Could those motifs be regarded as universal agents of mystification and

manipulation in the Western world? Or, rather, do they expose the complicity of capitalism and fascism?

20 See, among others, Bernardo Bertolucci's *1900* (1976) and *The Conformist* (1970), Lina Wertmuller's *Love and Anarchy* (1973), and Ettore Scola's *A Special Day* (1977) and *We All Loved Each Other So Much* (1974). Related as well are Luchino Visconti's *The Damned* (1969) and Lilliana Cavani's *The Night Porter* (1974), which deal with German Nazism. See also Hay, *Popular Culture*, esp. xv–xvii.

21 The death of Titta's mother coincides with the protagonist's emergence from the maze of confusion and ignorance of his adolescent years. Significantly, the motif of the maze, which recurs throughout Fellini's filmography (literally in *Satyricon* and *Casanova*, and metaphorically in *8½*, *Juliet of the Spirits*, and *Roma*) is present in *Amarcord* as a maze created by shovelled paths on the piazza in the aftermath of a snowstorm, where Titta loses track of Gradisca. This image is also associated with Titta's loss of his mother.

22 *Variety Lights* (1950), often considered Fellini's first film, was co-directed with Alberto Lattuada.

23 From a technical point of view, the relationship among *Amarcord*, *I vitelloni*, and *The White Sheik* is most clearly revealed through editing.

24 *Fellini's Casanova* is perhaps the most powerful and cathartic expression of the filmmaker's abhorrence of automatism and fixity. Entrapped within an institutionalized and mythical identity, Casanova is doomed to a perennial sense of absence, claustrophobia, and failure, and spellbound in the mechanical sterility of a simulated world where authenticity and creativity have become merely impossible desires. See my '*Il Casanova di Federico Fellini*: Exorcising the Loss of the Baroque Circle.'

25 For an opposed reading of *Amarcord* as a demagogic enterprise meant to please and cajole the Italian public, see Codelli.

References

Bondanella, Peter. *The Cinema of Federico Fellini*. Princeton: Princeton UP, 1992.
– ed. *Federico Fellini: Essays in Criticism*. New York: Oxford UP, 1978.
– *Italian Cinema: From Neorealism to the Present*. New expanded edition. New York: Continuum, 1994.
Bondanela, Peter, and Cristina Degli-Esposti, eds. *Perspectives on Federico Fellini*. New York: G.K. Hall, 1993.
Bonnigal, Dorothée M. '*Il Casanova di Federico Fellini*: Exorcising the Loss of the Baroque Circle.' *Il Veltro* 1–2 (1996).

Burke, Frank. 'Federico Fellini: From Representation to Signification.' *Romance Languages Annual 1989*. Vol. 1. Ed. Ben Lawton et al. West Lafayette: Purdue Research Foundation, 1990. 34–40.

– 'Fellini: Changing the Subject.' *Film Quarterly* 43.1 (Fall 1989): 36–48. *Perspectives on Federico Fellini*. Ed. Peter Bondanella and Cristina Degli-Esposti. 275–92.

Codelli, Lorenzo. '*Amarcord*: Nuit et Gel.' *Federico Fellini*. Ed. Michel Ciment Paris: Editions Rivages, 1988. 91–3.

Dalle Vacche, Angela. *The Body in the Mirror: Shapes of History in Italian Cinema*. Princeton: Princeton UP, 1992.

De Felice, Renzo. *Fascism: An Informal Introduction to Its Theory and Practice* New Brunswick: Transaction Books, 1976.

Fellini, Federico. '*Amarcord*: The Fascism within Us – an Interview with Valerio Riva.' *Federico Fellini: Essays in Criticism*. Ed. Peter Bondanella. 20–6.

– *Comments on Film*. Ed. Giovanni Grazzini. Trans. Joseph Henry. Fresno: California State UP, 1988.

– 'Fellini dit *Amarcord*.' *Cinéma* (Québec) 4.1 (1974): 43–4.

– *Fellini on Fellini*. Ed. Anna Keel and Christian Strich. Trans. Isabel Quigley. New York: Delacourte/Seymour Lawrence, 1976.

Fellini, Federico, and Tonino Guerra. *Amarcord: Portrait of a Town*. Trans. Nina Rootes London: Abelard-Schuman, 1974.

Genette, Gérard. *Palimpsestes: La littérature au second degré*. Paris: Editions du Seuil, 1982.

Hay, James. 'Godfather Fascism and *Amarcord*.' *Perspectives on Federico Fellini*. Ed. Peter Bondanella and Cristina Degli-Esposti. 166–79.

– *Popular Culture in Fascist Italy: The Passing of the Rex*. Bloomington: Indiana UP, 1987.

Keyser, Lester J. 'Three Faces of Evil: Fascism in Recent Movies.' *Journal of Popular Film* 4.1 (1975): 21–31.

Kezich, Tullio. *Fellini*. Milan: Biblioteca Universale Rizzoli, 1988.

Marcus, Millicent. 'Fellini's *Amarcord*: Film as Memory.' *Quarterly Review of Film Studies* 2 (1977): 418–25.

– 'Fellini's *Ginger and Fred*, or Postmodern Simulation Meets Hollywood Romance.' See pp. 169–187 in this book.

Metz, Christian. *The Imaginary Signifier: Psychoanalysis and the Cinema*. Trans Celia Britton, Annwyl Williams, Ben Brewster, and Alfred Guzzetti Bloomington: Indiana UP, 1982.

Parshall, Peter F. 'Fellini's Thematic Structuring: Patterns of Fascism in *Amarcord*.' *Film Criticism* 7.2 (1983): 19–30.

Renzi, Renzo. *Il Fascismo involontario e altri scritti*. Bologna: Cappelli, 1975.

Spivak, Gayatri Chakravorty. *The Postcolonial Critic: Interviews, Strategies, Dialogues*. New York: Routledge, 1990.

Stubbs, John C., ed. *Federico Fellini: A Guide to References and Resources*. Boston: G.K. Hall, 1978.

Tassone, Aldo. 'From Romagna to Rome: The Voyage of a Visionary Chronicler (*Roma* and *Amarcord*).' *Federico Fellini: Essays in Criticism*. Ed. Peter Bondanella. 261–88.

8

Memory, Dialect, Politics: Linguistic Strategies in Fellini's *Amarcord*

COSETTA GAUDENZI

One day I would like to make a film about Romagnolo farmers: a western without shootings, entitled *Osciadlamadona*. A blasphemy, but its sound is nicer than *Rasciomon*.

– Fellini, *Fare un film* 14[1]

Fellini made special use of verbal signs throughout his filmmaking career, and it is somewhat surprising that scholars have paid so little attention to the linguistic structure of his works. Over the years, Fellini moved away from a neorealist approach to spoken sounds as social descriptors,[2] toward a more elaborate use of language as symbol. Fellini fused the realistic, the symbolic, and the fantastic in his later films, and employed language as both tool and object of representation. In this essay I explore the linguistic strategies of *Amarcord* (1973), Fellini's film about his hometown of Rimini. I also discuss the implications for film and beyond film – for example, issues of postcoloniality – suggested by the use of dialect in *Amarcord*. Fellini uses language to recount and reinvent his own memory, and as a tool for asserting his subtly political discourse against levelling systems of culture such as fascism and capitalist Hollywood.

Amarcord opens with a dialect proverb uttered by an old man, Aurelio's father: '*S'al manin a li è arrivé, da l'invern a se scapé*' ('If puffballs have arrived, we have escaped winter'). The camera then moves to the town idiot, ironically named Giudizio ('man of wisdom'), who describes in Italian, with a strong dialectal accent, the dizzying flight of puffballs throughout Rimini. This combining of dialect and Italian at the very beginning of the film hints that informal language will play an important role. This role, as I will show, is significant to the general design of *Amarcord*, in that Romagnolo is one of the means the director employs to escape from the aesthetic of orthodox neorealism. Although the use of informal language in the film recalls previous neorealist and comic endeavours in Italian cinema, I will point out that Romagnolo is employed in *Amarcord* to lead the audience away from older, neorealist representations of reality toward a new vision of the world expressed with Fellini's own grammar.

The opening of *Amarcord* also shows that Fellini will not rely exclusively on dialect, unlike some neorealist directors (for instance, Luchino Visconti in *La terra trema* (1948), or at times Roberto Rossellini, who even eschewed professional actors in favour of local nonprofessionals). Like Pier Paolo Pasolini in *Decameron* (1970), Fellini in *Amarcord* prefers to employ a mixture of dialect and Italian; this choice enables him to better reflect the complex social stratification of reality, and helps him render his work more accessible.

Throughout *Amarcord*, Fellini is constantly preoccupied with the linguistic intelligibility of his film. When his characters utter dialect expressions, he often resorts to what might be termed 'oral footnotes.' Just as a translator might explain the meaning of particular culturebound terms in footnotes printed at the bottom of the text, so does Fellini disambiguate Romagnolo words and expressions in his film by preceding or following them with more or less orthodox Italian versions. In *Amarcord* this cinematic device is used mainly to introduce the speeches of the grandfather. After the grandfather asks in Italian, '*Buona, eh?*' he reiterates in Romagnolo, '*L'è bona, vera?*' ('It is good, isn't it?'). On another occasion, when the grandfather speaks of his own grandfather, he says in dialect, '*E bà dé mi bà*' and then translates into Italian, '*Il babbo del mio babbo*' ('The father of my father').

This cinematic technique is effective both linguistically and politically. While helping the spectator comprehend the film immediately, it also mimetically reproduces a behaviour that we find in Fellini's Romagna even today: attempts by older people like Aurelio's father to comply with the linguistic practices of a 'new age.' The grandfather, accustomed to speaking only dialect, seems to feel compelled to give an Italian version of his words, not only for the benefit of the younger generations, but also, at a more general level, in order to adhere to a contemporary ethos that models Italian as the most appropriate linguistic means of communication. (This prejudice was especially evident in the fascists' attempts to centralize power through cultural unification.)[3] From this perspective, the grandfather's words acquire appropriate status only when uttered in Italian.

Before investigating Fellini's adoption of local expressions and inflection in *Amarcord*, I turn to the homonymous poem 'A' M'Arcord,' written by Tonino Guerra in 1973, the year that Fellini's film on Rimini was produced. Guerra, a dialect poet and screenwriter, was born in Santarcangelo di Romagna – a fact that undoubtedly enhanced his collaboration with Fellini, who also was Romagnolo by birth.[4] When Guerra was asked to identify his contribution to the screenplay of *Amarcord*, he claimed that he did not remember how much was his and how much was Fellini's: 'I swear that I do not really know if in *Amarcord* there is more of mine or of his. I swear, I do not remember what is mine in it' (Faldino and Fofi 251). Guerra's poem 'A M'Arcord' not only bears the same title as Fellini's film on Rimini (though spelled differently), but also shares the same emphasis on youthful recollections:

A M'ARCORD	I REMEMBER
Al so, al so, al so,	I know, I know, I know,
Che un om a zinquent'ann	That when a man is fifty
L'ha sempra al meni puloidi	His hands are always clean.
E me a li lev do, trè volti e dè.	I wash mine several times a day.
Ma l'è sultent s'a m vaid al meni sporchi	But when I see my hands are dirty
Che me a m'arcord	It's [only] then that I remember
Ad quand ch'a s'era burdell.	My carefree boyhood days.

(Fellini and Guerra, *Amarcord, Portrait of a Town* 5)[5]

   The poet needs some special sign. Only when his hands are dirty can he remember his youth, the time when he was a *burdell* (dialect for 'boy'). Just as in Marcel Proust's *A la recherche du temps perdu* the little *madeleine* cake, when dipped in tea and tasted by the narrator, calls up a whole train of reminiscences about Combray, so does the sight of dirty hands evoke in Tonino Guerra his boyhood. Dirty hands, improper and imperfect, may also symbolize the inappropriate and indecorous behaviour of children and adolescents, which the poet counterpoises with the propriety of mature adults, who always have clean hands.

In *Amarcord* the director portrays the childhood and adolescent recollections mentioned by the poet. Guerra needs improper and imperfect dirty hands to recall his childhood memories; Fellini seems to
require the expressions and inflection of Romagnolo to mediate the
narration of his recollections. The Saussurian strain of poststructuralist
thought, the so-called language paradigm, emphasizes the idea that
human perception, cognition, and behaviour are structured and in part
determined by language.[6] The writer Italo Svevo, who like Pasolini
and Fellini made some use of dialect in his works, attributes the following linguistic reflection to Zeno, the protagonist of one of his most
successful novels: 'We prefer to recount all those things for which we
have the phrase ready and ... we avoid those that would compel us to
refer to the dictionary. In the exact same way, we choose the events of
our lives worth recounting. It becomes clear that our lives would
appear differently if told in our dialect' (445).

Not only is Romagnolo the idiom spoken in the particular geographical area that Fellini depicts in *Amarcord* (and thus mimetically reproduces reality),[7] but it is also the language in which he experienced his
youth. Feelings of love and hate are preferably expressed by individuals in their mother tongue, this being the language through which they
have learned to demonstrate such emotions since their infancy.[8] In cinematic situations that reproduce these intense feelings, Fellini often
employs dialect expressions. For instance, the grandfather tenderly
says in Romagnolo *'E mi fiol'* ('My son'), when he meets his son Teo
outside the madhouse. Aurelio, angered at the possibility that one of
his family members might have betrayed him to the fascists, screams,
'Me a mi magn la testa, a mi magn i cuaió' ('I'll break his head, I'll break
his balls').[9]

Fellini's decision to use some dialect in recreating a dear memory
has not only emotional but practical overtones. If the director were to
depict the Romagnolo society strictly in Italian, he would have had to
leave out some of its peculiarities. Regarding Italian versions of his
dialect poetry, Guerra maintained that 'a translation from Romagnolo
into Italian often cancels certain fundamental features of the original'
(West 171). Indeed, some Romagnolo terms cannot be rendered
directly into Italian because no correspondence exists. Fellini often
leaves such culture-bound expressions untranslated.

1. *La fogarazza* (a big bonfire on St Joseph's day, 19 March) is a festival
   dedicated in Romagna to the coming of spring, during which a

witch is burned in effigy. This festival has no precise equivalent in standard Italian culture, so Fellini maintains its dialect term.

2. *Pataca* is a term used in Romagna to describe, roughly, an arrogant boaster. There is no corresponding Italian term.[10] When Lallo tries to distinguish himself from the other Riminesi by adopting unusual behaviour, Aurelio tells Miranda, '*Certo che tuo fratello è proprio un pataca*' ('It is clear that your brother is a real asshole'). Likewise, the adolescent Titta says, '*Son rimasto come un pataca*' ('I felt like an ass-hole') when describing his speechless and hesitant behaviour in the cinema Fulgor toward the mature woman La Gradisca, with whom he is infatuated.

3. *Calzinaz* means 'mortar' in Romagnolo, and in *Amarcord* is the nickname of a mason. To change this appellation into its Italian equivalent, '*Calcinaccio*' would be to erase the relation between the actual person and his social identity. Calzinaz is a poor worker whose dialect name represents his social standing. For this reason, Fellini does not translate Calzinaz into Italian. Likewise with the characters. *Scureza* ('Fart'), the obnoxious man who rides the loud motorcycle, and *Carnaza* ('Big Meat'), the virile centenarian described by Aurelio's lubricious father.

In one scene in *Amarcord*, Fellini highlights the pitfalls of translating from Romagnolo into Italian, when he affirms indirectly that translations may jeopardize the content and sound of a source text. Once each month in the summer, Titta's family goes in a carriage to fetch Aurelio's crazy brother, Teo, who is kept at a mental institution. On the particular occasion recounted in *Amarcord*, Teo is taken out for a short trip to Aurelio's *podere* ('farm house'). At a temporary stop, the grandfather accompanies Teo into a field, and while they are relieving themselves, he utters a proverb: '*Per campé sen bsogna pisé spes come i chen*' ('To live healthy you need to piss as often as a dog does'). He then reiterates it in an Italianesque form: '*Per campare sano bisogna pisciare spesso come il cano.*' The rhyme '*sen ... chen*' of Romagnolo is reproduced in Italian as '*sano ... cano.*' Here the second term has obviously been distorted: instead of the correct Italian noun 'cane,' we hear 'cano,' a hybrid form that underscores the impossibility of finding a completely equivalent translation of the Romagnole proverb into Italian.

This episode suggests the limitations of translation; at a more obvious level it also humorously points to the Italian 'illiteracy' of the grandfather. This scene between the grandfather and his mad son also calls to mind the linguistic practices of the period (practices that to some extent are still alive in Romagna, as well as in other places where class distinctions correspond to linguistic-cultural divisions). Because the Romagnolo dialect has long been regarded as the language of poor and illiterate people, Romagnoli have often urged their children to speak only Italian, in order to elevate their own social status.[11] This custom has given birth to an awkward, hybrid idiom through which uneducated people try to reproduce Italian. One way of constructing such an idiom has been to add Italian suffixes to dialect words. For example, the Romagnolo past participle *imbrané* ('loser') has been transformed into *imbranato* – a word that does not actually exist in Italian but that tries to respect its grammatical rules.

In *Amarcord* Fellini records many similar hybrid expressions, most notably in Calzinaz's poem 'I Matoni':

I MATONI	BRICKS
Mio nono fava i matoni,	My grandfather made bricks,
mio babo fava i matoni.	My father made bricks,
Fazo i matoni anche me.	I make bricks too.
Ma la casa mia, dov'è?	But where is my house?

Calzinaz, the poet, seems to be reaching for a literary Italian that is beyond his powers. Half the words of 'I Matoni' are 'mispronounced': the double-consonants of the proper Italian words *mattoni* and *babbo* are missing (Calzinaz says '*matoni*' and '*babo*'), and the correct Italian form faceva is reduced by Calzinaz to '*fava*.' Because of these linguistic twists, 'I Matoni' sounds awkward to the ear of an Italian audience and adds a comic touch to *Amarcord*. At a deeper level the poem bestows a socio-political message, since it informs us that Calzinaz realizes that he and his family have been exploited for generations. 'I Matoni' compresses history and ideology and in Bakhtin's terms is richly heteroglossic. Bakhtin considers carnivalesque all the manifestations of a popular and democratic counterculture that oppose the formal and hierarchical official culture. The heteroglossia of *Amarcord* – a combination of Italian with dialect and dialectal inflections – is highly carnivalesque.[12] This mixture is not only humorous but also politically subversive. Fellini often makes sociopolitical observations in a light-hearted way. He rejects Zavattinian neorealist orthodoxy to some extent, believing that to make good films, ideology is not enough: 'Good intentions and honest feelings, and a passionate belief in one's own ideals, may make excellent politics or influential social work (things which may be much more useful than the cinema), but they do not necessarily and indisputably make good films' (Fellini, *Fellini on Fellini* 151).

In *Amacord*, Fellini employs not only the words but also the sounds of Romagnolo. As the epigraph of this essay informs us, the director was fascinated by the sound of his native dialect: the sound of *Osciadlamadona* was for him more pleasing than that of *Rasciomon*.

The dialect spoken in Romagna is a Gallo-Italian tongue that shares many linguistic features with French: for example, apocope (the cutting off) of final vowels (e.g., *ven!* instead of the Italian *vieni!*), and of endings of the past participle (*magné* like the French *mangé*, unlike the Italian *mangiato*; and *durmi* like the French *dormi*, unlike the Italian *dormito*). Another typical feature of Romagnolo involves the 's' sound. Romagnoli pronounce 's,' especially when doubled, as an unvoiced prepalatal fricative 's' For instance, they pronouce the words *sasso* ('stone') and *assassino* ('murderer') with a sound similar to that of the double 's' in the English word 'mission.'

In *Amarcord*, words such as *sasso* or *assassino* are repeated several times for the purpose of introducing a sort of amusing self-irony. Italians who want to characterize and also gently make fun of the way Tuscans speak, utter the initial consonant 'c' as a velar fricative 'h' in the phrase *'una coca cola con la cannuccia corta'* ('a coke with a short straw'); so too, do Romagnoli (and other Italians in referring to Romagnoli) use words like *sasso* and *assassino* when describing and mildly deriding the way Romagnoli speak. In the school sequence of *Amarcord*, when the physics teacher asks his students to identify an extremely rudimentary pendulum, one of the students replies, *'Mo è un sasso'* 'Well, it's a stone' (emphasis mine). Besides providing a diverting soundplay, the student's reply in strong dialect ridicules the 'proper Italian' taught at school. A similar situation arises later, in the *emarpsamen* scene, when Ovo makes fun of *'la bella lingua greca'* ('the beautiful Greek language') by deliberately mispronouncing the 's' sound of *emarpsamen* and turning it into a 'razzberry' or 'Bronx cheer.'

Fellini uses dialect expressions or inflections to underscore the absurdity of some situations in *Amarcord*, but this does not mean that he is deriding Romagnoli and their idiom. Rather, I agree with Peter Bondanella's statement that Fellini is representing the characters of *Amarcord* 'in the usual nonjudgmental manner typical of [his] portraits of Italian life' (284). On the one hand, soundplays and wordplays are naturally meaningful in a work that focuses on the ridiculous aspects

of reality and on those aspects which most impress children and adolescents. (To represent these situations, Fellini draws on the comical
tradition of Italian theatre and cinema, which uses dialect for entertainment, e.g., the cinema of Totò.) On the other hand, as I discuss in the
next section, the mockery inscribed in soundplays and wordplays is a
carnivalesque expression that aims at undermining the rules of society.
In *Amarcord*, soundplays and wordplays are making a political statement directed primarily against two Italian institutions: fascism and
schooling.

The first scenes of *Amarcord* reveal that the film is set in the 1930s, during Mussolini's reign. In the school classrooms, religious symbols such
as the crucifix and the image of the Pope are placed between secular
pictures of the Duce and the king. *Amarcord* thus seems to be following
the trend of the 1960s and 1970s, when Italian film directors such as
Bernardo Bertolucci and Marco Bellocchio harshly condemned fascism. But in contrast to those 'political' filmmakers, Fellini approaches
the subject indirectly. First of all, *Amacord*'s story is refracted through
the eyes of an adolescent, Titta; the result is a disingenuously naïve
narration of events. (This cinematic device, as Fellini himself pointed
out, is also a means of depicting fascists as adolescents – that is, as irre-
sponsible and immature ['Amacord' 20–1].) Second, instead of focusing on the physical violence perpetrated by fascism, Fellini looks for
concealed signs of its destructive influence. To carry out this project, he
employs not only special visual cinematic devices, as Bondanella has
pointed out (284), but also linguistics.[13]
    The school sequence provides a starting point for our investigation
of Fellini's use of language in relation to fascism. This sequence has
eleven scenes and shows us teachers who speak with a dialect inflection that is mostly not local (principally southern). In one of the scenes,
Titta purposely causes the history professor's cigarette ashes to fall; the
teacher then shouts at Titta in Neapolitan, '*Tu mi fa ascì paz! tu mi fa ascì
paz*' ('You are driving me crazy! You are driving me crazy!'). Given that
the school has so many non-local teachers and that they are generally
portrayed unsympathetically, we have reason to think that Fellini is
intentionally depicting the purveyors of culture as outsiders – a quality
that links (as I will later explain) schoolteachers to fascists.[14] The bond
between fascism and education is also evident in the elements of political indoctrination in the teachers' lectures and in the teachers' active
participation in the fascist parade of 21 April.

The arrival of the fascist *federale* on 21 April – the traditional anniversary of the founding of Rome and a holiday celebrated by Mussolini's regime – provides another significant instance of Fellini's cinematic use of language. Obscured by a great puff of smoke – a visual expedient perhaps used to point out the obscurantism of the period – the *federale*'s pompous entrance is warmly received by the Riminesi, who cry with joy when they recognize their leader among the crowd. The *federale* speaks perfect Italian, uttered with a distinctive French-like 'r' – a rhetorical device that underscores his haughty affectation and aristocratic descent, and thus his natural right to lead: '*Camerati ... il saluto di Roma imperiale che ci addita la via del destino dell'Italia fascista*' ('Comrades ... the salute of imperial Rome which points out for us the path of destiny of Fascist Italy'; emphasis mine).

The fascists who accompany the *federale* use dialectal inflections that are not local. There are a Tuscan and a Neopolitan among the soldiers who accuse Aurelio and others of playing the Socialist hymn atop the Campanile.[15] When Aurelio enters the courtroom, a soldier speaks to the previous defendant in a Tuscan tone and dialect: '*Sei libero, puoi andare a casa. Hai visto, eh? I Fascisti tanto cattivi! Un ti s'è fatto nulla! Un ti s'è torto neanche un capello!*' ('You are free, you can go back home. You see? Fascists are so bad! We didn't do anything to you! *We didn't even touch a hair on your head!*'; dialect emphasized). The soldier who encourages Aurelio to toast the victory of fascism with castor oil speaks with a Neapolitan inflection and dialect: '*Devi brindare alla vittoria dei fascisti, amico mio*' ('You must make a toast to the victory of the fascists, my friend'). Later, when Aurelio shows his reluctance to drink, the soldier continues: '*È questo che c'addolora, quest'ostinazione a non voler capire.* Ma pecché? Ma pecché: ('It's this which makes us sad, this refusal to understand. *But why? Why?*'; dialect emphasized).

The fascist *federale* is told that 99 per cent of the Riminesi have enrolled in the party, yet no Riminese takes any serious political action in the film. As Bondanella has observed: 'Fellini avoids dividing Riminesi into "good heroes" (the anti-fascists) and "bad villains" (the Fascists)' (267). Instead, Fellini represents the 'bad villains' as outsiders, as intruders into the world of *Amarcord*. The rough and cold violence of the sequence in which non-local fascists compel Aurelio to drink castor oil is eloquent testimony to this.

When Fellini portrays violence as something brought to Rimini by pretentious fascists who speak either a different dialect or an impeccable Italian, he is taking the same radical position as we often encounter among postcolonial writers. Fellini certainly remembered that Musso-lini regularly broadcast his speeches on radio to Italian *piazze* ('town squares'), and that he was known by Italians as *la voce* ('the voice'). He was thus aware that the fascists used language to oppress and alienate the Italian people. In *Amarcord* he attempts to represent that oppression by manipulating the film's linguistic structure. At the same time, though, in *Amarcord* he wanted to show that sound and language can also be instruments of liberation. It is not by chance that the resistance to fascism in *Amarcord* is symbolized by the sound of the socialist hymn played by the gramophone from the bell tower overlooking the town square. Furthermore, the dialect expressions and inflections adopted in the film represent a challenge to the conventionality and formality advocated by fascism. Borrowing from the terminology of Gilles Deleuze and Felix Guattari, the function of Romagnolo in *Amar-cord* becomes that of a minor literature refusing to submit to an exter-nal entity that would dictate the choices, tastes, and life of its people.[16]

Fellini's resistance to the cultural unification sought by the fascist regime becomes more explicit in the sequence in which La Gradisca meets with the Principe at Rimini's Grand Hotel and thereby earns her nickname. Here, Fellini describes the fascist politics of language in the words of one of the Amarcordians. While being driven to the Grand Hotel by a friend, La Gradisca is advised, half in dialect and half in Italian: 'Ninola fas fé 'na bela figura, a m'aracmand. *O, il Principe è bel-lissimo, sai. Sut ved che rimane contento, diglielo dei lavori sul lungomare. Lui con una parola mette a posto tutto, sai. Sii educata, parla italiano. È un principe, sai, non è mica un pataca qualunque*' ('*Ninola, please, do it for us, be sure to make a good impression.* Listen, the Prince is a very handsome man, you know. If you see that he is happy afterwards, tell him about the works on the water-front. With a word he can put everything in order, you know. Behave properly, speak in Italian. He is a Prince, you know, not any old *asshole*'; dialect emphasized).

La Gradisca, who comes from a lower class, is being told she must change register if she wants to impress a prince: she must behave prop-erly and speak in Italian. Pasquale Verdicchio has pointed out that a dominant culture often resorts to excuses such as 'public decency' whenever it intends to negate the presence of alternative cultures (370). The words of Ninola's friend are clearly the product of an ethic influ-enced by fascism, which in order to pursue a totalitarian design, dis-misses dialect as a product of ignorance and poverty.

In the scene that follows, in a Hollywood-like setting – a luxurious room filled with romantic music – La Gradisca is the only character whose words we hear. (The Prince's conversation with one of his attendants is completely covered by the music.) She utters only three words: '*Signor Principe ... gradisca*' 'Your Highness ... help your*s*elf'; emphasis mine). La Gradisca pronounces the words very slowly, so as to create a romantic atmosphere, but she speaks them with some dialect inflection (with the Romagnolo 's') so that they sound antiphrastic to the ears of the Italian audience. Furthermore, *gradire* ('to help oneself'), an Italian verb used mainly for food, becomes comically ambiguous when employed in a sexual context such as this. As a result, we cannot avoid laughing at the character's failed attempt to hide her provincial mannerisms. Yet Fellini is not being harsh toward her; again, his intentions are subtle and are directed toward institutions rather than individuals. During the romantic meeting with the Prince, the dialect inflection of La Gradisca's words not only shows how farcical people can become when rejecting their real selves, but also parodies similar scenes in romantic Hollywood films, which in Italy were dubbed in impeccable formal language.

La Gradisca provides an interesting focal point for concluding this study and for highlighting the links in Fellini's filmmaking between the linguistic, the visual, and the narrative. The 'gradisca' episode links up with the scene between Titta and La Gradisca at the cinema Fulgor and with her marriage at film's end. These scenes reveal how Fellini uses visual and narrative techniques to stress the same point: when La Gradisca's dreams and aspirations disappear, room is left for the ironically unsuitable word 'gradisca,' which she utters to the Prince, to the immature admirer Titta in the cinema Fulgor, and to the ordinary *carabiniere* ('officer') who becomes her husband in the film's finale.

Most important, La Gradisca embodies the dreams of greatness and success inspired by fascist Rome and capitalist Hollywood, both massive exporters of ideologies that tended to level society to an illusory optimism.[17] Fellini emphasizes La Gradisca's attraction to fascism in the scene in which the fascist federale arrives, when she nearly faints with apparent sexual excitement. She cries: '*Fatemelo toccare! Io lo voglio toccare! Viva il Duce!*' ('Please, let me touch him! I want to touch him! Long live the Duce!'). Her love for American films is most evident in the cinema Fulgor, when she cannot take her fascinated eyes off Gary Cooper. (Her attraction to American films is so strong that at her wedding, which is also the film's final episode, her friends say, '*La Gradisca ha trovato il suo Gary Cooper*': 'La Gradisca has finally found her Gary

Cooper.')[18] Her dream of a 'Prince Charming' has not been fully realized, and the director, who gently mocks her pretensions throughout
the film, is evidently employing her character to criticize the doctrines
of capitalist Hollywood as well as those of Fascist Rome. To systems
that would level society to the same ethical, political, and cultural values, Fellini counterposes the world of *Amarcord*, a self-contained space
where marginalized classes and cultures become the protagonists of a
beautiful memory.

Notes

1 *Osciadlamadona* is Romagnolo for 'Host of the Virgin Mary.' *Rasciomon*
  (Roshomon) is a film by Akira Kurosawa (1951). All translations of Italian
  into English are my own, unless otherwise stated.
2 For example, in *Lo sceicco bianco* (*The White Sheik*, 1952), ragioniere (accoun-
  tant) Ivan speaks an impeccable and elaborate Italian, while the film troupe
  members communicate in the more natural Romanesco, and the recep-
  tionist at the hotel where Ivan and Wanda are staying speaks with a
  Napoletano inflection.
3 Italian, the medium-level *koine* (common language) born of national unification, was the language of the *piccola borghesia* (lower middle-class) and
  thus the product of the conservative bureaucracy that laid the foundations
  for fascism.
4 'Con Tonino Guerra ho scritto *Amarcord* e *E la nave va*. Ci lega lo stesso
  dialetto, un'infanzia passata tra quelle stesse colline, la neve, il mare, la
  montagna di San Marino' ('I wrote *Amarcord* and *E la nave va* with Tonino
  Guerra. We are linked by the same dialect, a childhood spent among the
  same hills, the snow, the sea, the Mountain of San Marino'). See Fellini,
  Intervista sul cinema 150.
5 Rootes's translation of line 5 of 'A m'arcord' seems to ignore the word
  'sultent' ('only'). I have therefore added it to the text.
6 See Culler.
7 *Amarcord* seems to be Fellini's most autobiographical work, since nearly all
  the major characters in the film are discussed in his essay *La mia Rimini*. The
  director, however, felt that 'authorizing a viewing of the film with an autobiographical "key" would have been a grave error' (Fellini, *Amarcord* 24).
8 See Steiner 121.
9 *Magn* equals 'to eat.' I have translated it as 'to break' to better fit the English
  idiom.

10 *Pataca* is also a slang term used in Romagna to refer to the female sexual organ.

11 Behind such prejudice was the fascist attempt to centralize power through cultural unification, but also, as Chiesa and Tesio have pointed out, the fact that dialect is generally considered a low and unliterary language because it is prevalently oral: '*Si apprende dal colloquio e non da grammatiche e da modelli scolastici*' (7).

12 My study draws on Stam's *Subversive Pleasures*. Stam (115) finds echoes of the carnivalesque in *Fellini-Satyricon* (1969), *Ginger and Fred* (1985), and 8½ (1963).

13 Bondanella calls *Amarcord* 'one of Fellini's most complex visual representations of a political theme' (284).

14 The fact that most teachers represented in the film are not Romagnoli may also be explained historically. For years, public competitions in the field of education have resulted in the redistribution of Italy's teaching resources. Since there have been more positions available in the North, which is economically richer than the south, many southern teachers have moved to the north.

15 One soldier who accuses Aurelio speaks with a Bolognese inflection, an accent that could be misinterpreted for Romagnolo.

16 See Deleuze, and Deleuze and Guattari.

17 Many Italian scholars and statesmen of the 1930s underlined the link between fascist politics and the ideology promoted by Hollywood. For instance, Luigi Freddi, the General Director of Cinematography in the Ministry of Popular Culture, claimed that American films were most compatible with the needs of the national market and with fascist ideology: 'The American film industry produces films that are youthful, serene, honest, optimistic, enjoyable, generally of a high moral value and most often of a noble meaning' (Hay 71).

18 Cooper, a Hollywood star who played in several Westerns, becomes the ideal love of La Gradisca in *Amarcord*, Fellini's 'western senza revolverate.'

References

Bondanella, Peter. *The Cinema of Federico Fellini*. Princeton: Princeton UP, 1992.

Chiesa, Mario, and Giovanni Tesio. *Le parole di legno: poesia in dialetto del '900 italiano*. Milano: Mondadori, 1984.

Culler, Jonathan. *On Deconstruction: Theory and Criticism after Structuralism* Ithaca: Cornell UP, 1982.

Deleuze, Gilles. *Kafka: Toward a Minor Literature*. Minneapolis: U of Minnesota P, 1986.

Deleuze, Gilles, and Felix Guattari. 'What Is a Minor Literature?' David H Richter. *Falling into Theory: Conflicting Views on Reading Literature*. Boston: Bedford, 1994.

Faldino, Franca, and Goffredo Fofi, eds. *Il cinema italiano d'oggi 1970–1984 raccontato dai suoi protagonisti*. Milano: Mondadori, 1984.

Fellini, Federico. '*Amarcord*: The Fascism within Us – An Interview with Valerio Riva.' *Federico Fellini: Essays in Criticism*. Ed. Peter Bondanella. New York: Oxford UP, 1978.

– *Fare un film*. Torino: Einaudi, 1980.

– *Fellini on Fellini*. Ed. Anna Keel and Christian Strich. Trans Isabel Quigley. London: Eyre Methuen, 1976.

– *Intervista sul Cinema*. Ed. Giovanni Grazzini. Bari: Laterza, 1983.

– *La mia Rimini*. Ed. Renzo Renzi. Bologna: Cappelli, 1987.

Fellini, Federico, and Tonino Guerra. *Amarcord: Portrait of a Town*. Trans. Nina Rootes. New York: Berkley Windhover Books, 1974.

Hay, James. *Popular Film Culture in Fascist Italy*. Bloomington: Indiana UP, 1987.

Stam, Robert. *Subversive Pleasures: Bakhtin, Cultural Criticism, and Film*. Baltimore: The Johns Hopkins UP, 1989.

Steiner, George. *After Babel*. New Edition. Oxford: Oxford UP, 1992.

Svevo, Italo. *La coscienza di Zeno*. Milano: Dall'Oglio Editore, 1981.

Verdicchio, Pasquale. 'Censoring the Body of Ideology: The Films of Pier Paolo Pasolini.' *Fiction International* 22 (1992): 369–78.

West, Rebecca. 'Tonino Guerra and the Space of the Screenwriter.' *Annali d'Italianistica* 6 (1988): 162–78.

9

Fellini's *Ginger and Fred*: Postmodern Simulation Meets Hollywood Romance

MILLICENT MARCUS

Ginger and Fred (1985) has been commonly read as two films in one: the bittersweet romance of a pair of aged vaudeville dancers brought together after a thirty-year separation to perform their imitation of Fred Astaire and Ginger Rogers on the special Christmas installment of the TV show 'Ed Ecco a Voi' and the satire of postmodern image culture typified by mind-numbing media spectacles and ubiquitous messages to consume.[1] Much of the film's critical reception has hinged on the perceived compatibility or imbalance between its two rival parts. Thus Cattielli faults *Ginger and Fred* for its 'disequilibrium,'[2] while Kezich argues that 'the pharaonic frame, that is, the mega-show in which the two protagonists participate, does not detract from the story and above all does not disturb the delicate half tones.'[3] Critical disagreement goes beyond the question of structural balance, however, to the very nature of the film's core dichotomy. For Cattielli and Grazzini,[4] the opposition is generic, involving the tension between satire and parody on the one hand and romance tinged with irony on the other. For Moravia, Bruno, and Kezich, the film is traversed by a nostalgia for a past perceived as authentic and irretrievable in the face of a brutal and mechanized present.[5] For Bondanella, Zanzotto, and Cielo, *Ginger and Fred* represents a struggle between competing types of spectacle, where such older and more 'innocent' forms as vaudeville and cinema, are pitted against the corrupt, all-devouring medium of contemporary TV.[6]

My focus, instead, will be less on what tears the film apart than on what brings it together – on the continuity that Fellini establishes between his representation of postmodern media culture and the story of the two elderly vaudevillians reunited for their final *pas de deux*. Such a correspondence can best be understood in the context of Fellini's 'hyperfilm' – the unitary, ongoing creative project that links the artist's biography to his cinematic corpus at a relatively high level of abstraction, where the author's *life in filmmaking* comes to coincide with the *film of his life*.[7] The term 'hyperfilm' is not meant to suggest the kind of horizontal movement between related writings made possible by the technology of *hypertext*, but rather to suggest the construction of an elevated or heightened film that hovers above Fellini's works like a Platonic ideal. This virtual film may be defined as a series of points where mytho-biography[8] and meta-cinema converge, where the progress of Fellini's fictionalized life story comes to signify the creative struggles of the filmmaker at any given stage in his aesthetic itinerary. The most transparent example, of course, is *8½* (1963) in which film and hyperfilm come to intersect in the almost total identification between Guido and his author, but other obvious examples would include *I vitelloni* (1953), where the story of Moraldo's attempts to outgrow a belated adolescence allows Fellini to reflect on his own efforts to liberate himself from the baggage of a cinematic and cultural past, or *La dolce vita* (1960), which dramatizes how Fellini's relocation to Rome occasioned a revolution in his aesthetic vision, or *Fellini's Casanova* (1976), whose aged and decrepit narrator enables the filmmaker to vent his own anxieties about the decline of a career dedicated to crowd-pleasing but transgressive spectacles. It is not my purpose here to trace the workings of the hyperfilm throughout Fellini's career, but rather to posit its existence and to demonstrate how it is central to an interpretation of *Ginger and Fred*, for it is in the hyperfilm that the satire of postmodern culture and the evolution of the love story will find their common ground.

One of Fellini's foremost strategies in constructing the hyperfilm is the recycling of motifs from his cinematic past to locate the current work in relation to an ongoing autobiographic/metacinematic process. *Ginger and Fred* abounds in such self-reflexive recalls, from the invasion of the motorcyclists at the discotheque Satellit, resembling the new barbarians who take over the city in *Fellini's Roma* (1972),[9] to the surrealistic beacon that presides over the night like the sci-fi tower of *8½*. The film incorporates an entire history of Fellinian allusions to the circus (*La strada* [1954], *I clowns* [1970], *Giulietta degli spiriti* [1965]) and the variety show (*Luci del varietà* [1950], *I vitelloni*, *Le notti di Cabiria* [1956], *Roma*) in the procession of midgets, eccentrics, superendowed women, and other grotesques who parade across the stage of 'Ed Ecco a Voi' while the world of photoromance (*Lo sciecco bianco*, 1952) is invoked in the description of Fred as 'overwhelming in his gypsy-cossack pot-pourri: acrobatic, languid, tender, and savage' (168). But most indicative of this impulse to conjure up a cinematic past is Fellini's choice of Giulietta Masina for the part of Amelia Bonetti (alias Ginger), Marcello Mastroianni for the part of Pippo Botticella (alias Fred), and Franco Fabrizi for the part of the TV host. When all three appear on the stage of 'Ed Ecco a Voi' they stand as a living filmography, a *tableau vivant* of the author's career.[10]

'This is the fourth film that Giulietta Masina and Marcello Mastroianni have made with me as protagonists, but never together,' explains Fellini. 'Two filaments of my cinema that thus come together in *Ginger and Fred*; they unite. They tell a single story' (45). This impulse to synthesize and coordinate hitherto separate strands of his cinematic past puts *Ginger and Fred* in a privileged relationship to the hyperfilm, where the collaboration between the two characters in the narrative enables Fellini at once to reflect on his own life with Giulietta Masina, and to unify the elements of his filmography. Mastroianni's credentials as the author's on-screen surrogate, established in *La dolce vita*, *8½*, and *La città delle donne* (1980), are clearly reaffirmed by his assumption of the stage name Fred, his wearing of the trademark Fellinian hat,[11] and his personification of 'the right to live irresponsibly ... to flee maturity, understood as renunciation, extinction, surrender'(45).[12] Masina herself has a double-referential valence in Fellini's filmography, signifying both the wife/other, 'fated projection of wounded innocence' (45), and autobiographical self-reflection as the feminine principle within his own psyche, the Jungian *anima* so cryptically inscribed in the Asa Nisi Masa episode of *8½*.[13]

Of the two elderly vaudevillians, Amelia is the privileged partner in a number of ways. It is her personal itinerary that formally bounds the narrative – her arrival at Stazione Termini sets the film in motion and her departure signals its closure. Amelia immediately becomes the film's focalizer, mediating our view of the TV world through her astonished, disappointed, or disbelieving eyes. Most importantly, her dual status as Fellinian self-projection and feminine *other* enables her to play out, on several levels, the author's own drama of creation in *Ginger and Fred*. Fellini's ambivalence toward TV is repeatedly enacted by Amelia, who admits to an irresistible fascination for the medium when asked by a journalist why she accepted the invitation to appear on 'Ed Ecco a Voi,' but who is scandalized by the tacky and unprofessional preparations for the show. 'It's disgusting, a madhouse, an equestrian circus,

midgets, transvestites,' she complains to her daughter on the telephone the night before the performance. It should come as no surprise
that the very terms Amelia uses to denounce the TV mega-show have
been applied repeatedly to Fellini's cinema itself, which has been variously described as the 'circo felliniano,' the 'Fellinian caravan of midgets, admirals, transvestites, impersonators, violinists, intellectuals,
imbeciles, angelic bandits,' the usual 'Fellini circus and freak show,'
and so on.[14] On another level, Amelia's resistance to appearing on TV
may be read as Giulietta Masina's often-stated resistance to appearing
in a Fellini film. 'At a certain point,' explains Fellini, 'Giulietta, as
always happens when she makes a film with me, begins to resist'
(110).[15] Despite the considerable tensions it generates on set, such resistance can be productive. 'I often accept Giulietta's objections,' Fellini
admits, 'because I must take heed that certain of her rebellions, certain
of her resistences, also serve to improve the character, to make it more
human, given that they come from the psychology of the actress who
interprets it' (111).[16]

At its most obvious, *Ginger and Fred* portrays the struggle between
the cinematic past and the televisual present as a battle between good
and bad, between innocence and decadence, between memory and
oblivion. Fellini plays out this duality in Amelia's hotel room as he jux-
taposes the TV monitor with the mirror on her closet door. Casting a
look of distinct disapproval at her reflection, Amelia proceeds to
smooth back her skin and to conjure up her old performing self – the
'Ginger' of her days with 'Fred.' With this gesture, Masina's face
becomes a living archaeology, a palimpsest of performances written
over earlier ones whose traces nonetheless show through to give her
presence on screen a thickness and a layered quality that reaches back
in time. The broad, clownesque visage, illuminated to make its surface
screenlike in such films as *La strada* and *Le notti di Cabiria*, becomes a
text for Fellini, a repository of filmographic memory.[17] What obliterates
the past of cinema, what erases the historicity of Masina's face, is the
series of images flitting across the TV monitor reflected in the mirror;
each impression cancels out its predecessor in a kind of moving vacuum, denying any cumulative meaning or progressive truth. To put it
in schematic terms, horizontal movement through the image chain pre-
cludes the vertical movement through memory – television montage
denies the palimpsest of film. To make explicit how TV denies the
workings of time, Fellini concludes Amelia's channel hopping with a
show on facial calisthenics, led by an elderly German gym teacher who

insists that 'old age exists no longer' as she screws her wrinkled features into a variety of senile deformations.[18]

Space as well as time is obliterated by Fellini's television, which pokes fun at its 'global village' pretensions by showing that the medium works less to open out local minds to worldwide information channels, than to reduce the world to the level of a provincial sideshow. The many *sosie* or impersonators who populate the cast of 'Ed Ecco a Voi' and who should ideally demonstrate the international and transhistorical dimensions of video culture, from Gandhi to Verdi to Queen Elizabeth to Pope Pius XII, really dramatize the shrinkage of perceptual horizons to the familiar confines of one's own backyard. Thus we have Ronald Reagan who hails from Grottaferrata, Clark Gable and Marcel Proust who speak impeccable Sicilian, and Woody Allen who complains of a room without a loo. TV culture works not only to provincialize, but to reduce all its personalities to the same cognitive level, so that everyone emerges as a prodigy or a star and evokes the same brand of prurient curiosity as that cultivated by *People Magazine*, *Gente*, and *Ripley's Believe It or Not*. Thus no analysis of the social determinants of crime is accorded to a kidnap victim whose importance resides solely in that he commanded the highest ransom in recent history. A parliamentarian's hunger strike to legislate an end to hunting and fishing is presented as a mere PR tactic. The Mafioso Don responsible for nefarious crimes is greeted as a star – 'in his own way, he's a *divo* too' – and obliges his fans by composing a song for the show. The transformation of all TV personalities into what I would call 'celebrity bites' brings with it an obvious moral levelling: the Mafioso Don = the war hero = the saintly friar, as they all take their place in the paratactic procession of personalities who will command absolute public attention for the two minutes of screen time allotted them. This makes Fellini's TV a quintessentially escapist medium dominated by sports, quiz shows, thrillers, music videos, and age-denying calisthenics, while serious social problems are either ignored or given the most perfunctory consideration.[19] The network pays lip service to the need for responsible reportage in the show 'On the Margins of the Metropolis,' which features two token paupers, but the broadcast itself is relegated to the margins of *Ginger and Fred*, and all we learn of it is the studio president's pious approval – '*È doveroso, è doveroso*' ('It's our duty') – when he is informed of the project by his lackeys. Fellini's television also collapses the hierarchy of culture by exploiting Dante to sell watches and by equating Proust, Kafka, and Verdi with the likes of Andrea Celentano, Marty Feldman, and Kojak.[20]

Of course, Fellini will save his most scathing critique for commercials and for their colossal power to disrupt:

> The arrogance, the aggression, the massacre of advertisements inserted in a film! It is violence done to a human creature: [the TV commercial] strikes it, wounds it, mugs it. A film, an artistic creation where everything is calculated to have that certain breathing pattern, rhythm, cadence, musicality, subjected to a brutal external intervention, hammered out, this strikes me as indeed criminal. (75)

In *Ginger and Fred* the violence done to programming by such intrusions is not only rhythmic but also thematic: the most infelicitous juxtapositions subvert, trivialize, and counteract the emotional power of TV drama. The gory image of Reginald's victim, shot in the head, precedes an ad for risotto, and the plea of the emaciated Parliamentarian on a hunger strike is followed by a commercial featuring giant rigatoni. Even more disturbing is the placement of a polenta ad, accompanied by the jingle, 'What more do you want from life?' after the interview with the ex-clergyman who gave up the priesthood for love.

On Fellini's part, this hyperbolic and grotesque vision of TV is historically as well as personally motivated. *Ginger and Fred* bears witness to a precise cultural circumstance – the radical change in Italian television that took place in the 1980s when the state monopoly on broadcasting gave way to the unbridled freedom of private channel offerings at the initiative of media magnate Silvio Berlusconi. More than any other country in Europe, Italy went on a kind of televisual binge – an orgy of indiscriminate consumption provided by a medium subject to no apparent regulation.[21] The policy of limiting advertisements to a few discrete intervals between programs (the celebrated 'Carosello' from 9 to 9:20 p.m. comes to mind) was replaced by one that gave free rein to commercial interruptions.

In *Ginger and Fred*, Fellini's parody aims beyond the mere surface proliferation of ads in the wake of Berlusconi's deregulation; it also targets the deep structural mechanisms by which these messages generate desire. In so doing, Fellini targets advertising strategies that use sex to sell their products, whether bath soap, mortadella, or flavoured panties. The eroticism of these commercials enables Fellini not only to exploit the phallic imagery of his products (mostly gastronomical, with a high density of delicatessen) but also to construct a paradigm of desire that depends entirely on mediation. The fact that the model of desire within the commercial – often a gorgeous woman salivating over a Lombardoni sausage – displays an attraction to the product entirely inappropriate to the object itself, suggests that advertising works on René Girard's principle of triangulation.[22] In Girardian terms, what we as subjects really want is to have or to become the model of desire, so that our attraction to the ostensible object is really an alibi, a deflected and displaced version of the transgressive wish (in the case of Fellini's ads) to identify with the sex bomb on screen or to possess her. The commercial's underlying message is that if we buy the Lombardoni product we will be magically transformed into the phallic object of the kind of sexual desire the model displays, or that we will become her and thereby arouse those desires in others. By the same Girardian logic, it follows that the apex of all desire is *to be on* TV – to perform as the model of desire, to stand as the paragon of perfection that advertisements promise us we will become once we accept their messages to consume. For Girard, the attainment of the object itself will be fraught with disappointment, failing as indeed it must, to transform us into the handsomer, stronger, richer creatures of the advertising slogans. Thus, the medium's power is based on creating a need that only it can satisfy – the consumer's hidden dream of 'modelling' on TV. In so doing, television keeps its viewers bound in a system of displaced consumerism; whose built-in dynamics of disappointment propel them to ever higher levels of spending and enslave them ever more thoroughly to mediation.

It is in this hermetically sealed system of televisual signification that Fellini's satire reaches metaphysical seriousness, where the notion of an external referent, lying outside the play of signifiers and guaranteeing the gold standard of semiotic currency, is replaced by the infinite specularity of signs reflecting other signs in 'a simulacrum never again exchanging for what is real' according to Baudrillard, 'but exchanging in itself, in an uninterrupted circuit without reference or circumference.'[23] There is nothing arbitrary about Fellini's decision to construct the set of the mega-show entirely of mirrors and to clothe the host in a mosaic of reflective surfaces. His doing so makes the space of spectacle – like architecture itself in Jameson's interpretation – partake of a 'privileged aesthetic language [in which] the distorting and fragmenting reflections of one enormous glass surface to the other can be taken as paradigmatic of the central role of process and reproduction in postmodernist culture.'[24] Fellini dramatizes the way that television feeds on itself by showing crowds of journalists hovering around the studio cafeteria in search of a scoop about the mega-show, as if this spectacle constituted a primary source of news, a referent on the order of a military event, a legislative occurrence, or a major crime. Indeed, on the level of narrative structure, Fellini exemplifies the self-containment of video spectacle by constricting his time frame to the twenty-four-hour period defined by the logistics of rehearsal and broadcast, and by limiting himself to the series of closed spaces – train station, van, hotel, bus, cafeteria, dressing room, broadcast studio, and train station – needed to usher the performers through the television process.

Fellini's impersonators offer further evidence of television's aspirations to recreate the world as self-enclosed simulacrum. When Amelia first encounters the two *sosia* of Lucio Dalla, exclaiming '*Siete identici!*' it is unclear whether she is marvelling at their resemblence to the real-life celebrity, or at their resemblance to each other in a mirroring relation that privileges the lateral contiguity of signs and ignores the referent entirely.[25] 'TV makes fun of itself,' Fellini comments:

> with these imitators who imitate characters from politics or entertainment, then with other imitators who imitate the imitators in a kind of play of mirrors, an infinite specularity that gives a sort of demented vertigo and distances ever more the authentic, the original. Everything is at second hand, everything is reflected, alludes, in this saga of approximation. (96)

In media culture even gender is simulated: the transvestite Evelina Pollini emerges as the undisputed star of the show, and her mystical calling to alleviate the sexual needs of prison inmates participates in the ersatz religiosity of the entire Christmas special.

But Fellini's attitude toward television is far more ambivalent than this surface condemnation would suggest. To begin with, he had already made two TV films: *A Director's Notebook* (1969) for NBC and the documentary *I clowns* (1970), as well as several commercials, shot in the 1980s. 'It is not by chance that Fellini arrives at *Ginger and Fred* full of mortadelle and giant rigatoni,' observes Mario Giusti, 'after his two celebrated spots for Campari and La Barilla, and [it is not by chance] that many of his own collaborators on the film are also very active in commercials.'[26] Needless to say, the glimpses of rock concerts, thrillers, commercials, and announcements of forthcoming programs that flicker across the monitors located in virtually every set in the production are not drawn from real Italian broadcasts. They are entirely of Fellini's invention, and they fall under the general rubric of *fegatelli* –

snippets of film that Fellini always shoots before and after making the movie proper, and that he may or may not incorporate into the final cut.[27] It soon becomes clear that these *fegatelli* are not merely parodies of their TV counterparts; emerging instead as highly distilled, densely packed nuggets of Fellinian creativity. Unconnected to narrative context, unbound to any overarching structure, the videoclips provide occasions for unfettered imaginative play, allowing the filmmaker to indulge his love of hyperbole, of gags, of excess, of exuberant flashes of originality. They also permit him to retrace his own aesthetic itinerary, to regress to the level of his apprenticeship in the humour magazines of the late 1930s and early 1940s, and to merge the adolescent sexual imaginary with the gastronomic wish-fulfilment fantasies of an advanced consumer age. When arranged in close succession, as in the channel-hopping scene where Amelia flips from a thriller to a risotto commercial to a music video to a demonstration of facial calisthenics, the *fegatelli* reveal Fellini's preference for loosely episodic narrative structures and his propensity for inserting gratuitous images according to personal whim.

The presence of at least one TV monitor on each set also provides the carnivalesque clutter and frenzy that is so integral to Fellini's aesthetic. These monitors divide the visual field into two planes, each vying for the viewer's attention. Much like the celebrated Insula Felicles sequence in *Fellini-Satyricon* (1969), in which Encolpio and Gitone walk past a series of openings affording glimpses of prurient scenes and invitations to partake of their pleasures, the monitors in *Ginger and Fred* offer windows onto another order of experience. The television window gives onto a world where 'you too will be handsomer, stronger, richer if you use ...,' according to the generic ad slogan flashing across the train station in Rome. The glimpses of a heightened reality in *Satyricon* and *Ginger and Fred* may be seen as degraded versions of the mysterious beyond which beckon so many of Fellini's protagonists throughout his filmography. The transcendent place with which Gelsomina is mystically connected in *La strada*, with which Giulietta has paranormal contact through seances and hallucinations in *Giulietti degli spiriti*, and with which Ivo can communicate when he hears voices from a well, and talks to the moon, in Fellini's last film, *La voce della luna* (1990) – such a place is equated in *Ginger and Fred* with the privileged existence promised by postmodern enticements to consume.

A number of critics have argued that Fellini does not represent television in *Ginger and Fred* so much as reinvent or transfigure the medium,[28] taking what lends itself to his own aesthetic needs and exaggerating those elements to the point where satire and self-parody intersect. It is here that another casting choice – that of Franco Fabrizi to play the role of Aurelio, the TV host – reveals its logic. The actor's previous performances as senior *vitellone* Fausto and bumbling *bidonista* Roberto serve to implicate Fellini's filmography in this critique of TV spectacle.[29] With his facile smile that disappears as soon as the camera switches off, with his bonhomie that gives way to cowardice during the power failure, and with his glib chatter that degenerates into expletives, this grown-up ex–con man/*vitellone* is the *'vero divo della trasmissione'* (20), the centre around which the Centro Spaziale Televisivo revolves. But Aurelio is more than just a divo, he is also an *auteur*, capable of imposing his own vision on the viewing public through mass media technology, just as the quiz show host Mike Bongiorno is, according to Fellini, 'the only TV author in so far as he proposes over and over again with his little shape so distorted and delirious an image of our own country, or perhaps of the human condition.'[30] And it is precisely in his role as TV *auteur*, as host of the mega-show of TV, 'this grand deposit, this mastodontic ark brim full, regurgitating, overflowing, with all the materials of which spectacle has always been nourished' (44), that Fellini cannot help but find in Aurelio a vulgarized alter ego. In identifying with the TV host, Fellini is acknowledging his own participation in postmodern cultural practices, as well as admitting that any critique he levels at the medium will ultimately redound to himself.

There is another way in which Fellini complicates his position in the film-versus-television dichotomy. Not only does his hidden complicity with television call into question any absolute allegiance to older forms of entertainment over new, postmodern ones, but so too does the cinema's own failure to live up to an implied standard of authenticity. For Fellini, cinema is also a medium of simulation, offering a transfigured image of the world, at many removes from any 'objective reality,' just as *Ginger and Fred*'s protagonists are themselves impersonators whose stage identities derive from the highly constructed mythic personas of two American film stars. In fact, the dance sequence at the centre of 'Ed Ecco a Voi' – the moment that has been cited as the film's only instance of authenticity, and as the point where TV artifice melts away and genuine emotions shine through[31] – is itself highly derivative, standing at a considerable distance from anything we could call an originary experience. Pippo and Amelia's 1985 dance on television re-enacts their routine of thirty years before, which in turn reflects the filmed performance of Astaire and Rogers in the the 1930s, which in turn records the original on-location dance, and so on. The distinction between TV and the cinema on the grounds of authenticity is therefore less one of kind than of degree. Fellini's sympathies for the cinema may be obvious, but he cannot bring himself to celebrate the medium in absolute moral terms as the apotheosis of the genuine and the true, just as he cannot bring himself fully to condemn television for its failure to signify. If anything, he locates the two media on a continuum extending from referentiality to simulation. On a scale like this, the cinema comes closer to the referential pole, though never coinciding with it, while TV moves ever farther toward self-signification.

But Fellini does not accept the 'fallen' status of all spectacle without a struggle, and that struggle is played out with great poignance in *Ginger and Fred*. It is Pippo who gives voice to the filmmaker's longing for the referent, to his nostalgia for an art form that can signify. 'Tap dancing is not only a dance,' he tells an interviewer before the show:

> it is something more ... It was the Morse Code of the black slaves. A kind of wireless telegraph ... In the cotton plantations ... the black slaves could not talk among themselves, because if they spoke instead of working, the overseer whipped their skin off ... so what does the black slave do? He communicates with the comrade of his plight in this way ... [Mastroianni makes hand gestures to demonstrate the footwork of the dance] ... Watch out, there's the guard ... I have a knife ... They're doing him in. Or rather ... I love you ... and I too.

In his insistence on a performance that exceeds the level of its signifiers, Pippo lays the groundwork for an art that not only refers beyond itself, but actively intervenes to change its historical context. Tap dancing originated when the Slave Act of 1740 prohibited the use of drums because they could be heard from plantation to plantation and could be employed – so the white slavemasters feared – to incite rebellion. By substituting intricate footwork for the outlawed drumbeats, slaves created a secret language of subversion in the guise of entertainment.[32] The relationship between the Morse code of dance and the slaves' real-life oppression is thus direct and dynamic. 'Tip tap' is both a response to historical injustice and an appeal to act in a way that will bring about its alleviation.

Pippo's manifesto of an art that refers beyond itself to the real circumstances of the performers' lives has a powerful impact on Amelia, whose reaction suggests a possible happy ending for their romance: 'We'd been tip tapping together for fifteen years and you never told me anything! But look, Pippo, this is something very important, very beautiful. I have goose bumps.' It had not occurred to Amelia until now that Pippo might have been proclaiming his love to her all those years through dance. His declaration also hints at how the upcoming television performance could rekindle their relationship, especially when read in light of the Hollywood film on which the dance sequence is modelled. Mark Sandrich's *Follow the Fleet* (1936), starring Astaire and Rogers, is a powerful example of how spectacle can modify performers' lives. It tells the story of two dancing partners reunited after a separation of several years, who put on a benefit show and thus succeed in reconciling several pairs of lovers. By making the spectacle itself the agent of plot resolution, *Follow the Fleet* reflects Astaire's own insistence that dance be an organic part of the narrative, advancing and promoting it in significant ways:

> I think the audience always slumps ... even more in movies than on stage
> – when they hear an obvious dance cue, and both the picture and the
> dance seem to lose some of their continuity. Each dance ought to spring
> somehow out of character or situation, otherwise, it is simply a vaudeville
> act.[33]

The spectacle that is mounted at the end of *Follow the Fleet* is precisely what resolves all the film's narrative predicaments. In the aftermath of the show-within-the-film, Sherry Martin (played by Rogers) is convinced by the triumph of their professional reunion that her partnership with 'Bake' Baker (played by Astaire) should be continued offstage. The climactic routine, 'Let's Face the Music and Dance,' is itself a performance within a performance within a performance: the inner dance is surrounded by a pantomimed narrative, which the choreography addresses and resolves. In this frame story, an elegant gambler who has just squandered his fortune meets a desperate society lady about to leap to her death. Rather than self-destruct, the two decide to 'face the music and dance.' Thus *Follow the Fleet* comprises several layers of embedded spectacles, each of which remedies the interpersonal dilemmas of the surrounding narrative in a triumphant affirmation of art's power to intervene in life. Will Amelia and Pippo, like their exemplars Bake Baker and Sherry Martin, decide to renew their personal and professional collaboration as a result of their broadcast triumph? 'It would have been better if you were married ... It works better,' the assistant director of the TV show had remarked on learning that Amelia and Pippo had never wed. 'The public always likes love stories. Companions in art and in life.'

In two scenes near the end of *Ginger and Fred*, the protagonists seem on the verge of the kind of breakthrough that would indeed make them 'companions in art and life.' A power failure takes place at the very start of the televised dance, transporting the two performers back in time to the blackouts of the 1940s and clearing the air of all the light waves, sound bytes, and emissions that clutter the postmodern world. Here, in this oasis of calm, Amelia and Pippo can share an unguarded moment of intimacy. Freed from all their defence mechanisms and from the need to project their public personas, Amelia and Pippo withdraw into a secret space of authenticity deep within the self, 'as in dreams, far from everything,' says Pippo. 'A place that you don't know where it is, how you arrived.' The darkened stage allows the couple to become characters in a hypothetical Golden Age Hollywood romance. Two possible mini-films emerge – one ending in tragedy as the couple dies in a terrorist attack ('They broke up thirty years ago and are reunited to die together,' fantasizes Pippo) – and the other concluding happily as they run off together to start a new life in love. But the electric power is restored to thwart these romantic scenarios.

The blackout sequence provides a moment of stylistic repose in a film otherwise governed by the audiovisual techniques of TV.[34] During this welcome interlude, the crowded surface of the screen gives way to a space of true depth, whose various planes are no longer defined by the organizing presence of a video monitor competing with the narrative action of the foreground, but rather by the genuinely engaging intimacy of the couple which silences and stills everything around them. With the return of power to the set, the audiovisual values of TV are restored, and Pippo and Amelia must go on with the dance, forgoing the temptation to escape that the momentary darkness had held out to them.

A second near-breakthrough takes place at the railway station when the partners bid each other farewell after the show. Only now does Amelia learn that Pippo's wife has left him and that he is free of emotional attachments. But two young people who had seen the couple on TV insist on getting autographs at the very moment when the mutual feelings raised during the blackout scene could have been explored.[35]

Pippo, who cannot come right out and say, 'Amelia, I need you,' must resort to the code language of their show: 'Amelia! ... Vuuuuuuuu.' With this sound effect, he recalls the framing narrative of their own climactic dance routine in which Ginger, about to depart forever on an ocean liner, runs down the gangway into her lover's arms, vowing never to leave him. For Pippo, this re-evocation is a plea for renewal, an appeal to make life imitate spectacle, to 'follow the fleet' of their Hollywood paragons in becoming once more 'companions in art and life.' Amelia pretends to run back to him with open arms, but for her, it is all a charade. Pippo's inability to say, 'Amelia, I need you,' re-enacts the communicative failure of their entire relationship, and she is unwilling or unable to read his gesture as an encoded plea for love.[36] There will be no carryover from stage to life – for Amelia, the boundaries between the inner spectacle of the dance and the outer narrative of the sentiments are fixed and inviolate. Unseduced by their performance, she will not play Ginger to Pippo's Fred, but instead will go back to her hometown on the Italian Riviera to be the widow of the staid Enrico, with whom it was all 'molto diverso.'

Fellini could have ended his film right here, just as he could have ended it after the dance sequence, or after the backstage denouement. Instead the film survives the departure of its protagonists: the camera bids Amelia farewell on the receding train, and withdraws from Fred in the bar. At this point, Fellini lingers on an antenna salesman who boasts Rome's receptivity to sixty-six channels, and then settles on a TV monitor featuring a commercial for Scolamangi, the pasta that makes you lose weight. With these final frames the film comes full circle, bringing us back to where we began, with Amelia's arrival at the train station. But in so doing Fellini transforms that setting – traditional site of cinematic romance – into a quintessentially postmodern media space of antennae sales and television advertisements.[37] In contemporary video culture, romance is reduced to gastronomic lust, story to sound bites, and life-altering spectacle to videoclips.

The question of causality remains deliberately ambiguous in Ginger and Fred. Did the failure of the TV reunion to bring about an offstage happy ending spring from the couple's emotionally flawed relationship? Or is postmodernism at fault for thwarting the progress of an old-fashioned Hollywood romance? In other words, is the obstructed love story a mere allegorical expression of the antihuman workings of contemporary media culture? Or does the sentimental plot have its own integrity and logic, which find analogies on the level of culture critique but are not exhausted by it? Recourse to the hyperfilm sug-gests the second conclusion, in the sense that *Ginger and Fred* allows Fellini to advance both his own fictionalized life story and his aesthetic investigation without subordinating one to the other. In the moral principles embodied by Giulietta Masina and Marcello Mastroianni throughout Fellini's career – those of 'wounded and triumphant inno-cence' on the one hand, and of 'the right to live irresponsibly and flee maturity understood as renunciation, extinction, surrender' on the other – the filmmaker projects the eternal dilemma of his mythobiogra-phy. It is this human failure, this inability to script a happy ending to the couple's story, that provides Fellini with the occasion for pitting older forms of spectacle – those of vaudeville and 1930s Hollywood cinema – against those of postmodern media culture, as a way of dra-matizing his own quest for a genuinely communicative and referential art in the age of simulation.

For one brief, Utopian moment, that quest meets with success in *Gin-ger and Fred*. This moment occurs, of course, in the dance sequence, for it is here that past and present, audience and performers, cinema and television, all come together in a moment of imaginative transcen-dence. Most of all it is Amelia who personifies the transfiguring power of spectacle as she 'lets herself be carried away by the sweetness of the music' (264), and as Fellini's camera reveals to us her own process of self-mystification, her own belief that she has become, for the space of this dance, both the legendary Ginger and her own younger self. Like La Saraghina in *8½*, whose grotesqueness was tempered by her own sheer joy in being transformed into the graceful creature of her dreams, Amelia is at once pathetic and sublime, the aged relic who makes a fool of herself for public consumption, and the heroic trouper who believes in the transformative power of spectacle.[38] It is at this point that the rivalry between television and film aesthetics gives way to a unified vision within which the video and movie cameras merge in joint cele-bration of a spectacle that transcends its technological means.

Unlike the corresponding scene in *Follow the Fleet*, this visionary moment is finite and will have no repercussions in the world beyond the stage. Art's power of renewal does not survive the limits of the per-formance, and the dance spectacle is helpless to alter the course of two lives consigned to loneliness. But this does not signal Fellini's surren-der to the insignificance of spectacle and to the consequent triumph of postmodern simulation over an art that aspires to something beyond the mere proliferation of signs. Unable to attain the truth at the end of the signifying chain, but unwilling to renounce the quest for it, Fellini's cinema takes the only position it can – an oppositional one – to record its own struggle for authenticity in the face of great personal and cultural odds. In the final analysis, the place where art and life will converge for Fellini will be in the hyperfilm alone, in the privileged exchange between mythobiography and the filmmaking process that transfigures and redeems it.

Notes

1 The film was originally to be part of a television miniseries starring Giulietta Masina and involving a number of prominent directors (Michelangelo Antonioni, Carlo Lizzani, and Luigi Magni). When the project fell through, Fellini decided to expand his own proposed contribution into the full-length feature film, *Ginger and Fred*. Initially drafted to meet the requirements of a one-hour TV program, the script had to undergo a considerable process of amplification: the television show '*Ed Ecco a Voi*' ('We Are Proud to Present') had to be expanded without making it the protagonist of the film, and the elderly performers had to be given enough depth of character and background to sustain the weight of a full-length feature. Fellini describes this procedure in the material published in the prefatory section of the screenplay (Federico Fellini, *Ginger e Fred*, ed. Mino Guerrini [Milan: Longanesi, 1985] 82). All translations of these prefatory materials are mine. Henceforth page references to this edition will be included in the body of the text. Quotations from the film's dialogue are based on this text and on the Italian language of the film itself (translations mine).
2 For the comments by Giulio Cattielli, see Claudio G. Fava and Aldo Viganò, *I film di Federico Fellini* (Rome: Gremese, 1991) 178.
3 Tullio Kezich, *Fellini* (Milan: Rizzoli, 1988) 520.
4 See Fava and Viganò 178, 176.
5 For Moravia's comments, see Fava and Viganò 177. Edoardo Bruno's review, 'Ciao Pippo,' is in *Filmcritica* 37 (1986): 94. For Kezich's remarks, see *Fellini* 521.
6 See Peter Bondanella, *The Cinema of Federico Fellini* (Princeton: Princeton UP, 1992) 222; the review by Andrea Zanzotto reprinted in 'Critica dossier,' *Cinema sessanta* 227 (March–April, 1986): 51; and Silvana Cielo, 'Qualche minuto al buio,' *Filmcritica* 37 (1986): 95.
7 I am very grateful to my student Dorothée Bonnigal, whose many conversations with me on the subject of the hyperfilm have helped enormously in

the elaboration of this idea. Her own contributions to the notion are found in 'Federico Fellini's *Amarcord*: Variations on the Libidinal Limbo of Adolescence' in this volume.

8 For the term 'mitobiografia,' see Kezich, *Fellini* 17.

9 See Kezich, *Fellini* 515.

10 See Fava and Viganò 180. On the occurrence of a number of Fellinian *luoghi comuni* in *Ginger and Fred*, see Fava and Viganò 175.

11 This is Bondanella's observation in *The Cinema of Federico Fellini* 223.

12 Numerous critics have remarked on the status of Pippo as Fellinian self-projection. See, for example, Vittorio Giacci, 'Ballo. Non solo,' *Filmcritica* 37 (1986): 95; Francesco Tornabene, *Federico Fellini: The Fantastic Vision of a Realist* (Berlin: Benedikt Taschen, 1990) 122; and Pauline Kael, 'Lost Souls,' *The New Yorker* 62 (21 April 1986): 100.

13 See Carolyn Geduld, '*Juliet of the Spirits*: Fellini and Jung,' in *Federico Fellini: Essays in Criticism*, ed. Peter Bondanella (New York: Oxford UP, 1978) 137–51. In Amelia, Masina exhibits that combination of 'shyness, curiosity, vulnerability, tolerance, impatience, anger, and resolve' that mirrors an aspect of Fellini's own psychology according to Kezich, *Fellini* 522. On the roles of Masina and Mastroianni as alter egos of the director, see Kezich's *Fellini*, as well as his comments in *Cinema sessanta* 227: 54; and Jack Kroll, 'Last Waltz in Roma,' *Newsweek* 107 (31 March, 1986): 72.

14 See Bruno 94; Stefano Reggiani in *Cinemasessanta* 227: 50; and Kael 97.

15 What emerges from the actress's own account of the collaboration is that any attempt on her part to actively formulate a reading of her character is perceived by her husband as a usurpation of his authorial control: 'With other directors it is easier for me to have a dialogue. With him, instead, perhaps because I know that he doesn't listen to me (nor does he listen to anyone else), I have a greater, almost inexplicable shyness. With Federico I know that one must not talk, that it's useless to ask explanations, I know that he seeks the character "upon you" [*te lo cerca addosso*] on set, and thus, at the beginning of the film, the things that I feel that I need to tell him, well, I get some paper and think and I write them down for him' (61).

16 For the way in which the problematic relationships between director/husbands and actress/wives are internalized in the cinema of two prominent *auteurs*, see Dorothée Bonnigal, 'Restrained Women and Artistic Emancipation: Authority and Resistance in Federico Fellini's *Giulietta degli spiriti* and John Cassavetes' *A Woman under the Influence*,' *Romance Languages Annual* 5 (1996): 204–11.

17 From a feminist point of view, this erasing of the identity of Masina is

rather disturbing, as is Fellini's above-mentioned assertion that he, and not his wife, understands the effectiveness of her facial expressions.

18 In this sequence, Fellini may be making a grotesque allusion to the TV program on eye exercises that Giulietta watches with her maids, where a beautiful young model demonstrates ocular movements that 'helped your favourite actresses to achieve their success.' See the screenplay, published in English as Federico Fellini, *Juliet of the Spirits*, trans. Howard Greenfeld (New York: Ballantine, 1965) 211. I am grateful to Marguerite Waller for calling my attention to this analogy.

19 On TV's subordination of serious journalism to the overriding goal of entertainment, see Federico Fellini, *Fare un film* (Turin: Einaudi, 1980) 142.

20 For the satiric implications of Fellini's Dante allusion, see Bondanella, *The Cinema of Federico Fellini* 225.

21 See Fava and Viganò 174.

22 See René Girard, *Deceit, Desire and the Novel*, trans. Yvonne Freccero (Baltimore: Johns Hopkins UP, 1965).

23 Jean Baudrillard, *Simulations*, trans. Paul Foss, Paul Patton, and Philip Beitchmann (New York: Semiotext(e), 1983) 10–11. On Fellini's portrait of TV as a medium dedicated to self-representation, see Mino Argentieri, 'No, non è di TV che si tratta,' *Cinemasessanta* 227: 51 and Riccardo Rosetti, 'La fuga dalle cose,' *Filmcritica* 37 (1986): 99–101. Frank Burke has provided a number of valuable insights into the way in which Fellini's television works by simulation. For Burke, *Ginger and Fred* occupies an important step in Fellini's signifying itinerary, as the filmmaker moves ever farther from the non-problematic representation of his early filmography, to an even more deeply felt loss of the referent and consequent focus on self-signification in his later work. See 'Federico Fellini: From Representation to Signification,' *Romance Languages Annual* 1 (1989), esp. 38–9.

24 Frederic Jameson, *Postmodernism, or the Cultural Logic of Late Capitalism* (Durham: Duke UP, 1991) 37.

25 On the essential *ripetitività* and indistinguishability of TV messages, see Umberto Eco's remarks in *Cinemasessanta* 227: 50; Rosetti 101; and Fellini's own comments in Tornabene, 121. As a result of the semiotic indistinguishability of the video process, interpretation is rendered impossible by the failure of any privileged element to 'occupy the position of "interpretant."' See Jameson 90.

26 See Giusti's review for *Il Manifesto* excerpted in *Cinemasessanta* 227: 50.

27 See Kezich, *Fellini* 512.

28 See, for example, Kezich, *Fellini* 512, and the reviews of Reggiani and Argentieri in *Cinemasessanta* 227: 50 and 52 respectively.

29 On the filmographic consequences of this casting choice, see Bondanella, *The Cinema of Federico Fellini* 222.

30 See Federico Fellini, *Essays in Criticism*, ed. Peter Bondanella (New York: Oxford, 1978) 15.

31 See Bondanella, *The Cinema of Federico Fellini* 225; and Rosetti 101.

32 See Marian Hannah Winter, 'Juba and American Minstrelsy,' in *Chronicles of the American Dance*, ed. Paul Magriel (New York: Holt, 1948) 40.

33 Quoted in Jerry Ames and Jim Siegelman, *The Book of Tap: Recovering America's Long Lost Dance* (New York: David McKay, 1977) 57. See also Mary Clarke and Clement Crisp, *The History of Dance* (New York: Crown, 1981) 238.

34 See Paolo Vernaglione's excellent discussion of Fellini's mimesis of TV aesthetics in 'Variazioni minime sul sonoro,' *Filmcritica* 37 (1986): 107. Cielo remarks that *Ginger and Fred* was shot like a made-for-TV film (95); so does Kael (97).

35 On the televisual interference in the sentimental plot, see Burke 39.

36 Burke predicates the failure of this gesture on its very basis in simulation. 'Their farewell turns into a recreated piece of business from their televised *Ginger and Fred* routine: now an imitation of an imitation of an imitation' (39).

37 For Burke, this ending proves Fellini's case against the self-referentiality of TV: 'Unable to refer, it can only signify its will to ceaselessly signify' (38).

38 It is interesting to note that Fellini sought to exaggerate the pathos of the performance by having Amelia and Pippo dance far below their level of training and expertise. See Masina's comments in the preface to the screenplay for *Ginger and Fred*.

10

Cinecittà and *America*:
Fellini Interviews Kafka (*Intervista*)

CARLO TESTA

In the *république des lettres*, all artistic sympathies have equal dignity, but some seem warmer than others. It is hardly surprising to see with what love Francesco Rosi, a southern European to a fault, is attracted to the southern heritage that inspired his rendition of *Carmen* and of García Márquez's *Chronicle of a Death Foretold*. Likewise, the artistic affinity that led Luchino Visconti to go beyond the borders of Italian culture and to delve into the inner struggles of the 'poor folk' who are the protagonists of Dostoevsky's *White Nights* requires little hermeneutic effort, nor does his magnificently personal version of Thomas Mann's *Death in Venice*. Fellini's interest in the world of Petronius's *Satyricon* is another case in point among the many that could be mentioned. It seems that some artists were simply born with a manifest destiny to meet one another and to shed light on one another in the realm of creation, and there seems to be something inevitable about the works of art that result from such encounters.

On the face of it, no such inevitability seems to arise when we compare Federico Fellini's artistic universe with that of Franz Kafka. On one hand we encounter a Prague intellectual, an introvert raised in the strict discipline of the conservative family of a Jewish merchant, a loner in a lonely group that attempted to acquire social recognition in a hostile environment but could rarely interact successfully with the Czech and German communities. On the other hand we have a child of the archetypically, stereotypically exuberant Romagna, later adopted by the eminently social, cosmopolitan city of Rome – possibly the first and most significant cultural melting pot (*vide* Petronius's novel) in the history of Western civilization.

On one hand we have the stern world of perceived guilt and

expected punishment, where the chain of logical causality is suppressed and replaced by the chains of an inscrutable necessity, in a twi-
light zone of silence and doom; on the other we find a carefree
atmosphere in which even sin smacks of pleasure (especially so, it goes
without saying, for the sin *par excellence* of modern Christianity, the
carnal one), because sin too, as an index of biological effervescence, is
an instrument of nature, and thus ultimately a tributary of and witness
to the sanctity of Creation. On one hand we have a hidden God, one
who has vanished from the world and has with his disappearance
occulted the key to the meaning of an orphaned universe: a God who
has left behind – whether by the narrator's oversight, Freudian slip, or
deliberate hint to readers in the future – only a threatening sword
where one would expect the flame of liberty: 'As Karl Rossmann ...
stood on the liner slowly entering the harbour of New York, ... he saw
[the Statue of Liberty] in a new light, although he had sighted it long
before. The arm with the sword rose up as if newly stretched aloft, and
round the figure blew the free winds.'[1] On the other hand we see a pli-
able God, utterly uninterested in punishment, who seems to place a
number of (often grotesque) representatives on earth – as Goethe's
God places Mephisto – for the sole purpose of stimulating the Good by
spurring it on by means of the thorn of Evil, as if prohibition alone
could endow action with the ultimate attribute in the exercise of freedom: transgressivity. In Fellini, the presence of guilt and sin, even
when most keenly felt (I am thinking, to mention but one obvious episode, of Juliet-the-child's ordeal on the grill in *Juliet of the Spirits*), is
never a reason for paralysis and closure. Quite the contrary – in Fellini's world noncompliant behaviour is a powerful instrument on the
way to assertion of the ego and ultimately also a device allowing for a
lively, exuberant narrativity.

That Fellini should draw on Kafka for *Intervista* therefore seems to be
a bet running against many odds, and the revelation within the film
that Fellini is shooting screen tests for the film version of Kafka's
American novel comes as a surprise to all spectators who presumed
they knew what Fellini and, respectively, Kafka are all about. Discern-
ing how the two improbable bedfellows can be brought under a common sheet is, on the face of it, no slight challenge.

To be sure, Fellini knew and admired Kafka for reasons that are easy
to explain within the cultural history of twentieth-century Europe. It
was at a time when fascism still stood that the Italian director – then
only an obscure journalist in Rome – became acquainted with the uni-

verse of the absurd created and popularized by the man from the Jewish-German-Czech 'freezing pot.' Fellini recalls:

> One day a colleague, Marcello Marchesi, came from Milan with a book, *The Metamorphosis* by Franz Kafka ... The unconscious, which Dostoevsky had used to probe and analyze emotions, became, in this book, material for the plot itself ... Here was the individual unconscious, a shadow zone, a private cellar suddenly clarified ...
>
> Kafka moved me profoundly. I was struck by the way he confronted the mystery of things, their unknown quality, the sense of being in a labyrinth, and daily life turned magical.[2]

However, at this stage we are still in the period 1941–3, almost half a century before the film *Intervista*, and fully in the shadow of the European dictatorships that make Kafka's 'magical' (or nightmarish) anticipations seem perfectly adequate to, and in tune with, the European *Zeitgeist*. Furthermore, the text that came in from the cold – Fellini was in Rome, Marchesi brought the book with him from Milan – was not the novel about America, but the novella *The Metamorphosis*. So there must be more at stake in the broad Kafka/Fellini relationship than is revealed by Fellini's extant statements on the subject. What exactly?

The knot begins to unravel when we take a closer look at the information contained in two dependent clauses that Kafka's narrator adroitly ensconces in the opening paragraph of the unpublished manuscript that posthumously came to be known as both *America* (*Amerika*) and *The Lost One* (*Der Verschollene*): 'As Karl Rossmann, a poor boy of sixteen [sic] who had been packed off to America [by his parents] because a servant girl had seduced him and got herself a child by him, stood on the liner slowly entering the harbour of New York ...' (*America* 1).

Ecce homo. The decisive link between Kafka and Fellini, between *America* and *Intervista*, can be established, I surmise, not so much – or at any rate not only – by way of the aura of a 'daily life turned magical,' but also through a specific thematic analogy between Kafka's preoccupations in the novel and one of Fellini's favourite leitmotifs: the coming of age of the (male) adolescent, an autobiographical double of the artist-director. Fellini's interest in Kafka's novel is overdetermined; it is in the field of existential education (especially of sentimental education), in the area of the trials and apprenticeship of life undergone by adolescence, that they find a demonstrably common theme. It is their shared interest in the *Bildungsroman* that brings the two artists together.

Kafka's Novel of Education

'So then you're free?' she asked.
'Yes, I'm free,' said Karl, and nothing seemed more worthless to him.

– America: 120

The fragments now collectively referred to and published as *America* (*The Lost One*) belong to Kafka's early production. They are the closest thing to a *Bildungsroman* that Kafka's works can offer us. In the novel we can observe tentative attempts on the protagonist's part to come to terms with the social dynamics of a comparatively 'realistic' world, and to develop strategies aimed at evolution and growth. Based on evidence from his letters, I believe that Kafka's ideal model – though not necessarily his immediate blueprint – was Flaubert's peculiar and somewhat perverse masterpiece in the genre, the novel *L'Education sentimentale* (1869), a text devoted to the dubious glory of a provincial youth whose sole claim to excellence is the dedication with which he pursues his own superfluousness to the world.

In 1912, the same year he was working on his American novel (and, among other things, *The Metamorphosis*), Kafka unequivocally wrote to Felice Bauer: '*L'Education sentimentale* ... is a book that for many years has been as dear to me as are only two or three people; whenever and wherever I open it, I am startled and succumb to it completely, and I always feel as though I were the author's spiritual son, albeit a weak and awkward one. Tell me at once whether you read French.'[3]

The fame of *L'Education sentimentale* rests on the fact that it evacuates the traditional genre of the novel of education and consecrates an alternative tradition, destined to great fortune in the twentieth century, which explodes the notion of the individual's meaningful insertion into a well-ordered society. It seems safe to assume that this was why the book had such an impact on the avid young reader Franz Kafka.

It can be argued that as Kafka continued to develop his art, he brought the descending curve of the modern novel of education to something very close to its terminal point. *The Trial* and *The Castle* complete the subversion of the entire spectrum of premises on which the concept of growth through education and 'trial' (in an entirely different sense) had been predicated since the times of Goethe's *Wilhelm*

Meister, or Rousseau's *Emile*, or Fénelon's *Télémaque*. Kafka's American text shows unequivocal signs that the disarticulation of certain historically connoted optimistic assumptions in Western literature is about to enter its final stage; the novel's atmosphere is a recognizably 'Kafkaesque' one, in the sense that we lend the word today,[4] and the lack of a clear thrust in the ending leaves Karl's fate, at best, in the balance. All that is certain is that by the time Kafka altogether stopped working on the novel in 1914, he had drafted six numbered and titled chapters, followed by two more unnumbered and untitled ones that seem to be complete and in sequence, plus three fragments of unequal length that were probably destined to be part of the novel's conclusion. Unlike the canonical novel of education, Kafka's American text shows a protagonist whose development spirals increasingly downward as the plot thickens, with only a remote possibility of improvement in his situation in the last major fragment.[5] A brief summary of the novel will help set the stage for our sustained look at the intriguing links between Kafka and Fellini.

At the beginning of the novel the protagonist, Karl Rossmann, lands in New York for the reasons already cited. Instead of pursuing his family connections there, he stops at an inn at the extreme outskirts of the city. There he meets two youths: Robinson, an Irishman, and Delamarche, a Frenchman. The two, who also are jobless, are slightly older than he is; they have no scruples, and they are able to use and abuse him at will, taking advantage of his complete social and financial naïvete. During their march inland they steal Karl's money, take his parents' photograph, and exploit the connection he is able to make with the stocky, maternal figure of the Head Cook in Ramses's Hotel Occidental. At one point Karl breaks up with the two and takes a job as a lift boy in the hotel, working hard in a noisy and lonely environment. Because of their meddling, however, he eventually loses that job. Pursued by the police, he is even forced to flee the hotel.

Karl has abandoned all his personal belongings, including his papers, at the hotel, and when a policeman stops him and inquires about his status, he flees again. Only Delamarche's intervention opens an escape route for him – one, however, that results in his permanent dependence on his saviour's hardly generous good will. The apartment that Delamarche and his lover – a buxom former singer named Brunelda – share with Robinson now becomes Karl's domicile as well. The young Rossmann and Robinson take turns serving and humouring the despotic couple, with Karl – the more recent acquisition in the *ménage à quatre* – sitting decidedly lower on the hierarchical scale of power.

'Such a heat, Delamarche,' are the first words we hear from Brunelda. Lazy, capricious, vain, tyrannical, and irascible – all characteristics she shares with her younger lover – Brunelda does little but sit or lie around on her sofa, complaining about the discomfort of an East Coast summer evening. True to their personalities, the two order their servants out onto the balcony so as to protect the privacy of a cooling bath for Brunelda. Robinson and Karl oblige, and in a peculiar reenactment of the Oedipal triangle agree to jointly remove themselves to the liminal position of the outside observer, offering two complementary interpretations (respectively, the eager and the uncomprehending) of the voyeur role. Neurotic exchanges between the two inside and the two outside pepper evening life on the balcony; so does the hardly abundant meal consumed by the two outsiders, which consists of a hodgepodge of leftovers: a blackened sausage, an open sardine tin, a number of squashed sweets. A little later the manuscript shows an interruption similar to that of a chapter ending. This 'chapter,' then, suspends and delays Brunelda's cooling relief: she falls asleep, sighing and tossing about on her couch, 'apparently troubled by bad dreams' (*America* 252).

The next (also unnumbered) chapter is Kafka's *pezzo di bravura* about Brunelda's bath, into which we are plunged as abruptly as Karl is: '"Get up! Get up!" Robinson screamed, when Karl had barely opened his eyes.'[6] The bath foregrounds, under a thinly veiled allegory, the sexual act, which Delamarche and Brunelda interpret as a protracted game, showing a marked penchant for a to-and-fro of dominance and submission.

Mere pawns in this comedy, in which they are in turn teased and rebuffed, Karl and Robinson eventually prefer the straightforwardly servile task, imposed on them later on in the afternoon, of procuring breakfast for the two despotic parental figures: 'Karl ... realized that one could only hope to have any influence on the powers-that-be by showing them unswerving labor' (*Der Verschollene* 370). This part, which could be termed Chapter Eight, comes to an end with the adult couple's ludicrous satisfaction with the breakfast the two youths manage to scrape together for them by revamping disgusting leftovers. This is also the end of the continuous part of the novel in the manuscript.

In most recent editions, two long fragments and a shorter one are appended. The first fragment indicates that a dramatic upset has occurred in the intervening blank space of narration. Robinson and Delamarche have both disappeared, and in an about-face of paramount symbolic significance, Karl and Brunelda are now left to struggle for survival together. Brunelda has swollen to monstrous proportions. No longer even able to walk, she must be transported in a wheelchair, at the cost of stoical efforts on her part and Karl's. In this fragment she appears as a sweaty lump of flesh, covered with a cloth (why exactly, we are not told), resembling in size and shape 'ten sacks of potatoes,' 'a whole harvest of apples' (*Der Verschollene* 380, 382). She urgently needs to be moved out of her apartment, is intercepted by a policeman in the process, and only receives permission to proceed by submitting to a despising grimace: 'Meeting with the contempt of the police was better than eliciting their attention,' Karl muses (*Der Verschollene* 381).

Where is Brunelda so secretively moving to? She is taking up residence in a vaguely defined 'Institution #25' located in a dark, narrow alley – most likely a cheap brothel. Karl once more ignores the abuse he receives, this time from the administrator of Institution #25, and focuses instead on something that is incomparably more significant to the narrator – namely, the dirt in the building, which materializes and objectifies the nausea permeating Karl's relationship to the world. This closes the section titled 'Brunelda Moves Out.'

Kafka's novel of education then takes an even more enigmatic turn with what is presumed to have been the core fragment of its concluding chapter, which centres on the symbolical institution called in the manuscript 'The Theater of Oklahoma' ('Das Teater von Oklahama' – *sic* in the original), which combines images of North American plenty – freely available in contemporaneous travelogues for the benefit of hungry European would-be emigrants – with apocalyptic figures of a decidedly Biblical inspiration.[7] In this gigantic *theatrum mundi* Karl finally gains some form of acceptance, albeit at an infinitesimal level: though he still has no 'legitimacy papers' (*America* 262) to prove his hardly existent qualifications, the great Theater of Oklahoma accepts him too, because it needs and wants everyone to join its fold.

The manuscript's last fragment, barely one printed page long, fleetingly describes the train journey by which Karl and his fellow workers are transported from the coast to the inland location (Oklahoma, presumably), where the 'theater's' promise of unconditional acceptance – professional, to be sure, but by implication metaphysical – is to be fulfilled. It is on this train that Karl, having in rapid succession been lost sight of by his European family, his American uncle, and his sadistic 'friends,' vanishes from our view as well.[8] As foreshadowed in the original title of the novel, with the interruption of the manuscript he becomes 'the lost one' for us in name and in fact.[9]

What, then, of Karl's education, sentimental above all? I think it is fair to stress that Kafka's *The Lost One* pushes to an extreme the paralysis of the *Bildungsroman* that had first so convincingly been carried out by Flaubert's *L'Education sentimentale* – minus, crucially, the Flaubertian irony. Kafka's novelty consists in his injecting into the world of adolescent experiences that tragic sense of life, that suffocating perception of powerlessness in the face of an unscrutable universe, that is the hallmark of his poetic world. Only the formal structures of the literary form remain. Gone is the nucleus, the contents; these have vanished on the way to Oklahoma along with the concept of evolution ('*Entwicklungs*roman' as synonym of *Bildungsroman*) that had originally inspired the genre. Work, friendship, politics, sex are for Kafka's Karl no longer subject to a dialectical process of error and apprenticeship; instead they have become dehumanized spaces for the practice of unsubtle and at times outright brutal strategies of power. The drive toward psychological depth is relayed and replaced by the quest for a metaphysical goal that remains invisible beyond the transcendental horizon.

What knowledge are we left with as we turn the last page of Kafka's all-American jamboree? There seems little doubt that the American novel represented for Kafka an incursion into a symbolic land of freedom – a freedom promised, though not quite achieved in fact – paralleling that undertaken during the same years, at a different metonymical level, by millions of European immigrants. A spiritual rather than an economic migrant, Kafka sought in the locus he calls 'America' an experimental space in which to test fictional ways of lightening, or possibly overcoming, what can variously but equivalently be termed the crushing burden of guilt (to put the matter in theological terms), the Oedipal complex (to use the language of psychoanalysis), and the absence from the world, now perceived as a system of signs, of an ultimate and certain guarantee for meanings (to invoke recent deconstructionist theory). Finally, to couch the matter in terms of cultural history, it could be argued that Kafka was seeking to overcome in his metaphysical North America the intolerable prejudice of European nineteenth-century philosophical teleology, internationally adopted by the bourgeoisie, according to which all that is real is rational and all that is rational is real – a theory the logical conclusion

of which is that any form of thought questioning the real is, by definition, madness.

It is precisely into this hoped-for fictional testing ground that Karl
Rossmann finally vanishes, as he attempts to redeem the Old World
by travelling west. Surprisingly, he eventually resurfaces – if only as a
tentative narrative space – in Fellini's Cinecittà.

Fellini's Novel of Education

Yes, I believe that, in the last analysis, everything one writes is of an autobiographical nature. But this can be said: 'I was born in such and such a year, in
such and such a place,' or 'There was a king who had three sons.'

– Jorge Luis Borges[10]

Literary autobiographies have become suspect since at least the times
of Rousseau and Stendhal; and even work prior to theirs is almost
daily being taken to task. One of the complaints most often heard is
that the more authors write and publish in the autobiographical genre,
the more difficult it becomes to disentangle fact from fiction and to
offer a reliable reconstruction of the events in their lives. At the
extreme, autobiography as a genre is (perhaps by definition) always a
deliberate forgery. After all, why would authors attempt to cajole us
into exploring one particular direction in their lives, unless they had
strong reason to distract us from others that they wished not to be vio-
lated? It must be precisely what is *not* said that matters the most.

If that is in fact the case, future generations may find it well-nigh
impossible to read (or write) a reliable biographical account of Federico Fellini, for the simple – and maddening – reason that autobiography ostensibly is, in one way or another, all that Fellini's filmmaking is
about. We are, and will always be, in danger of confusing him with his
protagonists, whatever their names: Marcello Rubini, Guido, Sergio
Rubini – or Federico Fellini. It is paradoxical but true that Fellini's penchant for exhibitionism on the screen leads to the disappearance of an
empirically verifiable self; he is engaged in a circuitous but undeni-
ably effective strategy of camouflage.

To this ironic hide-and-seek strategy, *Intervista* is an outstanding contribution. There are three strands to the film's structure. The first – the
inverview – represents the frame narration. The person to be interviewed is a Famous Italian Director (henceforward FID), impersonated
on screen by the actor Federico Fellini; the interviewers are a group of

Japanese film fans eager to see the FID at work and to ask him questions about his art. The second strand arises from the fact that the FID, ever creatively engaged, is now hard at work on a rendition of Kafka's American novel (which in accordance with the editions available to the general public at the time in Italy and elsewhere, he calls 'America' *tout court*). He is presently selecting the cast, shooting screen tests, and coordinating other sundry aspects of the project. The third fictional stand centres on the FID's own recollections of his maiden trip to Cinecittà many years in the past, and on a number of episodes surrounding that visit. We thus have a triple source of narrative impulses that interact with one another, plus – as Peter Bondanella rightly emphasizes – a wealth of cinema-within-the-cinema intuitions that make for a truly cornucopian audiovisual experience.[11]

And yet, put this way, it all looks and sounds neat and clear: too neat and too clear for our FID. First, it should be noted that the three narrative areas are not treated symmetrically. The interview (strand 1) and the reminiscences (strand 3) have both a cinematic *and* a metacinematic component – that is, we get to see the final products along with the deictic gestures that unveil their respective modes of production. We witness the director's encounter with the Japanese visitors, as well as the events that surround it; we enjoy the reconstruction of the director's memories, as well as the preparations necessary to shoot them (or rather, such preparations as the director deems artistically suitable).

However, the same is not true of the film about America, which is never presented to us. The slot to be allotted to Kafka's narrative – which is the generative pretext for the whole project – remains an empty one (a 'lost one'?). In other words, there is no solid, ultimate *matriozka*[12] at the core of the last hollow one. One possible way of charting all this is shown on page 198.

A second complicating factor is that there are internal links between the three protagonists, each of whom mobilizes complex literary and cinematic echoes. For example, the FID plays a classic mentor role vis-à-vis his younger self, the protagonist of the prewar memories, whom he treats with paternal protectiveness. This entails a splitting of roles – a dual personality of sorts – whereby father and son 'are' the same person in an externalized reenactment of the duality between trainer and trainee that may well be taken as a symbolic figuration of a fundamental view of poiesis: namely, that the art of narrating is the artist's painstaking conquest of self-education by means of his or her fission into two separate entities – one, the narrator, and the other, the character.

Metafilm in Cinecittà

— —

Interview with the Japanese

Metafilm on the production of memories

— —

Memories

Metafilm on America

— —

X

Another issue of theoretical relevance suggested by the film is that of the defamiliarization tangibly created by the presence of the 'uncomprehending glance' of the outside observer visiting the main scene of the events: traditionally the *pícaro*, the clown, or the holy fool, but here the structurally equivalent group of urbane Japanese documentarians. Almost proverbial in Italy for the (supposed) remoteness of its *forma mentis* from the local one, Japanese culture is used by Fellini as an alternative vantage point from which to relativize the natives' experience. Through this relativization, the *vissuto* of everyday life becomes available to the artist for fictional fruition, thus affording a passage through æsthetic representation that is essential to the process through which art lifts individuals, however temporarily, out of their time; allows them to suspend, however transitorily, their transitoriness; and presents them with a *sub specie æternitatis* perception of their own impermanence.[13] Clearly, both the mentor/character, trainer/trainee split and the passage through representation by way of the outsider's glance are strategies aiming at implementing something that could be called the artist's *dream of omnipotence*.

Third, the FID's film 'about Kafka' is enormously complicated by

the fact that the director doesn't stick to his plans and constantly tres-
passes on the boundaries between narrative areas in his story. The
most glaring and recurrent of these transgressions is the one related
to the meant-to-be protagonist of the *America* film. The situation is as
follows: Sergio Rubini – a person called Sergio Rubini who in the film
plays the role of an aspiring actor by the same name – is hired to play
the adolescent FID's role in the Cinecittà film in preparation.[14] In contrast, the Kafka film does not yet have an assigned leading actor.
Thanks to this preferential treatment, the film about the Cinecittà
memories can be shot, while the one from Kafka's American novel
cannot; betrayed by its own director, deprived of a protagonist, the
fragment remains a fragment once more. Kafka's Karl, lost in America, resurfaces at the antipodes, but not as a solid semantic entity: he
lives only as a potentiality, as an empty space to be endowed with
meaning. He 'exists,' and can be detected, only as a series of relations. It is in a long string of ironic digressions – of 'permanent parek-
baseis' – that the FID's film wanders about and along, spinning on to
its conclusion.[15]

Thus it is that in *Intervista* autobiography wins out over the transpo-
sition of literature into film – at the empirical level, that is. In a deeper
sense, a direct form of autobiography takes over from the indirect one
that had been its pre-text (prior text). Ultimately, it is the self-unveiling,
self-concealing ironic interaction between the two that lends to the
narration the impetus necessary to proceed.

Fellini Interviews Kafka

All you put in front of the camera is yourself.[16]

What are the specific questions that, in *Intervista*, Fellini has asked of
Kafka? What are the answers he has obtained? How does he convey
them? The material in *Intervista* that is directly related to the Kafka
project can be subsumed under three rubrics: (A) encounters with, and
instructions to, individuals actually or potentially involved in the
screen tests for what the FID calls *America*; (B) recognizable reproductions or modifications of situations present in Kafka; and (C) allusions
to and oblique loans from the original – that is, transpositions from
Kafka that have undergone varying degrees of displacement, re-elabo-
ration, and camouflage.

(A) The first group of references shows an interesting overall picture of how the FID perceives his main characters. In light of what we know from Kafka, these are revealing because they allow us to see how the FID intends to transpose the verbal into the visual and the spiritual into the physical.

For Karl, he considers signing on a young Englishwoman, whom he would dress as a boy.[17] He then approaches 'two graceful and respectful youths' at the Rome music conservatory (*Block-notes* 121).

The director also hires an agent, who shows up in Studio 5 of Cinecittà with a day's catch, which she proceeds to peddle: 'I've been all over the place: music conservatories, libraries, religious institutions; Polish embassy, Hungarian embassy, Czech embassy, I've been through all of them, and well, if you can't find your character among these ones, then I sure don't understand what it is that he wants!' (*Block-notes* 153).

For Brunelda we have a few similar episodes that convey the FID's reading of the character and the particular interpretation he gives of her capricious, lazy sensuality. To the person who brings him the first candidate, he objects: 'Maurizio, Brunelda is blond, you know' (*Block-notes* 92). This does not prevent him from later opening up the search to brunette Bruneldas, as his assistant admits when all candidates are congregated in the studio for a general briefing session. The (female) secretary of production gallantly remarks as she clarifies the character for one of the candidates: 'She eats, she sleeps, and she's always making love, no fool she!' (*Block-notes* 144). Two candidates object to the very idea that they may be asked to pose in the nude for the bathing scene. Maurizio, the assistant director, later explains to the aspiring actresses just what kind of sensuality is expected of Brunelda:

Maurizio: Look at me! A frightening mask: a mask of perversity, of ferocity, but also, of tenderness. [He shows the expression to a gorgeous young woman wearing a white blazer jacket generously open on the front and a pair of sunglasses over her forehead.] Listen to me – you have to be animal-like, beastly ... Ah, I've got it: the quivering nostril is *absolutely crucial*. Trust me; the quivering nostril can make the whole difference. [The young woman nods as a sign of good will.] (*Block-notes* 146)

(B) With respect to recognizable reproductions or modifications of situations from Kafka, for the reader of the novel the clearest change undertaken in the film – perceptible even before the Brunelda scenes are acted out in the screen tests – is that the FID intends to show the female leading character in full light, most notably during the bath scene.

In contrast, Kafka's narrator does not mention the colour of Brunelda's hair (though he many times alludes to the red dress she invariably wears), and keeps her – and Delamarche – hidden behind a screen throughout what is in his text a literally steamy episode. His text engages in a sophisticated *Fort!-Da!* game, in which garments and segments of bodies alternatively emerge from behind the screen, appearing and disappearing in the haze under Karl's eyes. The novel, in other words, gives a clear sense of a partition in the room's space. In the hidden half, Delamarche pants and sweats in a vain attempt to satisfy Brunelda's aquatic whims. From the part accessible to the reader, Karl observes the events, while a hypnotized Robinson glosses them for him. In the film, instead, the climactic scene is rehearsed with the entire room open to the youths' – and the public's – glance.

The FID's screen tests introduce a further surprise for the film's spectator: the four main events about Kafka's Brunelda sequence (the interjection 'Such a heat, Delamarche,' Robinson's sardine eating, Brunelda's bath, and her being rolled out by Karl on a wheelchair) are compressed in the film into a rapid continuum, whereas in the novel they occupy distinct successive moments.

The plot's evolutionary dimension is thus de-emphasized in the film (or rather, in the fragments of it that we see rehearsed in *Intervista*). The relationship obtaining in the book at the beginning of the chapter with the bath scene undergoes a radical break by the time Brunelda is transported to 'Institution #25' (which in *Intervista* becomes a brothel *tout court*).[18] The FID is, on one hand, obviously intrigued by the especially sensual visual opportunities offered by the multiple *ménage*; on the other hand, he is relatively uninterested in developing the diachronic psychological shifts that occur within Kafka's plot – in particular those occurring between the main text and the fragments.[19]

(C) Among what I have called the 'oblique loans,' or transpositions from the original that have undergone various degrees of deformation and displacement, there are five that seem especially worthy of notice.

1. The subway that Karl takes to the open-air Theater of Oklahoma appears in *Intervista* as the 'elevated railway of an American city' (*Block-notes*, 155.) The substitution may seem inspired merely by the FID's desire to convey the urban skyline surrounding Karl; however, it is a liberating experience for Karl to emerge, after long ordeals, from

the bowels of the earth into a realm of universal acceptance that has banished all discrimination. In disposing of the subway, the FID is choosing to de-emphasize the important soteriological element in the Kafkaesque atmosphere of the novel.

The subway we do get in *Intervista* is located in Rome instead; it is not haunted by seekers of salvation, but rather by the FID's talent scouts. The foregrounding is entirely changed.

2 & 3. During Sergio Rubini's impersonation of the young FID at the time of the latter's first streetcar ride to Cinecittà, a series of exotic, dreamlike landscapes arise – an obvious intrusion of cinematic fantasies into the drab cityscape to be expected in the Rome of fascist autarky. These panoramas, which belong to the 'Cinecittà film,' also are interpolations from Kafka's novel. They have been appropriated and reassigned from the *America* film, to which they were theoretically destined.

> Now the landscape changes. In the roar of tumbling water, we see the luminous spray of a grand waterfall spread over the intense green color of the vegetation. Sergio Rubini changes seats so as to admire the view from Antonella's window ... A veil of pulverized water reaches and fogs up the glass, behind which the young woman's face presently disappears ...
>
> **Notarianni/fascist bigwig**: Niagara, Niagara! As you can see, my dear young man, Italy is second to none! Even when it comes to waterfalls! [Author's note: The tongue-in-cheek stab at grotesquely misplaced nationalism deserves noticing.]
>
> The landscape has changed again. The jagged crests of a mountain chain parade past the windows. The little streetcar enters a sort of gorge, a narrow trench between two walls of bare rock ...
>
> Driver [to the passengers]: Ladies and gentlemen, look up there! The Indians! (*Block-notes* 103–4)[20]

Without a word of warning, Kafka's train has suddenly become Fellini's streetcar, and Karl's vistas become part of the FID's fantasies. To be sure, the intertextuality of imagery is emphasized by the references, added *ex nihilo* in *Intervista*, to Niagara Falls and American Indians respectively. But even without them the dialogical relationship recalls the novel's story line, and on occasion echoes its very wording.

The circulation of images is so strong in *Intervista* that it tends to obliterate internal barriers between plots and conflated protagonists: by way of one and the same process of daydreaming, the FID, Sergio

Rubini, Karl Rossmann, Kafka's narrator, the obscure young journalist named Federico Fellini and impersonated by Sergio Rubini – all begin to blur and blend into one another.

4. The fourth substantial displacement that occurs between novel and film consists in the fact that there is an ablution scene actually displayed in *Intervista*. This, however, happens neither in the Kafka/America sequence (where sexuality is interrupted) nor in the Cinecittà sequence (where it is merely alluded to; on which more *infra*). The locus where representation is finally allowed to triumph is the autobiographical sequence, in which the young FID-to-be is allowed to witness from as close as decency would allow the shower ritual enacted by a famous prewar diva immediately before *her own* interview.

5. This finally brings us back and around to Brunelda. The red-clad, archetypal literary 'man eater' (*Block-notes* 144)[21] simply cannot find her match among would-be Roman actresses. Why? The reason is simple: the FID is looking for her in the 'wrong' narrative strand. He gets closer to the truth when, allowing himself to float on the waves of anamnesis, he enlists the magician *par excellence*, Mandrake (impersonated by Marcello Mastroianni), for a task so delicate he cannot even bring himself to articulate it.

It is out of this Fellinian paradoxical sense of shyness that a professional visit to the potential female leading character turns into a straightforward (though by no means simple) sentimental journey into the FID's – *and* the Famous Italian Actor's – past.

The two, accompanied by Sergio Rubini, travel in a car that eventually reaches a villa in the Roman countryside purportedly inhabited by Anita Ekberg, impersonated by herself. When an aging but characteristically robust Ekberg, her body and (blond) hair tightly wrapped in bright orange towels after a shower, appears on the screen, we know that Brunelda's prototype had existed all along in a universe parallel to Karl's. We then understand that finding her was merely a matter of breaking through the conventional barriers of narration, of abolishing the boundaries of time and self that artificially separate life from life and plot from plot. All things considered, the reason why the FID does not ask Ekberg to star in his Kafka film may simply be that, because the distinction between one fiction and another is a fictional one, she *already* stars in it.

'She's mythical!' proclaims the FID about her (*Block-notes* 165). Myths have no beginning and no end; they are always, everywhere.[22] In his poetic universe there is little space for structured notions of time and identity based on the dualisms on which Western logic is posited: I/non-I, true/false, before/after, centre/periphery, inside/outside.

Abolishing Boundaries of Self, Time, and Textuality

I have already argued that although Fellini constantly denudes himself before our eyes in his films, there is no ultimate naked core to the *matriozka*. Or, rather, the multilayered doll *is* the core – which we have been inclined to disregard in our expectation of a climax. The strip is interminable; or rather, it is always already contained in each of its increments.

I suspect, however, that the wooden-doll image may not after all be the most satisfying among the many possible figurative renderings of Fellini's poetics. I would like to suggest another strip in particular as a possibly less inadequate metaphor for his artistic method: the Möbius strip.

In its simplest form, a Möbius strip is a three-dimensional solid obtained by joining the two ends of a ribbon into a ring-shaped object after twisting the ribbon, end to end, by 180° on the longitudinal axis. (If a model is made out of adhesive tape, this implies twisting it so as to join one glued end against the other glued end.) The result is a very approximately 8-shaped band on which an observer can move ahead and return exactly to the starting point after 'two' laps, having scanned the *whole* surface by moving continuously in the same direction. Put more simply, a Möbius strip is a solid that has only one surface; it is a three-dimensional object in which the notions of 'inside' and 'outside' are non-definable.

Interviewing a Fellinian text, I maintain, causes an effect similar to that which an insect – or, for that matter, a character out of a novel by Kafka – would experience while crawling along a Möbius strip. As one progresses, one gradually moves from discourse to metadiscourse, from narration to metanarration, from the 'inside' to the 'outside' of self, time, and text. In fact, in the Fellinian universe outside and inside no longer exist as distinct concepts.

Each time we return to the starting point (let us assume, for the sake of simplicity, Studio 5 at Cinecittà), we seem to have just moved in one direction along the surface of a band; in reality, however, we have accomplished a complex three-dimensional journey. This is the journey through which *Intervista* takes us, loading us onto the scenic platforms of its trains/streetcars, and leading us alternatively to the 'inner' and to the 'outer' sides of, respectively, autobiography and novel, fantasy and cinematic re-creation. At the end of the film, we return to the Cinecittà studio from which we had set out, and away from which we never really moved, having gone constantly ahead in one direction with each turn of the projector's wheel, exactly as we would have on a hypothetical Möbius strip. This strip is *Intervista*, in which *Bildungsroman* and fantasy, autobiography and myth, are made to collapse and coincide, forming one and the same genre.

What sort of *omiyage*,[23] if any, do then we – we strangers, we true Japanese tourists on a visit to Fellini's fantastic continent – bring back with us from this peculiarly stationary journey? Not much more, perhaps, than a sense of exhilarating playfulness; a meagre sense of euphoria, nothing more than the thin, corny 'ray of sunshine' that a producer of old used to beg Fellini to include in each of his films as an antidote to what he perceived as an excess of pessimism on the director's part. Yet it is clear that self-observation enacted through the prism of the mobilization of temporal and psychic boundaries can help achieve a certain levity and detachment from one's impermanence, and thus ultimately serve as an excellent tool for carrying out a form of training toward liberation. The opposite is true of obstinate insistence on self-analysis mediated by the traditional Western parameters of dualism.

In the third of the notebooks published posthumously with the novella *Preparations for a Marriage in the Countryside*, Kafka's aphorisms engage in a prolonged, chainlike dialogue with the notion of evil, and at one point unequivocally state: 'Only Evil has self-awareness.'[24] In interviewing him, Fellini implicitly corrects him: 'In that Oriental tale of *The Sorcerer's Apprentice* the book of knowledge that he arrives at after a long process of self-discipline is composed of pages made out of mirrors: which means, the only way of knowing is to know one's self.'[25]

Reflected and refracted through innumerable mirrors/sheets, Fellini's ray of sunshine – postmodernly portrayed in *Intervista* as coming from Cinecittà's floodlights – bounces back all the way to us, the 'lost ones' in America. The simpleminded producer may now rejoice, unaware that the artificial ray he finally got may well signify instead the inability of art to save anyone or anything, in America or elsewhere.

Notes

1 Franz Kafka, *America*, trans. Edwin Muir (New York: New Directions, 1946)
   1. Hereafter cited in the text as *America*.
2 Federico Fellini, *Comments on Film*, ed. Giovanni Grazzini (Fresno: California State UP, 1988) 53–4.
3 15 November 1912. In F.K., *Letters to Felice*, ed. Erich Heller and Jürgen Born (New York: Schocken Books, 1973) 42.
4 Kafka and Fellini share the curiously rare characteristic of having had adjectives – to be sure, of very different meaning – fashioned after their last names and adopted by common parlance, so successful has their brand of imagination been in the creation of distinctly definable universes.
5 'Optimism' or 'pessimism'? Kafka's intimate friend and first editor, Max Brod, emphasizes that Franz's intention was to lead Karl to final 'liberation' ('*Erlösung*') – albeit 'not a complete one' ('*nicht ganz vollgültig*') due to 'certain accessory circumstances' ('gewisse Nebenumstände'). F.K., *Amerika. Roman* (Frankfurt am Main: S. Fischer, 1953) 358.
6 Franz Kafka, *Der Verschollene*, in *Schriften Tagebücher Briefe. Kritische Ausgabe* (Frankfurt am Main: S. Fischer, 1983) 355. All translations from this volume are mine. (Translated sections are not included in the most common English translation.) Hereafter cited in the text as *Der Verschollene*.
7 For a useful cross-referencing of sources, see Hartmut Binder, *Kafka-Kommentar zu den Romanen, Rezensionen, Aphorismen und zum Brief an den Vater* (München: Winkler, 1976) 152–7.
8 Among the innumerable works that make up the critical corpus on Kafka, I have found the following ones particularly useful: Chris Bezzel, *Kafka-Chronik* (München-Wien: Carl Hanser Verlag, 1975); Wilhelm Emrich, *Franz Kafka* (Bonn: Athenäum-Verlag, 1958); and Ralf R. Nicolai, *Kafkas Amerika-Roman 'Der Verschollene.' Motive und Gestalten* (Würzburg: Königshausen u. Neumann, 1981).
   It goes without saying that I can lay no claim to having introduced here a novel reading of Kafka; my approach to *The Lost One* simply aims at emphasizing those aspects of the text which I believe are likely to shed the most light on Fellini's interpretation.
9 Kafka's novel belongs to a long-standing literary tradition depicting the 'journey of redemption,' consisting in the narration of an allegorical voyage through the canonical sequence Hell–Purgatory–Paradise, among whose specimens Dante's *Comedy* and Gogol's *Dead Souls* rank foremost. The project of *The Lost One* is reminiscent of Chichikov's travels through Russia, if only in consideration of the fact that in tackling 'Hell' both Gogol and

Kafka were extraordinarily successful, while both gave up trying to complete the paradisian part of their work.

10. Esteban Peicovich, ed., *Borges, el Palabrista* (Madrid: Editorial Letra viva, 1980) #1. Translation mine.

11 Peter Bondanella, 'Dreams and Metacinema,' *The Cinema of Federico Fellini* (Princeton: Princeton UP, 1992) 205–13, esp. 211.

12 A *matriozka* is a multi-layered Russian doll: a doll inside a doll, inside a doll, and so on.

13 The rationale for the artist's search for a defamiliarized 'Japanese glance' could be summarized as follows: if the outsider's eye can detect no tragedy about me, why should I?

14 Peculiarly, he bears the same (real) last name as the (fictional) protagonist of *La dolce vita*, the journalist Marcello Rubini played by Marcello Mastroianni.

15 Fellini's postmodernism and Friedrich Schlegel's ironic (philosophical) Romanticism link up as milestones in a long tradition of self-reflexive textuality. Bondanella's richly informative chapter on the subject, to which I have already alluded, can be complemented on the literary watershed by Robert Alter's *Partial Magic: The Novel As Self-Conscious Genre* (Berkeley: U of California P, 1975), as well as by Jorge Luis Borges's 'Magías parciales del Quijote,' in J.L.B., *Obras completas* (Barcelona: Emecé, 1989) 2:45–7.

   Schlegel's definition of Romantic irony as 'a permanent digression' ('eine permanente Parekbase'), to be found in Friedrich Schlegel, *F. S.s Kritische Ausgabe*, ed. Ernst Behler (München: Schöningh, 1963) 18:85 (668), is discussed at some length in De Man's well-known 'The Rhetoric of Temporality,' in his *Blindness and Insight: Essays in the Rhetoric of Contemporary Criticism* (Minneapolis: U of Minnesota P, 1983) 218–22.

16 Fellini, *Comments on Film* 116. Translation reviewed and corrected.

17 Federico Fellini, *Block-notes di un regista* (Milano: Longanesi, 1988) 83. All translations of quotations from *Block-notes* are mine. Hereafter cited in the text as *Block-notes*.

18 Other slight differences worth mentioning:
   • Unlike Fellini's Robinson, Kafka's shows no particular sensual pleasure in eating sardines. He eats them just as any brute such as himself spontaneously would.
   • In the novel, Brunelda's transportation in the early hours of the day happens through the streets of a city. In the film, it occurs in the countryside.

19 The best Italian edition available to Fellini shows the bath drama and the 'Brunelda moves out' episode as appended fragments (i.e., out of sequence). It includes all events in Delamarche's apartment as 'Chapter Seven'; it leaps, without a transition, to the Oklahoma Theater, which it

numbers as 'Chapter Eight'; and it closes with the train ride episode. In other words, this particular edition discourages, or even defeats, all attempts at a diachronic reading of the psychological situation as it evolves in the (admittedly unfinished) novel. Franz Kafka, *America*, trans. Alberto Spaini, in F.K., *Romanzi*, ed. Ervino Pocar (Milano: Mondadori, 1969).

20 A subject of inquiry that is adjacent to but, I believe, not identical with the Kafka connection is Fellini's verifiable biographical interaction with 'America' (= the U.S.A.). Those interested in evidence about Fellini's relationship with, and opinion of, the real country (as opposed to Kafka's symbolic one) will find the director's own statements on the topic in *Comments on Film* 113–20. The original Italian appears reprinted as a separate chapter in *Block-notes* 61–5.

21 Nowhere is she so defined by Kafka, however.

22 In his real-life interview with Giovanni Grazzini, Fellini speaks at length about his deep involvement with Jungian philosophy. *Comments on Film* 162–7.

23 An *omiyage* in Japanese signifies a gift culturally typical of a faraway land, brought back by the voyager for the curiosity – but ideally also for the intellectual edification – of those back at home.

24 Franz Kafka, *Hochzeitsvorbereitungen auf dem Lande und andere Prosa aus dem Nachlaß*, ed. Max Brod (New York: Schocken Books, 1953) 84. Translation mine.

25 *Comments on Film* 19. I am approximating the Italian *ascesi* (Greek *askêsis*) with 'a long process of self-discipline,' rather than the translator's (incorrect) 'ascent.'

11

Interview with the Vamp: Deconstructing Femininity in Fellini's Final Films[1]
(*Intervista, La voce della luna*)

ÁINE O'HEALY

From the 1960s onwards, as Fellini moved away from the comic realism of his earlier films toward the carnivalesque excesses that characterize his later style, spectacular configurations of the feminine grew increasingly visible in his work. This variegated parade of female bodies ultimately became one of the most memorable features of his authorial signature. Yet there has been surprisingly little feminist analysis of the Fellinian feminine, and the handful of feminist critics who have engaged with his work have voiced sharply divergent assessments. On the one hand the director has been criticized for his misogynistic deployment of the feminine (de Lauretis). On the other, his films are said to implicitly resist the discourses of patriarchy by cleverly subverting some of the discursive strategies of mainstream cinema (Waller).

My interest in Fellini's work was prompted by the complicated and contradictory configurations of femininity that appear in his films from *8½* (1963) onwards. These configurations are often inflected with an ironic self-consciousness that foregrounds the cinematic construction of Woman as a projection of male fantasy and desire. In fact, Fellini's 'women' are almost always focalized by male characters, who are pointedly constructed as perpetual adolescents. In many of his films this approach allowed the director to have it both ways: that is, to criticize (apparently) the masculinist biases of cinematic practices while indulging in some of the voyeuristic strategies he was exposing. The textual ambivalence that arises from this self-reflexive exploration of cinematic femininity results in an unsettling viewing experience for the female spectator.

In this essay I focus on Fellini's last two films, *Intervista* (1987) and *La voce della luna* (1990), which offer some of his most complex and disturbing constructions of femininity. Both films resonate with the anxieties of a modernist auteur threatened by the proliferation of post-modern discourses and technologies – anxieties that were already present to varying degrees in Fellini's three preceding films: *La città delle donne* (1980), *E la nave va* (1983), and *Ginger e Fred* (1985). The anxieties that underpin *Intervista* and *La voce della luna* relate to the decline of cinema in the televisual age, the crisis of masculinity, the demise of the author/artist, and the social and cultural displacements brought about by globalization and the postcolonial moment. While noting the significant shift in tone that occurs between the penultimate film and the last, I propose to investigate how the deployment of the feminine in these films is interwoven with the discourses of sexuality and politics, fantasy and art.

These two films are in several respects quite dissimilar. *Intervista* provides a personal and highly idiosyncratic tribute to Cinecittà, the studio where the director spent most of his working life. Like *I clowns* (1970) and *Fellini's Roma* (1972) it is a pseudo-documentary in which Fellini plays himself on screen, and it offers a provocative commentary on the director's creative process and on his relationship to the cinematic apparatus itself. The film is laced with both irony and nostalgia. *La voce della luna*, on the other hand, is a narrative film loosely based on Ermanno Cavazzoni's whimsical contemporary novel *Il poema dei lunatici*, which is set in the Romagna region of Italy where Fellini grew up. In this, the director's final film, irony gives way to satire infused with resentment. What links both films is an implicit critique of the contemporary cultural landscape. In each film, however, the image of Woman bears a different relation to the director's darkly comic view of post-modernity.

In an early version of the *Intervista* screenplay,[2] Fellini referred to Cinecittà as '*una fabbrica per costruire le donne*' ('a factory for constructing women'), thus insinuating his awareness of the masculinist bias of cinematic femininity. His assertion that 'cinema is a woman,' or that 'woman is a series of projections invented by man'[3] had already been implicitly articulated in a number of his films through the strategy of mise-en-abyme. Nonetheless, with its insistent foregrounding of the 'manufacture' of femininity, *Intervista* offers Fellini's most sustained engagement with the relationship between cinema and Woman. This film's textual enactments of femininity are complicated on the one hand by the director's phantasmagoric evocation of life under fascism, and on the other by his view of contemporary culture as it has evolved under the regime of postmodern technologies.

The organizing fiction of *Intervista* is that we are watching a Japanese television crew preparing a documentary on Fellini's work at Cinecittà. At the same time, the *maestro* is supposedly involved in preparations for a new film, an adaptation of Franz Kafka's unfinished novel *Amerika*. Thus, throughout *Intervista*, the fictional Japanese videographers follow Fellini's activities as he begins the casting process for his (invented) adaptation. From the outset, the young Japanese woman who functions as spokesperson for the television crew questions Fellini directly about his career. This is presumably the interview to which *Intervista*'s title refers, but it is not the only interview in the film. In order to recount to his visitors the memory of his first visit to Cinecittà, the on-screen Fellini shoots a flashback sequence (virtually a film-within-the-film) set in the late 1930s in which the much younger 'Fellini' (Sergio Rubini), then a timid reporter, goes to interview a glamorous actress at the film studio.

These two interviews have an odd symmetry, with the director's youthful stand-in as the deferential interviewer in one, and the aging *maestro* as the imperious and somewhat distracted interviewee in the other. This sly juxtaposition pokes fun at Fellini's self-importance in the present tense of *Intervista*. Yet, like the narcissistic diva who casually accepts the adulation of the young reporter, the contemporary Fellini, assured of his status as a Great Artist, indulges the fascination of the Japanese crew. Although *Intervista* suggests that the author/artist is not yet completely dead despite postmodern reports to the contrary, it implicitly casts doubt on the current status of the filmmaker's art in a studio now dedicated almost entirely to television commercials. The persona of the aging *maestro* is thus tinted with self-mockery. For example, during the opening exchange with the visiting crew, Fellini tells his interlocutors of a recurring dream that, like the famous dream of his alter ego at the beginning of *8½*, concludes with his taking flight. He admits, however, that it is more difficult for him to fly nowadays, even in his dreams. This allusion to diminished potency implicitly marks *Intervista*'s construction of the contemporary *maestro*.

The long flashback through which Fellini reinvents the memory of his first visit to Cinecittà as a timid reporter around 1939 is intercut with shots from the present tense of *Intervista* that document the flashback's preparation and shooting. This allows for an exploration of the contrast between present and past, between the cheap vulgarity of contemporary Cinecittà and the glamorous pretensions of the film studio almost half a century earlier. Indeed, nothing in the present seems to measure up to Fellini's memories of his youth. When his assistant director and producer go to inspect the spot that functioned long ago as the starting point for the tram line linking downtown Rome to Cinecittà, they find themselves in a neighbourhood very different from the *maestro*'s cherished recollections. The realities of contemporary urban life – chaotic traffic, run-down buildings, and a multiethnic population that includes African street vendors – have made the area unsuitable for shooting the initial scene of Fellini's 'flashback,' prompting the director to construct his set in another location.

Besides highlighting the contrast between present and past, the film's movement between diegetic levels exposes the efforts underlying the representational process. This enables the spectators to observe the constructedness of roles and identities, as the actors move in and out of their fictional roles in the flashback. These moments of slippage are sometimes of special importance to the construction of sexuality in the film. One of the most interesting transitions occurs in the scene where Sergio Rubini prepares to play the younger Fellini in the flashback sequence. The *maestro* obliges the actor to wear a fake pimple on his nose, with the intention of inspiring a sense of mortification in Rubini as he re-enacts the young reporter's interview with the star. This visual flourish serves to feminize Fellini/Rubini, anticipating his abjection vis-à-vis the famous actress. Here and elsewhere in *Intervista* the feminization of Fellini in his various incarnations is a subtle but important trope.

Interwoven with its critique of contemporary culture and an accompanying nostalgia for the past, *Intervista* presents a host of references to the construction of female sexuality. In addition to the boyishly dressed Japanese interviewer and the effulgent diva, the film offers a kaleidoscope of female figures on different diegetic levels: a chorus line of majorettes making a lipstick commercial; a blonde ingenue courted by Fellini/Rubini on his tram ride to Cinecittà; the coquettish, 'real life' film archivist Nadia Ottaviani; and an assortment of large women recruited to audition for the part of the plump and lascivious Brunelda in the projected adaptation of *Amerika*. Finally, there is Anita Ekberg, whom we encounter in two different incarnations: as a middle-aged recluse in the present tense of *Intervista* and as the vivacious young blonde glimpsed in the screening of an excerpt from *La dolce vita*. These figures are deployed with the phantasmagoric exuberance that is characteristic of much of Fellini's later work, and are coded ideologically in interesting and unsettling ways.

The intersection of political and sexual discourses in the construction of the fascist-era diva who is interviewed by Fellini/Rubini offers an especially striking example of this process. The interview, which links the delusional aesthetics of fascist kitsch with the apparatus of cinema itself, is preceded by the depiction of the young man's tram ride to Cinecittà, in the course of which his relationship to fascism is clearly brought into question. As the tram leaves the heart of the city and heads for Cinecittà, a uniformed fascist *gerarca* strikes up a 'patriotic' conversation with Fellini/Rubini. Although the director's youthful alter ego is more interested in a pretty blond passenger than in the *gerarca*'s propaganda, he eventually falls under its spell. When, unexpectedly, the tram comes to a halt in the open countryside, the passengers watch as three peasant women dressed in the colours of the Italian flag advance through the fields bearing baskets of fruit. A ragtag group of followers is heard singing the fascist song 'O bella campagnola' as they approach the tram, and when the *gerarca* raises his arm in the fascist salute, the other passengers do likewise, including Fellini/Rubini. Meanwhile, declarations of patriotic sentiment are exchanged, and the official is enthusiastically embraced by the peasant women. The gendering of fascist spectacle in this scene is clear: the fertile Italian countryside is coded as feminine, and its fruits are offered in homage to the phallic, uniformed figure of the *gerarca*. What we see here is the staging of fascist ritual as primal scene, with Fellini/Rubini participating as mystified onlooker.

In Freud's theory of human development, the primal scene – that is, the imagined observation of parental coitus – is linked to the Oedipal and castration crises and is accompanied by a sense of the uncanny. Freud suggested that primal fantasies are not necessarily linked to actual events. Rather they are scenarios to which the child resorts when its own experience fails to provide answers to the mysteries of identity, origins, and sexual difference. Film theorists since Christian Metz have attempted to link the primal fantasies described by Freud to the processes of film spectatorship. For Metz the regressive state of the cinema spectator prompts the reactivation of the 'imaginary signifier' – that is, the various traumas associated with the development of subjectivity in childhood.

Fellini's construction of fascist pageantry as a regressive phenomenon has interesting analogies with the theorization of cinematic pleasure as a form of psychic regression. In fact, the sequence that follows *Intervista*'s fascist interlude sets up an analogy between the reception of fascist discourse and the experience of cinema spectatorship. As the music on the soundtrack conjures up a sense of the uncanny, the tram resumes its journey to Cinecittà and passes a variety of spectacular though unlikely sights, including dense woods, towering cliffs, and a majestic waterfall. When an Indian Chief and his attendants are sighted on a cliff – in a shot that seems to belong in an old-fashioned American western – the fascist official casually suggests the desirability of exterminating all Indians, adding, however, that a handful of them should be salvaged for use in the movies. Meanwhile, a mutual fascination with the passing spectacle draws Fellini/Rubini and the young blond passenger together. Side by side they gaze through the windowpane, which is dappled with reflected light. Enraptured as spectators at a movie theatre, both of them ignore the sinister implications of the *gerarca*'s speech. As elephants roam nearby, a fast zoom brings an elephant's head into a tight close-up, and in the counter-shot we see an expression of awe on the young journalist's face. The sight of these animals prompts the fascist official to announce the tram's imminent approach to Cinecittà. In fact, when the tram stops at its destination, the young reporter enters the studio on the heels of an elephant. Fellini's arrival at Cinecittà is thus associated not only with the promise of glamorous feminine beauty but also with the massive figure of the elephant, one of the conventional symbols of Mussolini's expansionist policies in Africa.

In several scenes of *Intervista*, the elephantine is implicitly juxtaposed with images of voluptuous femininity. In much of Fellini's later work the relationship between the alluring and the grotesque is one of uncanny fluidity and ambivalence. The young journalist's encounter with the diva in *Intervista* is rich in dialogical elements typical of the director's carnivalesque style. The film's construction of the interview, which takes place in the star's trailer, foregrounds the youth's fascinated voyeurism, his interest in surfaces rather than depth, his misreadings and misrecognitions. On entering the trailer, Fellini/Rubini catches sight of the diva's nude silhouette through the frosted door of the shower, a two-dimensional figure on a screen. Bashfully, he smoothes his hair in anticipation of the imminent encounter. This bashfulness is contrasted with the lewd behaviour of two middle-aged men also present in the dressing room, who are involved in a conversation prompted by their reading of the *Kama Sutra*. Clearly, the erotic energy circulating in the trailer's pink interior is generated by men, marking the diva's inner sanctum as the domain of the hom(m)osexual.[4] Momentarily forgetting the term used in the ancient text to describe the female genitalia, the men pause in their conversation until the actress casually supplies the word from behind the bathroom door. With her ready participation in this lewd exchange, the actress thus enters the scene as 'one of the boys.'

Although Fellini/Rubini sees the diva as 'a Tiepolo Venus' – an allusion lost on the unlettered actress – the film presents her as a vacuous vamp given to predictable posturing. The stage name assigned to her, Katia Devis, intended to suggest the exotic appeal of northern femininity, disavows her humble Neapolitan origins. These are nonetheless evident in her speech and mannerisms. Before submitting to the interview with Fellini/Rubini, she pauses to have lunch, loudly sucking the contents of an egg through a hole in the shell. Despite this lack of decorum in the presence of the journalist, the diva is intensely interested in supervising the construction of her star persona. As she proceeds to answer the questions posed by Fellini/Rubini, a make-up artist begins to work on her face in preparation for the afternoon shoot. 'Katia Devis' then preens for her interviewer, her arms above her head in a poster-perfect image of stardom, until a wardrobe assistant takes over the assignment of transforming her into an exotic princess. Thus the Neapolitan *popolana* is remade before our eyes as a haughty maharani. Rarely has a film so meticulously rendered the step-by-step construction of cinematic femininity.

The scene simultaneously demonstrates a shifting play of power along various axes of difference – notably those of gender, 'race,' and class. This destabilizes the signifiers of identity. At the beginning of the scene, the star is explicitly masculinized (she admits that one critic found her to be more like a man than a woman), while Fellini/Rubini, the bashful reporter with the pimple on his nose, is feminized and rendered abject. There is a corresponding ambivalence and fluidity in the diva's adopted identities. Coded by her accent as subaltern, this Mediterranean *popolana* likens herself to the glamorous Nordic beauty Greta Garbo, and, approximating what she imagines to be an air of superior elegance, reduces the young bourgeois reporter to stammering admiration. She is then further transformed for her role as Indian princess in a film set in the British Raj.

The shifting social and political valences of these performed identities become even more complicated when the costumed diva emerges onto the set of the elaborate spectacle-film in which she is starring. Here she immediately becomes embroiled in a bitter quarrel with her director. Irritated by his insulting remarks, Katia Devis sits on top of a fake elephant and refuses to continue her performance. Invoking her influence with the producer, she threatens to have the director sent into internal exile by the regime. Chaos ensues as the enraged director attacks the producer for the flimsiness of the fake elephants provided for the set – a gesture that associates by allusion the overblown diva with the poorly constructed props. Finally, from the present tense of *Intervista*, the *deus ex machina* voice of Fellini intrudes to offer direction to the cast of this film-within-the-film, rupturing the diegesis and immediately ending the flashback.

The sequence as a whole ties together the signifiers of woman, fascism, and cinema; all three are presented as pure spectacle, as a game of smoke and mirrors in which everyone seems equally complicit. In this, *Intervista*'s sunniest sequence, the darker side of life under fascism is alluded to only in passing. It is glimpsed in the *gerarca*'s casual racism, in how the star threatens the director with internal exile (the dreaded *confino*), and in the preposterous spectacle-films promoted by the state-controlled film studio. But it is played out as comedy. An unmistakable nostalgia simultaneously runs through Fellini's reconstruction of his first encounter with Cinecittà, extending even to the absurd pomposity of fascist-era film productions, which are recreated here with mocking but affectionate humour. *Intervista* transforms everything – the vacuous diva, the elephants real and fake, the magical tram ride, the encounter with the *gerarca* – into a dreamlike fantasy that contrasts sharply with the construction of contemporary Cinecittà as a territory that has been colonized by an apparently much uglier regime: television production.

It is against the implicit contrast between the gaudy excess of fascist spectacle and the cheap kitsch of contemporary television commercials that Fellini's effort to cast Brunelda unfolds. Brunelda – a colourful though minor figure in Kafka's tale – is a character that Fellini might have invented himself, and it is hardly surprising that much of the present tense of *Intervista* is devoted to the *maestro*'s attempts to cast this role. The fantasized but never realized Fellinian Brunelda – glimpsed only potentially in an assortment of female figures at the earliest stages of talent scouting and screen testing – seems antithetical to the bland images of femininity fostered by contemporary televisual culture.

Intervista begins its construction of Brunelda with a question from one of the Japanese crew: How does the *maestro* locate the 'strange faces' that populate his films? As if in response, the film cuts immediately to Fellini's assistant director, Maurizio Mein, as he travels on the underground train, carefully scrutinizing his fellow passengers in an effort to recruit candidates for the role of Brunelda. Mein singles out large-breasted or overweight women and invites them to Cinecittà for screen tests. Meanwhile, the train is passing through stations decorated exclusively with identical posters of a sleek 'televisual' beauty. This postmodern simulacrum, this endless repetition of the same, seems at odds with the varied assortment of faces and bodies that Mein considers for the maestro's proposed adaptation of *Amerika*.

The quest for the voluptuous Brunelda apparently triggers in Fellini's memory the image of an actress he had once constructed as an icon of feminine desirability: Anita Ekberg. Fellini recruits Ekberg's co-star in *La dolce vita*, Marcello Mastroianni (who has shown up at Cinecittà to play a magician in a television commercial), and sets off with him, Rubini, and the Japanese crew for an unannounced visit to the actresses's home. Just as the entrance of the diva was signalled in the flashback sequence by the lewd fantasies of two men lounging in the trailer, Ekberg's entrance is similarly preceded by a lewd exchange among men. On their way to Ekberg's home, Mastroianni and Rubini – seated with Fellini in the back of a chauffeur-driven Mercedes – joke about their enjoyment of masturbation and extol the superior pleasures of making love to imaginary women. Here again, Woman is invoked as a purely masculine fantasy generated within the hom(m)osexual imaginary.

The visit to Ekberg's home can be construed as *Intervista*'s third interview sequence. It has interesting parallels with Fellini/Rubini's visit to the fascist diva, as well as some telling differences. Like the star in the earlier flashback, Ekberg enters the scene wrapped in a large bath sheet and is regaled with assurances of her fame. What we see, however, is an aging, overweight matron who still, somewhat incongruously, retains her long blond hair and flirtatious mannerisms. The film's construction of the contemporary Ekberg bears only a passing resemblance to her famous image as a sex goddess of the 1950s and 1960s. The contrast between past and present is dramatized when Mastroianni, still wearing his magician's costume, conjures up a film screen in Ekberg's living room on which a sequence from *La dolce vita* is projected. Seated at Mastroianni's side, the teary Ekberg watches her youthful performance as the vivacious Sylvia who dances with Marcello at a nightclub and wades playfully in the Trevi Fountain. On screen, the younger Marcello earnestly addresses her. We hear nothing of their conversation, however, since the scene is projected without its original soundtrack. His eyes riveted on the black-and-white image of Ekberg, the aging Mastroianni resupplies the words spoken long ago: *'Ma chi sei tu? Sei una dea, la madre, il mare profondo, la casa; sei Eva, la prima donna apparsa sulla terra'* ('Who are you? You're a goddess, the great mother, the ocean, home. You're Eve, the first woman who appeared on earth'). Mastroianni thus reconsecrates the young actress of *La dolce vita* as the eternal, mysterious feminine. In the present tense of *Intervista*, however, he has only one query for the aging actress – where to find the booze – and they both repair to the kitchen to console themselves with alcohol.

The young journalist's encounter with Katia Devis in the *Intervista* flashback parodies the transformation of a supposedly ordinary woman into a film star; the episode at Ekberg's seems to suggest a similar process in reverse. In her theorization of the femme fatale, Mary Ann Doane has offered some interesting observations on the construction of the female star that may be usefully applied to an understanding of the Ekberg figure in *Intervista*. According to Doane (who refers to the protagonist of Max Ophuls's *La signora di tutti* as her example), the star's image betrays an impossible logic: she is presented simultaneously as unique and as the embodiment of a universal femininity.

> [The star] becomes the image of Woman because no other – ordinary – woman is like her ... [She] somehow represents all women through her incarnation as a generalized femininity, an abstraction or ideal of femininity. The monolithic category of Woman here is not even an alleged average or distillate of concrete women but their abstraction, their subtraction. Not like other women ... [the female star] is transformed into Woman, a position inaccessible to women. (77–8)

The scene at Ekberg's house seems to expose this very process. By positioning the aging, overweight actress as a spectator of her idealized image on screen, the film underscores the dichotomy between the contemporary Anita Ekberg and her other, unchanging, cinematic incarnation as a feminine ideal.

But it would be inaccurate to assert that Ekberg, as she appears in the present tense of *Intervista*, is simply an ordinary woman. Despite her voluntary participation as a 'real life' personality in Fellini's pseudo-documentary, she is only partially in control of how she is constructed by the film. The mise-en-scène repeatedly foregrounds her heavy physicality through camera angles and framing, even while the other, pre-filmic Ekberg intrudes on this construction. This is unwittingly signalled in the actress's efforts to conceal her weight, first under a huge orange towel and later under a lighter wrap. In the tension generated by Ekberg's apparent struggle to play the part of the still beautiful film star Anita Ekberg, the actress is transformed into something that approaches the grotesque.

While images of the female grotesque are a staple of the Fellinian repertoire, the construction of Ekberg in *Intervista* differs from that of Fellini's other grotesques, in that she appears on different diegetic levels within the same sequence as both an idealized figure of femininity and a disturbing image of aging and excess. In Fellini's deployment of the same actress at opposite poles of the patriarchal feminine, we find the typical ambivalence between the sublime and the grotesque noted by Mary Russo: 'The proximity of female grotesques to their attractive counterparts has a long history in the typology of Western art and theater, especially comedy, in which the whorish matron, the crone, the ugly stepsisters, and the nurse are brought on-stage for comparison and then dismissed' (40).

By encapsulating both the sublime and the monstrous connotations of femininity in the figure(s) of Ekberg, Fellini is exposing the motivations and effects of patriarchal representation, and showing how the desire to appropriate or fetishize and the tendency to reject or debase coexist in masculinist constructions of femininity. Tania Modleski has described precisely how the figure of the aging actress – a staple of camp aesthetics – reveals the 'double bind of patriarchal representations of the feminine, signifying decaying flesh and intimations of mortality on the one hand, and muting their terrors through hysterical excess and parody on the other' (103).

Here, anxieties about aging and decay are not simply displaced onto that perennial figure of jest, the fat lady. A note of pathos undercuts the parody inherent in the reconstruction of Anita Ekberg, partially foreclosing this process. As the camera concentrates on Ekberg's massive form, the effort made by the actress to disguise her bulk projects a sense of uneasiness, complicating the effects of the grotesque. The issue of male aging and mortality, though partially displaced onto the body of the present-day Ekberg, remains manifest in this crucial scene of *Intervista*. If Rubini stands in for Fellini's younger self, Mastroianni, in his absurd magician's outfit, heavy makeup, and fake whiskers, stands in for the aging auteur. Castration anxiety and the decline of vitality are the subtext of Mastroianni's preoccupations, from the first line he utters in *Intervista*, as he pretends to advertise a product that will restore sexual potency, to his joking remark about the possibility of his moustache falling off. Ekberg reinforces these implications by teasingly scanning his face for the telltale scars of cosmetic surgery.

But it is finally on the aging and imperfect body of Ekberg that the camera concentrates, while the narrative emphasizes her seclusion from the outside world. Her luxurious residence in an out-of-the-way location proves to be a gilded cage. Mastroianni, by contrast, despite his flabby form, aging features, and appetite for alcohol, is presented as a working actor, more in control of his world than the housebound Ekberg hiding behind bars and protected by vicious dogs. She is in fact as securely hidden away from the world as the unhappy soubrette in the harem scene of *8½*, banished upstairs and out of sight on reaching the undesirable age of twenty-six. (In fact she blatantly underestimates her years, but the point is clear: beyond a certain age, women are expendable.)

A note of intense nostalgia pervades the entire sequence, and cuts the pathos generated by Ekberg's minimal gestures of self-production, This is not merely the nostalgia performed by the aging actors as they mourn the loss of their youth. Rather, it is a distinctly Fellinian nostalgia echoed in a remark made by one of the Japanese crew: 'There are no women like her in Japan.' The film's construction of Ekberg – in both grotesque and sublime incarnations – is offered as a celebration of the kind of femininity that Fellini sees eclipsed by postmodern aesthetics. 'Japan' can be read as a signifier of the postmodern. Though the members of the Japanese crew offer homage to Ekberg by their very presence in her living room, they also remind us that the international mass media have hastened the demise of the modernist aesthetics exemplified by *La dolce vita*, and with it the freedom of the filmmaker as artist. The remark made by the Japanese interpreter underscores Fellini's own sense of loss in the postmodern landscape, which has been given over to mass-produced images and the endless replay of simulation. In this way, the contemporary Ekberg of *Intervista* ultimately becomes a figure of nostalgia for the kind of femininity that is in danger of being eclipsed by the postmodern imaginary.

Indeed, the film's construction of Anita Ekberg is one of the most interesting configurations of the feminine in all of Fellini's work. Although Mastroianni functions as Fellini's alter ego throughout the Ekberg sequence, the actress herself can be construed as an additional stand-in for the director in the same scene. Shortly after the visitors enter her home, Fellini drops out of sight, and the visit develops without any mention of him. Thus, in a sense, the *maestro* is replaced by the aging actress. This provides a marked contrast with the interview in *Intervista*'s flashback sequence, in which both the female star and Fellini/Rubini remain present on screen and the young man's emotional responses are highlighted as prominently as the vamp's affected posturing. Clearly, he is the subject and she the willing object of desire. In the present tense of *Intervista*, however, the older Fellini seems to recognize at least some aspects of himself in the aging female star. There are in fact significant similarities between the *maestro* and the contemporary Ekberg. In their initial appearances in the film, both are greeted by enthusiastic admirers offering homage. Yet Ekberg lives as a recluse who basks in past glories and is susceptible to empty flattery; in much the same way, Fellini is secluded behind the walls of the film studio, unable to acknowledge fully his own obsolescence. In this implicit parallel, the film again feminizes the director himself. Ultimately we could construe the *maestro*'s unseen presence in the scene of Ekberg's tears as an oblique identification with the actress: a kind of 'Mme Ekberg, c'est moi!'

The failure to cast Brunelda can be read as another tacit acknowledgment of the *maestro*'s vulnerability and loss of power. Although he seems to abandon his interest in casting Ekberg in this role, Fellini continues to interview various large-breasted women for screen tests, along with actors trying out for other roles in *Amerika*. In *Intervista*'s final sequence, the casting process is interrupted by a violent rainstorm that leaves both actors and crew stranded for the night in a makeshift shelter on a studio lot. Here they are attacked at dawn by an incursion of warriors, brandishing weapons uncannily similar to television antennae. The warriors who invade the present tense of *Intervista* include the 'Indians' glimpsed on the cliff in the earlier, fascist-era sequence, reminding us of the *gerarca*'s statement that this 'treacherous race' should be exterminated, leaving only a few 'for use in the movies.' An ironic twist complicates the identity of the intruders, however. The 'Indians' in this scene are no longer coded as noble savages and as potential victims of racial intolerance, but rather as agents of the colonizing forces of television sent to attack the survivors of a doomed cinematic civilization; the signifiers of colonizer and colonized are thus destabilized and collapsed. The irony is further compounded when the voice of Fellini abruptly intervenes to end the attack, announcing that the shoot is finished and ordering everyone to go home. Thus the *maestro* reasserts his own directorial status, divesting the 'Indians' of their role as allies of the postmodern media while disclosing that they are 'really' movie extras, hired to participate in the film we are watching. As they dismount, the warriors revert to their local, Italian identities and leave the studio along with the remaining aspirants for the part of Brunelda.

Fellini's self-construction in the concluding scenes of *Intervista* is marked with ambivalence. Despite the director's self-mockery and veiled admission of diminished power at several points in the narrative, the final moments of *Intervista* take a vaguely triumphalist turn. First, the *maestro*'s abrupt rupture of the diegesis draws attention to his authorial power and status. Then, having dismissed his cast and crew, he sits alone in a darkened sound stage playing God-the-film-director as he prepares again to summon light out of darkness.

The inability of the on-screen *maestro* to cast Brunelda is one of the most noticeable 'failures' we witness in this film. Fellini's next (and last) film *La voce della luna* demonstrates that even if Brunelda vanishes from *Intervista* before she has fully materialized, Fellini has salvaged at least one female figure 'for use in the movies.' Supposedly playing her real-life role as director (or 'vestal virgin') of the studio archives, Nadia Ottaviani first appears in *Intervista* at the moment that Fellini introduces her to the Japanese crew. Despite the *maestro*'s request that she assist them in their research, Ottaviani quickly evolves into a capricious siren, leading the perplexed visitors to an overgrown lot in search of wild chicory while postponing their more pressing interests. In each of her brief appearances in *Intervista*, the blond studio employee is coded as a figure of seduction with the help of framing, lighting effects, and minor costume changes involving furs, hats, pearls, and gloves. Although she is seen infrequently, and is easily outmatched by the preposterous fascist-era diva and the monumental Ekberg, Ottaviani is a visually memorable presence in the film. *Intervista* thus provides a wry commentary on Fellini's transformation of Ottaviani into a star image for his subsequent film, in which she plays the leading female role. This clearly suggests the director's ongoing ability to construct the feminine for his own, real cinematic ends.

Intervista concludes on an ambivalent note that is not entirely devoid of hope for the survival of cinema; Fellini's final film takes a much darker view of the postmodern scene and its effects on art, culture, and the collective imaginary. It also takes a darker view of femininity. *La voce della luna* reiterates the anxieties provoked by the contemporary cultural landscape that Fellini expressed in various ways in his last decade of work. But the film's narrative tone, its particular construction of femininity, and the way it introduces a new breed of male protagonist into the Fellinian repertoire – the slightly mad, slightly effeminate man/child – distinguish *La voce della luna* from all of the director's earlier films.

One of the most interesting aspects of this film's hermeneutic is the development of diverse focalizing characters through whose perspective the narrative unfolds so that the diegetic development is not continuously organized around a single, unifying subjectivity. Different plot lines are thus sketched out, and there is only a fragile narrative connection among the three male characters who all happen to inhabit the same small town. The film's protagonist, Ivo Salvini (Roberto Benigni), is a grave and gentle youth youth who is prone to psychotic fantasies and attentive to the voices that call to him in country fields and in an empty room of his childhood home. He is linked to the Romantic poet Giacomo Leopardi (whose invocations of the moon are quoted several times in the film) and also to Pinocchio (by whose name he was known as a child). Ivo is involved in the futile pursuit of an elusive blond named Aldina (Ottaviani), whose pale, incandescent beauty he associates with the moon. Not long discharged from a mental hospital, Ivo indulges in nocturnal ramblings through streets and fields. In the course of these wanderings he befriends Gonnella, a retired public official who struggles to ward off the specters of paranoid senility and isolation. Both men have only a tenuous relationship to sanity, the Law, and the Symbolic order. Both are treated as eccentrics by the town's other inhabitants. But a few fellow eccentrics offer company and affection. Chief among Ivo's friends is a balding youth named Nestore – the third focalizing presence in the film – who in a long sequence early in the film tells Ivo the details of his courtship and failed marriage to the sexually voracious Marisa, otherwise known as the Locomotive.

The three most important male characters are thus constructed as outsiders in the small town they inhabit. This town is an extraordinary jumble of petty provincialism and postmodern pretensions. In the piazza stands a hideous contemporary church run by an entrepreneurial priest. Signs of Americanization are much in evidence: a 'Bank of Tucson' in the piazza, a restaurant named 'Las Vegas' on the outskirts of town, and so on. Moreover, the townspeople are hooked on media culture and are happily awaiting the launch of their own television station. But this participation in the high-tech global village does not imply the acquisition of a more cosmopolitan outlook. On the contrary, these small-town Italians are motivated by pure materialism and remain uninterested in the larger world.

Like *Intervista*, *La voce della luna* fleetingly acknowledges the demographic shifts resulting from globalization and postcolonial migrations. In the town centre, as in the streets of *Intervista*'s contemporary Rome, African vendors ply their meagre trade. One of these traders accosts a passer-by with the question *'Vu' comprà?'* ('Wanna buy?'), a phrase adopted by Italians as a pejorative reference to the African immigrants who have thronged to Italy in recent years, many of them from Italy's former colonies. The passer-by responds with anger, dismissing the street vendor as a blight on the scene. The townspeople are hardly more welcoming toward the other, more affluent foreign visitors: a group of Japanese tourists who pause in the piazza to take snapshots as they pass through town on a bus tour.

The scene in *La voce della luna* dedicated to the arrival of the Japanese tourists links the growing presence of foreigners in Italy to the curse of postmodernity, and suggests a subtle intertextual reference to the Japanese documentarists in *Intervista*. As the visitors step out onto the piazza to take photographs of the ugly contemporary church, their bus obstructs the local traffic. In typical postmodern fashion, these tourists observe their surroundings principally through the camera lens, treating local sights as images to be carried home as snapshots, and oblivious to the disruption caused to the townspeople. The tourists' preoccupation with capturing the local sights as exportable simulacra is pointedly contrasted with Ivo's poetic fantasy of 'seeing' the sparkling sound of church bells. Clearly, Fellini is valorizing the young man's capacity for fantasy above the unsympathetic behaviour of the foreign visitors. The film's construction of these tourists betrays a note of resentment that is re-echoed at other points throughout the narrative, especially at moments dominated by the central female characters, and in sharp contrast to the sympathetic construction of the embattled male characters Nestore and Ivo.

It is ultimately on the two main female figures of *La voce della luna* that the heaviest burden of resentment falls. Marisa, the small-town vamp loved by Nestore, is the film's most prominent grotesque and constitutes one of the most spectacular configurations of a sexually desiring woman in all of Fellini's work. The sexually voracious woman is not a common character type in cinematic representation, although examples are found in other films by Fellini. In most film traditions, female desire is rarely shown as exceeding the economy of male desire, since women's sexuality is imagined in direct relation to male plea-sure. When female desire does exceed male need, it is almost always represented as threatening or grotesque. Fellini's representation of Marisa's all-consuming sexual demands vacillates between the subver-sive, the comic and the offensive. It is crucial, however, to observe how the deployment of Marisa's sexuality ties in with the construction of masculinity in *La voce della luna*.

Marisa – whose first appearance in the film is a chance encounter with Ivo after her separation from Nestore – quickly evolves from a benign seductress into an all-consuming grotesque in the course of Nestore's flashback. Even in her first scene, however, she is marked as a figure of excess: a tall, shapely woman wearing a tight red suit with a plunging fur collar, alternately tearful and flirtatious. Despite her tears, she proves to be a shrewdly calculating personality, as she waits in the piazza to supervise the emptying of the apartment she once shared with Nestore. Marisa's grasping attention to possessions distinguishes her from the dreamy, childlike Nestore. Her estranged husband is in fact happily despoiled of all his worldly goods, except for a single household item – a washing machine that he cherishes not for its usefulness but rather for the haunting, fantasy-provoking sounds it emits.

The contrast set up in this encounter prepares us for the flashbacks that follow, all of them corresponding to Nestore's memories. In the first of these we witness his initial encounter with Marisa in the local barbershop. While performing a manicure, Marisa reads Nestore's palm and coyly extracts a proposal of marriage. The palm reading con-structs her as a powerful sorceress under whose sway Nestore is com-pletely helpless. This impression is confirmed in the scene of their wedding reception, which takes place at a restaurant where a huge mural of the Milan soccer team forms a backdrop to the bridal table. Here Marisa towers over Nestore with her large headdress, often blocking him from view. He is further dwarfed by the 'real men' repre-sented on the wall behind him. As a photographer is about to take a picture of the bride and groom, Marisa pushes Nestore aside so that

the giant figure of Ruud Gullit, star of the Milan team at the time, will
appear next to her in the photograph. Another 'real man' looms close
by on the swing-door that leads to the restaurant kitchen, completing
the mural on the adjacent wall with the image of a referee. The referee's face happens to bear the features of Silvio Berlusconi,[5] Italy's
most powerful media tycoon and owner of the highly successful Milan
team. Fellini's invective against television and the politics of postmodern culture thus insinuates itself into the diegesis of La voce della luna.
What is most interesting here, however, is how this trope intersects
with a demonstration of the media's construction of masculinity, and
the suggestion (however comically expressed) of the consequences of
this ideological manipulation for actual men. By the time the bride and
groom dance away toward the waiting car, Nestore seems to have
shrunk in stature and Marisa looms even larger than before.

The final scene in Nestore's flashback, depicting his married life,
completes the transformation of Marisa into an all-consuming grotesque. A cloud of steam surrounds her as she hovers over the sleeping
Nestore, begging him for sex. Finally, in a climactic montage sequence
articulated in expressionistic style, Marisa insists on making love on
the sofa in the moonlit living room. Fast-moving close-ups and rapid
cross-cutting to images of a train in motion transform Marisa into a
powerful locomotive whose energy terrifies the defenceless Nestore.
Sound effects and the huge shadow of Marisa's flailing legs on the living room wall heighten the fantasy, as the panic-stricken Nestore
struggles to disengage himself from the momentum of the runaway
train. This scene was sharply criticized by a number of Italian women
after the film was released in 1990. Dacia Maraini and others condemned La voce della luna for its grotesque representation of female
desire.[6] The depiction of female sexual desire as preposterous seems to
continue a trend already present in La città delle donne. While some
female spectators were repelled by how femininity was deployed in
that earlier film, at least one critic has proposed a feminist recuperation
of Fellini's grotesques. In an analysis influenced by Julia Kristeva's
recuperation of the Bakhtinian carnivalesque, Christie Milliken has
proposed a feminist interpretation of the female characters in La città
delle donne. Milliken reads Fellini's figures of excess not as evidence of
misogyny but as part of a discursive strategy that subverts the models
of femininity proposed by the dominant representational regime. Yet I
would argue that representations of bodily excess are not always transgressive, since the carnivalesque can also be used in the service of

repressive ideologies. In my view, the grotesque transformations of femininity in *La voce della luna* are largely inspired by a reactionary sentiment, and are infused with a note of resentment that is more strident than the irony that underpins most of Fellini's earlier configurations of female excess.

When Ivo's beloved Aldina first appears in *La voce della luna*, she seems related to the muse figures found in Fellini's earlier work, most notably *8½*'s 'woman in white.' Aldina nonetheless undergoes important transformations, progressing from fetishized object of the gaze to punished grotesque. The construction of her character is complicated by clues that link her romantically to the moon on the one hand and repudiate her complicity with contemporary mass culture on the other. In Aldina's first scene, Ivo creeps into her bedroom to catch a glimpse of her sleeping face. Here she is immediately associated with the moon, both visually (a halo of moonlight surrounds her sleeping face) and verbally (Ivo quotes Leopardi's invocations of the moon). This Sleeping Beauty quickly turns into a negative version of Cinderella as she flings her silver slipper at Ivo, an object he treasures fetishistically for the remainder of the narrative. Ivo's invocation of the moon in this scene links Aldina retrospectively to the film's opening scene, in which the moon is also conspicuously present.

The opening shots of *La voce della luna* offer a guide to the deployment of femininity throughout the film, and to some of the psychoanalytic underpinnings of the narrative. As the film begins, we see a circular well in an empty field at night. Ivo enters the frame. Murmurings rise out of the well, and rustlings, twitterings, and other eerie noises are heard in the surrounding countryside. There is a cut to the full moon overhead, which mirrors the circular shape of the well and then a cut back to the well, as the murmurings begin to articulate Ivo's name. Ivo is thus interpellated as a subject by a disembodied voice apparently emanating from the well (the womb/tomb) and is simultaneously associated with that archetypal feminine figure, the moon. Ivo's encounter with these voices and his subsequent acoustic hallucinations are important to the film's articulation of sexual difference.

If Aldina is associated with disembodiment (with voices, the moon, and fairy tales) in the early part of the film, she gradually loses her lunar aloofness as the narrative progresses. In her next appearance we watch her strolling through the streets at night wearing a bright silver coat, with the rebuffed Ivo trailing behind. She is constructed simultaneously as consumer and consumer-object, and is clearly aware of her dual role as she checks her multiple reflections in a lighted store window featuring mannequins modelling wedding gowns. Visually, Aldina has evolved into a combination of Barbie Doll and Marilyn Monroe. Finally, in the film's central sequence that depicts the town's annual dumpling festival (the *gnoccata*), Aldina competes in a beauty pageant and is crowned Miss Farina (Flour) 1989. Accidentally trapped under the stage, Ivo must observe her triumph through a hole in the stage floor. As he watches from his lowly vantage point, Aldina's face is outlined by the halo-shaped peephole, thus reinforcing the lunar associations already attached to her image, while simultaneously evoking the icon of the Virgin Mary and a residual resemblance to Marilyn Monroe.

The ambiguities inherent in this vision are intensified when Aldina is sprinkled with flour to mark her coronation as the festival queen. As the flour pours down on her, Nadia Ottaviani is divested of the luminous beauty that characterized her looks throughout this film and the previous one. Her incandescent paleness suddenly becomes opaque, even dirty. Visually, this is a highly unsettling moment in Fellini's configuration of the feminine, and seems all the more powerful given that it occurs in one of the key sequences of his final film.

Richard Dyer has identified an enduring tendency in cinema to render femininity – white, Western femininity – as more luminous and ethereal than white masculinity. For Dyer, the exaggerated whiteness of female characters – constructed with the help of specific lighting effects in countless films produced in the West over the past century, connotes spiritual power as well as physical beauty. But he also notes that it suggests at the same time an unconscious anxiety about the physical fragility of the white race. For Dyer, the luminous quality that characterizes many representations of white women hints at a sense of insecurity regarding the reproductive capacity of white people relative to the world's darker peoples, with their allegedly superior physical strength and fecundity. Indeed, many of Fellini's female figures are marked with a special luminosity, from the pale, almost childlike Giulietta Masina in her various roles to the 'woman in white' in *8½*. In the central scenes of *La voce della luna*, however, this luminosity is dramatically disavowed. The opaque coat of flour that clings to Aldina's blond hair and white satin dress suddenly renders her abject – part person, part food product. The scene foregrounds Aldina's collusion with consumerism and mass advertising as she is soiled by the product with which she has become identified. Fellini's eternal feminine is now definitively desecrated. Aldina is exposed as no less grotesque than Marisa or the grossly obese woman designated as Queen Gnocca.

Ultimately there is nothing vulnerable about either of the two principal female characters in this film. Both Marisa and Aldina are constructed as calculating survivors; in contrast, the central male characters, Ivo, Nestore, and Gonnella, seem fragile and doomed to extinction. The women seem monstrous precisely because of their ability to adapt to the postmodern values of consumption, reproduction, and simulation – an ability that is lacking in the dreamy, imaginative male characters with whom the narrative point of view strongly identifies.

Significantly, the vulnerable Ivo is able to act out his resentment by contributing to Aldina's abjection. On his liberation from accidental captivity, the unrequited lover discovers Aldina dancing provocatively with a prominent local doctor, whom she allows to lick the sauce off her fingers. Dismayed, Ivo throws a plate of gnocchi at his rival, but the red sauce also splatters Aldina's white dress as she falls humiliated to the floor. Her pale, lunar beauty is thus definitively desecrated by Ivo himself, who turns her into a pathetic figure at the very moment that she reveals herself as a sexually desiring subject.

In a later scene, which seems to be part of Ivo's hallucinatory ruminations, the moon itself is debased and desecrated, following Aldina's trajectory. Functioning as a metaphor for the Other, the moon is captured by two local men, who use conventional phrases of seduction to lure it from the sky with a giant harvesting machine. As spectators we do not see the moment of capture; instead, like the townspeople, we learn about it through the mediation of high-tech reportage. While held prisoner in a nearby barn, the moon becomes the focus of a spontaneous media circus. The event is projected onto a huge video screen in the piazza, where the townspeople conduct a talk show on the significance of the sensational capture. At the moon's refusal to respond to a question regarding the meaning of life, however, the local barber shoots a hole in the giant screen, annihilating the moon's image and bringing the media event to an abrupt conclusion. When Ivo sees the moon in the final scene of the film, it has been restored to its usual place in the heavens. But it has now turned nasty, teasing Ivo in a voice that bears a suspicious resemblance to Aldina's. In fact, Aldina's face is now superimposed on the moon, and in the film's closing moments we see her announcing a commercial break from her new vantage point in the sky.

This final metamorphosis suggests the transformation of the moon itself – a timeworn locus of inspiration for poetry and myth – into a fetish-screen at the service of postmodern technologies. While the diva of *Intervista* is shown to be complicit with the fascist regime, Aldina demonstrates a comparable complicity with the imperializing regime of television. But Aldina's capitulation to the cheap celebrity of electronic advertising is constructed as a sadder betrayal than the diva's collusion with fascism, in the sense that advanced media technology threatens to annihilate the poetry of the moon – which has been celebrated in cinema at least since Méliès' *Trip to the Moon* – and with it the wonder of art.

If Aldina is the villain of *La voce della luna*, Ivo is presented as a true antitelevisual hero, looking for meaning in dead sparks, in the peal of church bells, in the murmuring of the country well. The film elevates these idiosyncrasies over the crass vulgarity of contemporary media technology, video games, and the high-tech hysteria of the mega-discotheque. But Fellini's invitation to reject postmodern technologies that prove threatening to his central male characters is a nostalgic, regressive one. His elevation of these socially marginal male eccentrics is linked to his self-celebration as an artist, simultaneously placing women in a position of complicity with the archenemies of consumerism and communication technology.

Like several American films from the same period, *La voce della luna* responds to the crisis of masculinity and the 'threat' of feminism by presenting childlike male heroes. Ivo can be linked to Roger Rabbit, PeeWee Herman, Forrest Gump, and other youthful protagonists we encounter in the Hollywood cinema of the late 1980s and early 1990s.[7] Ivo's yearning for a magical, infantile experience of the world locates him in the pre-Symbolic stage of psychic development – a stage at which the illusion of continuity between infant and mother still prevails and the paternal order of language has not yet separated the subject from the (m)other. Ivo's fascination with the world 'beyond' – with the hole leading elsewhere – mirrors the regressive fantasy of a return to the maternal realm. The sounds that call to him from wells and fields are like the sonorous blanket provided by the voice of the pre-Oedipal mother.

Ultimately the figure of the actively desiring woman functions in *La voce della luna* as a synecdoche for the threatening aspects of advanced technological communication. The female figures in this film thus fulfil a different signifying function than those in *La città delle donne*. That earlier film ended with enough ambiguity to invite a recuperative reading of Fellini's grotesques as possible models of resistance for feminists. *La voce della luna*'s construction of femininity forecloses this possibility – female sexuality has now become a signifier of a more threatening global disturbance.

Notably absent in *La voce della luna* is the gentle irony that underpins the female characters in *Intervista*, who are constructed with affection, even empathy, in contrast to those of Fellini's last film. In *Intervista* Fellini maintains the illusion of authorial grandeur, playfully hinting at his powerlessness and abjection while underscoring with *deus ex machina* interventions that he is ultimately the creator and arbiter of all his characters. *La voce della luna*, by contrast, is haunted by the terror of the artist's definitive loss of power and status, the vulnerability of age, and the transformation of the human imaginary by alien technologies. Just as the swaggering *maestro* of Fellini's penultimate film yields in the final film to the doomed idiot savant, the exuberant female characters of *Intervista* are replaced in *La voce della luna* with grotesque, grasping figures that encapsulate the resentment, disappointment, and loss at the heart of the film's inspiration.

Notes

1 The section of this essay devoted to *La voce della luna* has been published previously in a slightly different version (see O'Healy, 'Unspeakable Bodies').

2 I am indebted to Peter Bondanella for the opportunity to consult the collection of Fellini manuscripts in the Lilly Library at Indiana University.

3 In a much-quoted interview, Fellini described the relationship between cinema and femininity as follows: 'I think the cinema is a woman by virtue of its ritualistic nature. This uterus which is the theater, the fetal darkness, the apparitions – all create a projected relationship, we project ourselves onto it, we become involved in a series of vicarious transpositions, and we make the screen assume the character of what we expect of it, just as we do with women, upon whom we impose ourselves. Cinema being a series of projections invented by man' (Bachmann 8).

4 In her powerful critique of the dominant symbolic order, Luce Irigaray coined this term to categorize patriarchal sexuality, which exists only for men and in which the other (i.e., female) sex is defined solely in terms of its relation to men.

232   Áine O'Healy

5 When the film was made, Berlusconi was still to become founder of the
centre-right party Forza Italia and eventually Prime Minister of Italy.
Berlusconi's political success has been attributed largely to his substantial
control of the media.
6 Personal communication with Dacia Maraini. Rome, June 1990.
7 For a critique of the tendency to valorize male regression in contemporary
popular culture, see Modleski, chapter 6.

References

Bachmann, Gideon, 'Federico Fellini: The Cinema Seen as a Woman.' *Film
Quarterly* 34.2 (1988): 2–9.
Cavazzoni, Ermanno. *Il poema dei lunatici*. Turin: Boringhieri, 1987.
de Lauretis, Teresa. 'Fellini's 9½.' *Technologies of Gender*. Bloomington: Indiana
UP, 1987. 95–106.
Doane, Mary Ann. *Femmes Fatales: Feminism, Film Theory, Psychoanalysis*. New
York: Routledge, 1991.
Dyer, Richard. *White*. London: Routledge, 1997.
Freud, Sigmund. 'The Uncanny.' *The Complete Psychological Works: Standard Edi-
tion* 17. New York: Norton, 1976. 219–52.
Irigaray, Luce. *This Sex Which Is Not One*. Trans. Catherine Porter with Carolyn
Burke. Ithaca: Cornell UP, 1985.
Kafka, Franz. *Amerika*. Trans. Edwin Muir. New York: New Directions, 1962.
Metz, Christian. *The Imaginary Signifier*. Trans. Celia Britton, Annwyl Williams,
Ben Brewster and Alfred Guzzetti. Bloomington: Indiana UP, 1982.
Milliken, Christie. 'From Fair to Feminism? Carnivalizing the Carnal in Fel-
lini's *City of Women*. *Spectator* (Spring 1990): 28–45.
Modleski, Tania. *Feminism without Women: Culture and Criticism in a 'Postfemi-
nist' Age*. New York: Routledge, 1991.
O'Healy, Áine. 'Unspeakable Bodies: Fellini's Female Grotesques.' *Romance
Languages Annual* 4 (1992): 325–9.
Russo, Mary. *The Female Grotesque*. New York: Routledge, 1994.
Waller, Marguerite. 'Neither an "I" nor an "Eye": The Gaze in Fellini's *Giulietta
degli spiriti*.' *Romance Languages Annual* 1 (1989): 75–80.

Selected Bibliography

Screenplays, Projects, and Novelizations

Amarcord: Portrait of a Town. Federico Fellini with Tonino Guerra. Trans. Nina Rootes. London: Abelard-Schuman, 1974.

8½: Federico Fellini, Director. Ed. Charles Affron. New Brunswick and London: Rutgers UP, 1987.

Federico Fellini: Early Screenplays: Variety Lights, The White Sheik. Trans. Judith Green. New York: Grossman, 1971.

Federico Fellini: Three Screenplays: I vitelloni, Il bidone, The Temptations of Dr Antonio. Trans. Judith Green. New York: Grossman, 1970.

Fellini's Casanova. *Retold by Bernardino Zapponi*. Trans. Norman Thomas di Giovanni and Susan Ashe. New York: Dell, 1977.

Federico Fellini's Juliet of the Spirits. Ed. Tullio Kezich. Trans. Howard Greenfeld. New York: Ballantine, 1965.

Fellini's Satyricon. Ed. Dario Zanelli. Trans. Eugene Walter and John Matthews. New York: Ballantine, 1970.

La Dolce Vita. Trans. Oscar DeLiso and Bernard Shir-Cliff. New York: Ballantine Books, 1961.

La Strada: *Federico Fellini, Director*. Ed. Peter Bondanella and Manuela Gieri. New Brunswick and London: Rutgers UP, 1987.

Moraldo in the City and A Journey With Anita. Ed. And trans. John C. Stubbs. Urbana: U of Illinois P, 1983.

Bibliographies

Price, Barbara Anne, and Theodore Price. *Federico Fellini: An Annotated International Bibliography*. Metuchen, Scarecrow Press, 1978.

Stubbs, John C., with Constance D. Markey and Marc Lenzini. *Federico Fellini: A Guide to References and Resources*. Boston: G.K. Hall, 1978.

Biographies and Portraits
Alpert, Hollis. *Fellini: A Life*. New York: Atheneum. 1986.
Baxter, John. *Fellini*. London: Fourth Estate, 1993.

Critical and Background Studies
Bondanella, Peter. *The Cinema of Federico Fellini*. Princeton: Princeton UP, 1992.
– ed. *Federico Fellini: Essays in Criticism*. New York: Oxford UP, 1978.
Bondanella, Peter, and Cristina Degli-Esposti, eds. *Perspectives on Federico Fellini*. New York: G.K. Hall, 1993.
Boyer, Deena. *The Two Hundred Days of 8½*. New York: Macmillan, 1964.
Budgen, Suzanne. *Fellini*. London: British Film Institute, 1966.
Costello, Donald P. *Fellini's Road*. Notre Dame: U of Notre Dame P. 1983.
Hughes, Eileen Lanouette. *On the Set of* Fellini-Satyricon: *A Behind-the-Scenes Diary*. New York: William Morrow, 1971.
Ketcham, Charles B. *Federico Fellini: The Search for a New Mythology*. New York: Paulist Press, 1976.
Perry, Ted. *Filmguide to 8½*. Bloomington: Indiana UP, 1975.
Rosenthal, Stuart. *The Cinema of Federico Fellini*. South Brunswick: A.S. Barnes, 1976.
Salachas, Gilbert. *Federico Fellini: An Investigation Into His Films and Philosophy*. Translated by Rosalie Siegel. New York: Crown Publishers, 1969.
Solmi, Angelo. *Fellini*. Translated by Elizabeth Greenwood. Atlantic Highlands: Humanities Press, 1968.

Interviews/Writings by Fellini
Fellini, Federico. *Federico Fellini: Comments on Film*. Ed. Giovanni Grazzini. Trans. Joseph Henry. Fresno: California State UP, 1988.
– *Fellini on Fellini*. Ed. Anna Keel and Christian Strich. Trans. Isabel Quigley. New York: Delacourte/Seymour Lawrence, 1976.
– *Fellini on Fellini*. Ed. Costanzo Costantini. Trans. Sohrab Sorooshian. London: Faber and Faber, 1995.
– *I, Fellini*. Charlotte Chandler. New York: Random House, 1995.

Filmography

Major Screenplay Contributions

1943   *L'ultima carrozzella* (dir. Mario Mattoli). Co-scriptwriter.
1945   *Roma, città aperta* (dir. Roberto Rossellini). Co-scriptwriter.
1946   *Paisà* (dir. Roberto Rossellini). Co-scriptwriter.
1947   *Il delitto di Giovanni Episcopo* (dir. Alberto Lattuada). Co-scriptwriter.
1948   *Senza pietà* (dir. Alberto Lattuada). Co-scriptwriter.
1948   *Il miracolo* (dir. Roberto Rossellini). Co-scriptwriter.
1949   *Il mulino del Po* (dir. Alberto Lattuada). Co-scriptwriter.
1950   *Francesco, giullare di Dio* (dir. Roberto Rossellini. Co-scriptwriter.
1950   *Il cammino della speranza* (dir. Pietro Germi). Co-scriptwriter.
1951   *La città si difende* (dir. Pietro Germi). Co-scriptwriter.
1951   *Persiane chiuse* (dir. Luigi Comencini). Co-scriptwriter.
1952   *Il brigante di Tacca del Lupo* (dir. Pietro Germi). Co-scriptwriter.
1979   *Fortunella* (dir. Eduardo De Filippo). Scriptwriter.
1979   *Viaggio con Anita* (dir. Mario Monicelli). Fellini not credited.

Written and Directed

1950   *Luci del varietà* (*Variety Lights*)
1952   *Lo sceicco bianco* (*The White Sheik*)
1953   *I vitelloni* (*I Vitelloni*)
1953   'Un'agenzia matrimoniale' ('A Matrimonial Agency'), episode in *Amore in Città* (*Love in the City*)
1954   *La strada*
1955   *Il bidone* (*The Swindle*)
1956   *Le notti di Cabiria* (*Nights of Cabiria*)
1960   *La dolce vita*

1962   'Le tentazioni del dottor Antonio' ('The Temptations of Dr Antonio'),
        episode in *Boccaccio '70*
1963   *Otto e mezzo (8½)*
1965   *Giulietta degli spiriti (Juliet of the Spirits)*
1968   'Toby Dammit,' episode in *Histoires Extraordinaires,* also called *Tre Passi
        Nel Delirio,* and *Spirits of the Dead*
1969   *Fellini: A Director's Notebook*
1969   *Fellini-Satyricon*
1970   *I clowns (The Clowns)*
1972   *Roma*
1973   *Amarcord*
1976   *Fellini's Casanova*
1979   *Prova d'orchestra (Orchestra Rehearsal)*
1980   *La città delle donne (City of Women)*
1983   *E la nave va (And the Ship Sails On)*
1985   *Ginger e Fred (Ginger and Fred)*
1987   *Intervista*
1990   *La voce della luna (The Voice of the Moon)*

Contributors

Dorothée Bonnigal is a Professor of English in Paris, France, and a training psychoanalyst. She has published articles on Italian, American, and Italian-American cinema in the United States and Europe. Her current research is devoted to the cinema of Martin Scorsese. Her article 'Restrained Women and Artistic Emancipation: Authority and Resistance in Federico Fellini's *Giulietta degli spiriti* and John Cassavetes's *A Woman under the Influence*' was the winner of the *Romance Languages Annual* Lorraine K. Lawton Award in 1995.

Frank Burke is Professor of Film at Queen's University (Canada). He has published two books on Fellini: *Federico Fellini: Variety Lights to La Dolce Vita* and *Fellini's Film: From Postwar to Postmodern*, as well as many essays on Italian and North American cinema. He has also edited several film sections and one special film issue for the *Canadian Journal of Political and Social Theory*.

Cosetta Gaudenzi is Assistant Professor of Italian at Gettysburg College. She earned her Ph.D at the University of Texas at Austin. The title of her dissertation is 'Appropriations of Dante: 18th- and Early 19th-Century Translations of the Divine Comedy in Great Britain.'

Millicent Marcus is Mariano DiVito Professor of Italian Studies at the University of Pennsylvania. Her specializations include Italian cinema and medieval literature. She is the author of *An Allegory of Form: Literary Self-Consciousness in 'The Decameron,' Italian Film in the Light of Neorealism, Filmmaking by the Book: Italian Cinema and Literary Adaptation*, and *After Fellini: National Cinema in the Postmodern Age*. She has also published many articles on Italian literature and on film, and is currently working on an interdisciplinary, collaborative project titled 'Italy 1919.'

Áine O'Healy is Professor of Italian at Loyola Marymount University in Los Angeles. She is the author of *Cesare Pavese* and has published many essays on Italian cinema and on feminist issues in literature, cinema, and culture. Her articles have appeared in *Screen, Cinefocus, Women's Studies Review, Spectator, Annali d'Italianistica, Italica, Italian Culture,* and other journals.

Virginia Picchietti is an Associate Professor of Italian at the University of Scranton as well as Director of that school's Italian Studies Program and Assistant Director of Women's Studies. She has published a book and several articles on Dacia Maraini.

Christopher Sharrett is Professor of Communications at Seton Hall University. He has published *Mythologies of Violence in Postmodern Media* and edited *Crisis Cinema: The Apocalyptic Idea of Postmodern Narrative Film.* His work has appeared in *Film Quarterly, Persistence of Vision, Journal of Popular Film and Television, Cinéaste, CinéAction,* the *Canadian Journal of Political and Social Theory,* and elsewhere.

Helen Stoddart is a lecturer in English Literature and Film Studies in the Department of English at Keele University, United Kingdom. She has published *Rings of Desire: Circus, History and Representation* as well a number of articles on Gothic film and literature.

Carlo Testa is Associate Professor in French and Italian at the University of British Columbia. His research interests are Italian Studies and Comparative Literature. Among his publications are *Desire and the Devil: Demonic Contracts in French and European Literature,* (edited), *Poet of Civic Courage: The Films of Francesco Rosi, Italian Cinema and Modern European Literatures,* and *Masters of Two Arts: Re-creation of European Literatures in Italian Cinema.*

Marguerite R. Waller is Professor of English and Women's Studies at the University of California, Riverside, where she also teaches in the Film and Visual Culture Program. She is the author of *Petrarch's Poetics and Literary History* and the co-editor of *Frontline Feminism: Women, War, and Resistance.* Her articles on Italian and other cinemas, virtual reality, border art, Renaissance literature, and global feminism have appeared in many books and journals.

William Van Watson has taught at universities in Portugal, Italy, and the United States, and is currently a Visiting Assistant Professor of Italian at the University of Arizona. He has published *Pier Paolo Pasolini and the Theatre of* *the Word*, and contributed chapters to anthologies on Luchino Visconti and Shakespeare. His articles on theatre, film, MTV, opera, and poetry have appeared on both sides of the Atlantic in such journals as the *Romance Languages Annual*, *Il Veltro*, *Theatre Journal*, *Semicerchio*, *Literature Film Quarterly*, *Theatre InSight*, and *Annali d'italianistica*.